RE-IMAGINING THE TEACHING OF EUROPEAN HISTORY

This book explores the challenges of teaching European history in the 21st century and provides research-informed approaches to history teaching that combine civic education, historical consciousness, and the teaching of controversial social issues.

With contributions from researchers across Europe, the book includes both theoretical and case study chapters. The first part of the book addresses issues such as globalization and teaching in an interconnected world, using multicultural and critical approaches, decolonizing education, and teaching uncomfortable narratives of the past. The second part of the book showcases thematic chapters dedicated to teaching intersecting topics in the European curriculum such as violence and armed conflict, social inequality, gender equality, the technological revolution, and religion.

Ultimately, this volume promotes criticality, civic engagement, and reflection on social issues, thereby prompting methodological change in the teaching of history as we know it. It will appeal to researchers and students of history education, democratic education, and citizenship education, as well as teacher educators and trainee teachers in history.

Cosme Jesús Gómez Carrasco is Senior Lecturer, Social Sciences Teaching, University of Murcia, Spain.

RE-IMAGINING THE TEACHING OF EUROPEAN HISTORY

Promoting Civic Education and Historical Consciousness

Edited by Cosme Jesús Gómez Carrasco

LONDON AND NEW YORK

Designed cover image: © Getty Images

First published 2023
by Routledge
4 Park Square, Milton Park, Abingdon, Oxon OX14 4RN

and by Routledge
605 Third Avenue, New York, NY 10158

Routledge is an imprint of the Taylor & Francis Group, an informa business

© 2023 selection and editorial matter, Cosme Jesús Gómez Carrasco; individual chapters, the contributors

The right of Cosme Jesús Gómez Carrasco to be identified as the author of the editorial material, and of the authors for their individual chapters, has been asserted in accordance with sections 77 and 78 of the Copyright, Designs and Patents Act 1988.

The Open Access version of this book, available at www.taylorfrancis.com, has been made available under a Creative Commons Attribution-Non Commercial-No Derivatives 4.0 license.

This book is a result of project "HistoryLab for European Civic Engagement: open e-Toolkit to train History Teachers on Digital Teaching and Learning", funded by SEPIE on call ERASMUS + KA226 [2020–1-ES01-KA226-HE-095430]

This project has been funded with support from the European Commission. This publication reflects the views only of the author, and the Commission cannot be held responsible for any use which may be made of the information contained therein.

 Co-funded by the Erasmus+ Programme of the European Union

Trademark notice: Product or corporate names may be trademarks or registered trademarks, and are used only for identification and explanation without intent to infringe.

British Library Cataloguing-in-Publication Data
A catalogue record for this book is available from the British Library

Library of Congress Cataloging-in-Publication Data
Names: Gómez Carrasco, Cosme Jesús, editor.
Title: Re-imagining the teaching of European history : promoting civic education and historical consciousness / edited by Cosme Jesús Gómez Carrasco.
Description: Abingdon, Oxon ; New York, NY : Routledge, 2023. | Includes bibliographical references and index.
Identifiers: LCCN 2022042664 (print) | LCCN 2022042665 (ebook) | ISBN 9781032294261 (hardback) | ISBN 9781032294278 (paperback) | ISBN 9781003289470 (ebook)
Subjects: LCSH: Europe—History—Study and teaching. | Europe—History—Study and teaching—Historiography. | Europe—Historiography.
Classification: LCC D16.25 .R45 2023 (print) | LCC D16.25 (ebook) | DDC 907.1—dc23/eng/20221108
LC record available at https://lccn.loc.gov/2022042664
LC ebook record available at https://lccn.loc.gov/2022042665

ISBN: 978-1-032-29426-1 (hbk)
ISBN: 978-1-032-29427-8 (pbk)
ISBN: 978-1-003-28947-0 (ebk)

DOI: 10.4324/9781003289470

Typeset in Bembo
by Apex CoVantage, LLC

CONTENTS

List of figures viii
List of tables ix
List of contributors x

Introduction: re-imagining the teaching of European
history from historical thinking and civic engagement 1
Cosme Jesús Gómez Carrasco and Ramón López Facal

PART I
Teaching approaches on history education **11**

1 History education and democracy 13
  Ramón López Facal and Daniel Schugurensky

2 The origin and development of research into historical
  thinking: a key concept in the renewal of history education 25
  Cosme Jesús Gómez Carrasco and Jorge Sáiz Serrano

3 Digital resources for rethinking history education 42
  Juan Carlos Colomer Rubio and Anaclet Pons Pons

4 Narratives of the past: a tool to understand history 53
  Stéphane Lévesque

5 Controversial heritage for eco-citizenship education in Social Science didactics: Implications for initial teacher education 68
Sergio Sampedro-Martín, Elisa Arroyo-Mora, José María Cuenca-López and Myriam J. Martín-Cáceres

PART II
Cross-cutting topics on European history 81

6 Landscapes, agriculture, peasants and environment in the history of Europe 83
Lourenzo Fernández Prieto

7 Social and economic impact of technological revolutions in Europe 99
Raimundo A. Rodríguez-Pérez, Pedro Miralles-Martínez, Francisco Precioso-Izquierdo and Pedro Miralles-Sánchez

8 Bourgeoisie and peasantry: unequal but necessary to understand European history and its identity 112
Juan Ramón Moreno-Vera and José Monteagudo-Fernández

9 Family, daily life and social inequality in Europe 125
Raquel Sánchez-Ibáñez and Antonio Irigoyen-López

10 Power and powers in the history of Europe: oligarchies, political participation and democracy 136
María del Mar Felices de la Fuente, Ramón Cózar Gutiérrez and Álvaro Chaparro Sainz

11 Under a cloak of terror: violence and armed conflict in Europe 149
Cláudia Pinto Ribeiro, Luís Alberto Marques Alves, Helena Vieira, Ana Isabel Moreira, Diana Martins, Daniela Magalhães and Lara Lopes

12 Persecuted by justice and powers: outcasts, rebels and criminals in the history of Europe 162
Carla van Boxtel

13 Women, gender, and the fight for gender equality in Europe 179
Ingmarie Danielsson Malmros and Marianne Sjöland

14 Travel stories and travelers: transdisciplinary approaches
and proposals for a history of Europe 193
Beatrice Borghi and Rosa Smurra

15 Churches and religion in Europe: interdisciplinary
methods and approaches for a European history 206
Filippo Galletti and Manuela Ghizzoni

Epilogue: "we wanna learn like common people whatever
common people did" 219
Juan Ramón Moreno-Vera

Index 224

FIGURES

2.1	Annual scientific production	33
2.2	Corresponding author's country	33
2.3	Most relevant words	34
2.4	Trending topics	35
2.5	Top authors' production over the time	36
2.6	The intellectual structure of the field of knowledge	36
4.1	Munslow's act of narration	56
12.1	T'Rasphuys (around 1700), a workhouse where delinquents had to shave wood from the brazilwood tree, rasping it into powder which was delivered to the paint industry (City archive Amsterdam)	165

TABLES

4.1	Megill's narrative tasks	55
10.1	Historical concepts associated with the topic of power and powers in Europe	145
12.1	General and historical concepts related to the history of crime and punishment and violence against the powers, organized in periods and themes	173

CONTRIBUTORS

Elisa Arroyo-Mora
Fellowship in Social Sciences Education
University of Huelva, Spain

Beatrice Borghi
Assistant Professor of Education Studies
University of Bologna, Italy

Álvaro Chaparro Sainz
Associate Professor in Social Sciences Education
University of Almeria, Spain

Juan Carlos Colomer Rubio
Associate Professor in Social Sciences Education
Universitat de València, Spain

Ramón Cózar Gutiérrez
Senior Lecturer in Early Modern History
University of Castilla-La Mancha, Spain

José María Cuenca-López
Full Professor in Social Sciences Education
University of Huelva, Spain

Ingmarie Danielsson Malmros
Senior Lecturer in Society, Culture and Identity
University of Malmö, Sweden

María del Mar Felices de la Fuente
Associate Professor in Social Sciences Education
University of Almeria, Spain

Lourenzo Fernández Prieto
Full Professor in Contemporary History
University of Santiago de Compostela, Spain

Filippo Galletti
Doctoral Student of Education Studies
University of Bologna, Italy

Manuela Ghizzoni
Assistant Professor of Education Studies
University of Bologna, Italy

Cosme Jesús Gómez Carrasco
Senior Lecturer in Social Sciences Education
University of Murcia, Spain

Antonio Irigoyen-López
Senior Lecturer in Early Modern History
University of Murcia, Spain

Stéphane Lévesque
Associate Professor in History Education
University of Ottawa, Canada

Lara Lopes
Researcher in History and Political International Studies
University of Porto, Portugal

Ramón López Facal
Professor Ad honorem
University of Santiago de Compostela, Spain

Daniela Magalhães
Researcher in History and Political International Studies
University of Porto, Portugal

Luís Alberto Marques Alves
Associate Professor in History and Political International Studies
University of Porto, Portugal

Myriam J. Martín-Cáceres
Senior Lecturer in Social Sciences Education
University of Huelva, Spain

Diana Martins
Researcher in History and Political International Studies
University of Porto, Portugal

Pedro Miralles-Martínez
Full Professor in Social Sciences Education
University of Murcia, Spain

Pedro Miralles-Sánchez
Fellowship in Social Sciences Education
University of Murcia, Spain

José Monteagudo-Fernández
Senior Lecturer in Social Sciences Education
University of Murcia, Spain

Ana Isabel Moreira
Researcher in History and Political International Studies
University of Porto, Portugal

Juan Ramón Moreno-Vera
Associate Professor in Social Sciences Education
University of Murcia, Spain

Cláudia Pinto Ribeiro
Professor Auxiliar in History and Political International Studies
University of Porto, Portugal

Anaclet Pons Pons
Full Professor in Contemporary History
Universitat de València, Spain

Francisco Precioso-Izquierdo
Associate Professor in Early Modern History
University of Murcia, Spain

Raimundo A. Rodríguez-Pérez
Senior Lecturer in Social Sciences Education
University of Murcia, Spain

Jorge Sáiz Serrano
Senior Lecturer in Social Sciences Education
University of Valencia, Spain

Sergio Sampedro-Martín
Fellowship in Social Sciences Education
University of Huelva, Spain

Raquel Sánchez-Ibáñez
Associate Professor in Social Sciences Education
University of Murcia, Spain

Daniel Schugurensky
Professor of Justice and Social Inquiry
Arizona State University, USA

Marianne Sjöland
Project Researcher in Society, Culture and Identity
University of Malmö, Sweden

Rosa Smurra
Associate Professor of Education Studies
University of Bologna, Italy

Carla van Boxtel
Professor in History and Education
University of Amsterdam, Netherlands

Helena Vieira
Researcher in History and Political International Studies
University of Porto, Portugal

INTRODUCTION

Re-imagining the teaching of European history from historical thinking and civic engagement[1]

Cosme Jesús Gómez Carrasco and Ramón López Facal

What is Europe?

In 1959, General de Gaulle gave a speech in which he stated that the fate of the world would be decided by a Europe stretching "from the Atlantic to the Urals". With this theory, he sought to promote European autonomy, fundamentally that of France, to overcome the logic of the Cold War. He considered it necessary to move beyond or break with the subordination of European states to one block or another. This Gaullist initiative, formulated more than half a century ago, has aroused a certain degree of sympathy and is periodically taken up by political leaders such as Emmanuel Macron before Russian President Vladimir Putin in 2019: "I know that Russia is a European country deep down in its soul. We believe in a Europe that extends from Lisbon to Vladivostok".

But what are the limits of Europe? Is it a geographical unit, a continent, a geopolitical space, or a cultural unit? Is it possible to conceive of a united Europe from the Atlantic to the Urals? More than 40 million inhabitants live in Siberia, of whom 95% are ethnically and culturally the same as the inhabitants of St. Petersburg or Moscow. Are the Siberian Russians and Europeans who live west of the Urals Asian? Is Turkey a European country? Is Georgia, which is part of the Council of Europe and has applied to join NATO, a European country?

Europe is a historically constructed cultural concept (Fontana, 2013) born from a myth, the limits of which have changed considerably over time. As a geographical term, the Greeks of the Archaic Period used this name for the continental European territory of Greece as opposed to the Peloponnese and the coast of Anatolia. The concept of Europe as a continent is historically quite recent. In the later Roman Empire only the province located in the territory that currently comprises the European part of Turkey received this name. Only from the 18th century has Europe been imagined as a space with supposedly common characteristics. The idea of placing the limits of Europe in the Urals and in the Caucasus Mountains was formulated in the middle of the 18th century by the Russian geographer Tatischev and the Swede Strahlenberg. The latter's books, which included maps, were translated into English, French, and Spanish and achieved notable popularity among European cultural elites. This idea was also taken up by the tsars as part of their political project to transform Russia. Therefore, barely three centuries have passed since the consolidation of this image of the limits of Europe.

From a geographical point of view, Europe is nothing more than a large peninsula of the Asian continent or Eurasia. In the Cenozoic era, some 66 million years ago, an enormous geological process began, caused by the clash between the African and Indian tectonic plates against the northern Eurasian plate, giving rise to a succession of mountain ranges and massifs that extend from the Cantabrian Mountains in northern Spain through the Pyrenees, the Alps, the Balkans, the Caucasus, and up to the Himalayas, even extending as far as the island of Sumatra. These mountain systems did not separate differentiated human groups nor are they specific to Europe. There is continuity in the landscapes and the settlements on both sides of them. They delimit regions or bioclimatic areas from the Mediterranean area, with its mountainous Iberian, Italian, and Balkan peninsulas, to the Arctic regions. Various subareas can be defined and modulated by their latitude, relief, or degree of continentality (distance from the seas). The dynamics of the atmosphere and ocean currents in the northern hemisphere influence the western coasts of Europe and North America, which receive warm currents, while the eastern coasts are colder. Therefore, over the centuries greater populations have gathered in these more temperate zones than in colder areas.

Research on the origins and spread of humanity on Earth is providing new insights into the chronology of the different species that modify previous theories relating to the presence of humans in Europe. Increasingly earlier dates have also been suggested for the different species. However, there is still consensus on the African origin of humanity. Several species of humans have successively populated the European area for close to 900,000 years, including Homo antecessor (Atapuerca, Spain) and Homo neanderthalensis, from approximately 230,000 years ago during the fourth Ice Age and becoming extinct about 28,000 years ago. Homo sapiens, our direct ancestors, have their origins in Africa, like all human species. They have been present in Asia for about 100,000 years and in Europe for at least 46,000. Homo sapiens replaced the Neanderthal, although there is evidence of hybridisation between the two species and the survival of part of the Neanderthal genome among modern Europeans.

The entire world population, including the inhabitants of Europe, has been the result of miscegenation. Over the course of history, numerous migrations are known to have taken place in all directions throughout European territory, from the north to the Mediterranean, from the east, including the Asian plains, to the west, and from the south to the north. In many cases they have been presented as invasions by different peoples who replaced populations which had previously settled on the same territory. Violence was a common occurrence in many migrations, although not all of them were conflictive in nature. Miscegenation has been present in all European and non-European peoples, with intentional exterminations, the great genocides, being contemporary phenomena.

Romanticism helped spread mythical origins to today's European nations, in addition to Greco-Roman cultural roots (which are not ethnic), Celtic, Germanic, Nordic, and Slavic nations. There is no scientific basis for these national (or nationalistic) myths, with archaeology and, especially, genetics having dismantled the idea of the existence of alleged ethnically differentiated populations at any time in the past. The Mediterranean has always been a place of communication and exchange. The contributions of the Greeks and Romans to history were, above all, Hellenism and Romanisation, with miscegenation being present from the very origins, making cultural diffusion possible.

The vast majority of European inhabitants speak Indo-European languages, and evidence of linguistic affinities has frequently been confused with proof of ethnic and even racial identities. The linguistic hypothesis of the existence of a proto-Indo-European language that spread from the steppes between south-eastern Europe and central Asia about 4,000 years ago, from where it spread to India and mainland Europe, is plausible but has not been supported by evidence. In any case, this would have been more a process of acculturation by assimilation among pre-existing populations than of substitution, although there may have been violent events leading to the annihilation of certain populations. Among these linguistic families, in addition to Greek and Latin, the Celtic, Germanic, and Slavic languages have had a notable influence in Europe.

Beginning in the year 3,000 B.C., a migration of populations identified as pre-Celtic began from the Caucasus area to the north and west. The first true Celtic culture is associated with the iron metallurgy of Hallstatt (1,200 B.C.). The Celts did not constitute any kind of state, empire, or kingdom. Rather than a "conquest", this was more a process of the superimposition and assimilation of pre-existing populations with cultures that used neolithic and bronze technology. Indeed, it could be said to have been a process of acculturation. The European Atlantic coast from Scotland, Ireland, and Wales to the west of the Iberian Peninsula, were the last territories assimilated by the Celtic culture and the last areas in which it survived until the Middle Ages. For several centuries the cultural elites of Western Europe assumed that their peoples had their origins in biblical figures or in classical Greco-Roman culture. European Romanticism abandoned this tradition, replacing it with Celtic or Germanic origins, in a movement parallel to the rise of nationalism. Currently many inhabitants of Western Europe identify themselves with (and consider themselves the heirs of) Celtic culture. This identification is more emotional than material, even among the small populations that preserve a language of Celtic origin.

The Germans are also an ethnolinguistic group of peoples whose origins are usually located in the south of the Scandinavian Peninsula both shores of the Baltic. The first recorded mention of them was made by the Romans, with Publius Tacitus providing a description of them in the 1st century. Although he had never travelled through those territories, he recorded second-hand information about the populations settled north of the Danube and east of the Rhine. Tacitus presented them as a uniform group, although, in reality, they were quite diverse peoples who did not form a political unit. In an attempt to criticise the moral decadence of his compatriots, he contrasted them with the virtuousness of the "noble savages". Beginning in the 4th century, the great Germanic migrations took place crossing the borders of the Roman Empire. About 20 peoples arrived in the West: the Suebi, Vandals, Goths (Visigoths and Ostrogoths), Franks, Burgundians, Thuringians, Alemanni, Angles, Saxons, Jutes, and Lombards, among others. At times they allied themselves with the Romans and with Romanised populations and frequently clashed with each other.

The Romantic idealisation of some of these peoples as the germ of contemporary European nations ignored processes of acculturation. Perhaps the most significant aspect in this regard was that they soon assumed the official religion of the empire, Christianity. It would even appear that Clovis, the King of the Franks, had both Gallic (Celtic) and Frank ancestors. In the most intensely Romanised territories (present-day Spain, France, Italy, and Portugal), Latin prevailed over Germanic languages, while, in the northernmost, less Romanised territories, the Celtic languages prevailed and Germanic languages expanded (present-day United Kingdom, Austria, Germany, the Netherlands, Germany, etc.), in addition to the Scandinavian varieties in Nordic territories.

The Slavs today constitute the largest ethnolinguistic group in Europe with more than 250 million people. Their origins are said to lie between the Baltic Sea and the Carpathian Mountains. Their great migrations began around the 2nd century, and they diversified into different families from the 3rd century onwards due to the interference of other peoples (Goths in the 3rd century, Avars in the 6th), which led to their migration towards the West, up to the Elbe and the Saale, and southwards through the Balkans to the Peloponnese and Asia Minor: Western Slavs (Czechs, Moravians, Slovaks, Poles, etc.); Southern Slavs (Slovenes, Serbs, Croats, Macedonians, Montenegrins, Bosnians, and Bulgarians); and Eastern Slavs (Russians, Belarusians, and Ukrainians). These peoples also experienced a process of cultural fusion, adopting Christianity as their religion. Due to Byzantine influence, most adopted the Orthodox or Eastern variant along with the Cyrillic alphabet, derived from Greek, while the Croats, Slovenes, Czechs, Slovaks, and Poles adopted the Roman Catholic variant and use the Latin alphabet.

In the words of Benedetto Croce, all history is always contemporary as it always answers questions that we ask ourselves from the present. We are interested in knowing the genealogy of our problems because we are concerned about the future. History is a dialogue with the past to build the future. Hence, local history makes sense when we ask ourselves about the national and global stories of the future. These are always interpretations, albeit based on evidence, and constitute reasonable and argued interpretations to know and understand ourselves. Europe is a cultural construction in which many millions of people, aware of its plurality, believe. The search for an approach to a history of Europe is consistent and compatible with other approaches at different scales.

What is the approach of this book?

Several decades ago, studies on the teaching of history began to undergo a cognitive change, one which has not taken place at the same time nor at the same pace in all countries. Wilschut (2011) has situated the origin of this trend in the 1970s at a time in which Bruner's theories and Bloom's and Krathwohl's taxonomies of educational objectives began to have a decisive influence on proposals relating to the teaching of history.

The increase in research in the field of history education has, in recent years, led to the publication of many monographs. Particularly worthy of note among these publications are those by Counsell et al. (2016), Carretero et al. (2017), and Metzger and Harris (2018) which have examined key methodological concepts, current lines of research, teaching praxis, and the uses and objectives of the teaching of history (Grever et al., 2011). These reviews agree on the fact that there has been a significant increase in research in this area since the 1990s (Metzger & Harris, 2018). They show that historical thinking and historical consciousness are two fundamental axes of the research of recent decades (Seixas, 2017) and that these studies have focused mainly on the curriculum, textbooks, and, to a lesser extent, on interviews, learners' perceptions, observation records for the evaluation of intervention programmes, and case studies (Epstein & Salinas, 2018).

Research on history education has developed a paradigm for analysis and interpretation which is based on two concepts: historical thinking (studies based on students' use of sources and historical argumentation) and historical consciousness (studies based on the public use of history and on the construction of collective identities among students) (Seixas, 2017). Such a development involves moving forward from a previous stage that can be termed pre-paradigmatic. Subjects with a focus on history textbooks or history in general (both closely related to the analysis of historical discourse and the very discipline of history education) have gradually become less significant.

The differences between historical thinking and historical consciousness are vague. Currently the concept of "historical thinking" frequently emphasises the analysis of evidence, reasoning, interpretation, and argumentation. "Historical consciousness" is commonly linked to history in popular culture, media representations, and "uses of the past". However, historical thinking is no longer so closely "linked" to the work of the historian (although some scholars do still advocate "thinking like a historian", but this is far from universal). It now more frequently emphasises the analysis of evidence, reasoning, interpretation, and argumentation (Reisman, 2012). As Lévesque and Clark (2018) have pointed out, historical literacy has been commensurate with a growing body of research on students' reading and writing abilities related with the second-order concept of historical comprehension. This is of great importance in relation to the recent results of the

Stanford History Education Group (Wineburg, 2018). This research group has identified how U.S. students reason about historical and contemporary information they consume from the Internet and social media. Their initial findings suggest that students are ill-prepared and poorly skilled at judging the credibility of online information. What is more, Lévesque and Clark (2018) have also pointed out that current research has not made much progress from the History 13–16 Project in the United Kingdom or the expert–novice studies of the 1990s. However, we consider that the research carried out in the Netherlands (mainly by the research group of van Boxtel, van Drie, and de Groot) has made significant progress in terms of historical argumentation by making use of rigorous quantitative and qualitative methodologies.

Historical consciousness is not merely linked to the "public use" of history but also to history in popular culture, media representations, and "uses of the past" (in Northern European parlance). Indeed, Clark and Grever (2018: 192) have stated that

> Researching historical consciousness has a critically defining and influential role on history education – both as a philosophically inspired claim on students' connections to past, present, and future and, increasingly, as a possible empirical model for researching the teaching of history and for practical applications for teaching historical thinking in the classroom.

There are many studies that employ "historical thinking" with more of a learning psychology orientation, as was pioneered by British educational psychologists in the 1970s and popularised by Sam Wineburg (2001) in the United States. While "historical consciousness" may be more oriented towards cultural studies and memory, its origins are more linked to German critical historiography, fundamentally due to the work of Rüsen. His influence has progressively grown in other European and Latin American countries and has become popular in the English-speaking world, thanks to the work of Seixas (2017), among others.

This book originated from the project entitled "HistoryLab for European Civic Engagement", funded by the KA226 Erasmus + project for the improvement of digital competencies in higher education. The aim of our project was to put forward a proposal to bring together the two key concepts of historical thinking and historical consciousness via a consortium of six institutions: the University of Porto (Portugal), the University of Bologna (Italy), the University of Amsterdam (the Netherlands), the University of Malmö (Sweden), the University of Helsinki (Finland), and the University of Murcia (Spain), which would coordinate the project.

Following the Covid-19 pandemic, certain needs of history education, observed over the last decade (Miralles et al., 2019), have been exacerbated. First of all, there is a clear need for a methodological change, integrating active learning methods, digital resources and emerging technologies (Colomer et al., 2018; Cózar & Sáez, 2016; Gómez et al., 2020). Traditionally, history classes in secondary education have been spaces where the most successful students adopt the ways of reading, memorising, thinking, and writing demanded by the teacher (Nokes, 2010 and 2017). Faced with this traditional image of history classes, the aim was to promote an alternative model to enable students to interpret and use information appropriately. In this model, knowledge is seen as a construction based on real social problems and with interdisciplinary approaches. Active learning methods and the capacity to handle and evaluate digital resources play a key role in bringing about a far-reaching change in the globalised and hyperconnected society of the 21st century.

Secondly, there is a need for a multicultural approach to the history of Europe, based on inclusion and social and gender equality, far removed from dogmatic narratives. Teachers must change their conception of why and to what end they teach history (Seixas & Morton, 2013). This approach combines civic education, historical consciousness, and controversial social issues (Rüsen, 2012 and 2015). It is a perspective which promotes citizen participation via reasoning and reflection. This need to fight against manipulative and hateful discourse via argumentation and the critical analysis of sources has become more evident since the beginning of the Covid-19 pandemic. One of the aims of this approach is to avoid fake news and to develop learning based on reflection concerning historical evidence and sources (Fogo et al., 2019). Secondary education students should also be aware of the origin of social inequalities and the fight for equality.

Therefore, the proposal put forward in this book addresses, on the one hand, the need for a change in the epistemological skills of history teachers and, on the other, the need for a far-reaching change in terms of methodology and contents (Gómez & Miralles, 2016). The social and educational value of European heritage is examined in order to help bring about this epistemological change in the teaching of history. Topics which are more social in nature and more relevant for students must be addressed in the classroom with the aim of motivating them to learn about our history and our cultural heritage. This learning should aim to bring about a greater degree of civic commitment with European democratic values (Carretero et al., 2017; Counsell et al., 2016; Metzger & Harris, 2018; Sandwell & Heyking, 2014).

How is this book structured?

The chapters of this book have been written by 37 scholars from 11 universities and six different countries. The book is divided into two parts. The first deals with approaches to the teaching of history in the 21st century. These chapters enable teachers to understand the methodological tools necessary for introducing the cross-cutting issues proposed in the second part of the book into the classroom.

This first part consists of five chapters. The first, written by Ramón López Facal (University of Santiago de Compostela) and Daniel Schugurensky (Arizona State University) poses the question of how history education can contribute towards a democratic citizenship. In response to this question, the authors address the evolution of history teaching from the nation as a historical subject to the study of society and the common people. In an attempt to move beyond traditional teaching models, these authors propose possible pedagogical approaches based on multiculturality, equality, and the construction and development of democracy.

Historical thinking has become a central concept in the teaching of history in the 21st century. The second chapter, written by Cosme Jesús Gómez Carrasco (University of Murcia) and Jorge Sáiz Serrano (University of Valencia), addresses its theoretical origins, its main points of academic reference, and how proposals have been developed in different countries and research groups. The chapter contains a bibliometric analysis of research on history education which has employed historical thinking as a keyword. The results show the increase in such studies, a greater pedagogical focus in recent years, and the main points of reference.

In this globalised and hyperconnected society the use of digital resources is essential for the teaching of history. The third chapter, written by Juan Carlos Colomer Rubio and Anaclet Pons Pons (University of Valencia), explores two specific issues: Changes in the teaching of history as a result of the present-day online society and the different digital resources employed in the classroom and the problems which may arise from their use.

One of the preoccupations of current research on history education is students' comprehension of the narrative structure of the past. The chapter by Stéphane Lévesque (University of Ottawa) explores the notion of narrative competence in an attempt to understand what perspective can be offered to education by the study of narrative in history. The objective is to explain the need for including the narrative dimension if teachers want their students to develop an understanding and more powerful uses of the past in order to guide their daily lives.

The chapter by Sergio Sampedro-Martín, Elisa Arroyo-Mora, José María Cuenca-López, and Myriam J. Martín-Cáceres (University of Huelva) analyses the links between heritage education and controversial issues, ecosocial education, and citizen education. The authors suggest that heritage is an ideal framework for developing educational experiences for initial teacher training.

The second part of the book presents ten cross-cutting issues of the history of Europe which allow for the development of a different model of teaching. This proposal was evaluated by 17 experts in research on history and history education. The overall evaluation of the proposal was positive in terms of relevance, clarity, and sufficiency. Given the positive evaluation of the judges and their qualitative proposals, the following issues were put forward:

1 Landscapes, agriculture, peasants, and environment in the history of Europe.
2 The social and economic impact of technological revolutions in Europe.
3 The rural and urban worlds in Europe.
4 Family, daily life, and social inequality in Europe.
5 Power and powers in the history of Europe.
6 Under a cloak of terror: violence and armed conflict in Europe.
7 Persecuted by justice and powers.
8 Women and the change for gender equality in Europe.

9 Travels and travellers: economic, social, and cultural connections.
10 Churches and religions in Europe.

In addition, the committee of experts made a series of recommendations which made it possible to address these issues from a civic and social perspective, which, it is hoped, has been followed in this book:

- Communicative language has been used.
- Each topic ends with educational objectives or a proposal for new educational approaches.
- At the end of each topic, there is a list of key bibliographic references, websites, and digital resources to find out more about the topic in question.
- A multicultural approach has been taken to the language employed, along with the idea of bottom-up history. In other words, an attempt has been made to escape from Eurocentrism (demonstrating the interconnections and reciprocities with Muslim culture, Atlantic connections, etc.), presenting it over the course of time, not merely from the present-day perspective.
- The topics have been contextualised on a temporal and chronological level.
- The topics have been proposed from different areas of Europe, comparing and presenting the contents simultaneously.
- Those "forgotten" by history, who do not normally appear in most textbooks, have been taken into consideration when writing this book.

Note

1 This chapter is a result of projects "HistoryLab for European Civic Engagement: open e-Toolkit to train History Teachers on Digital Teaching and Learning", funded by SEPIE on call ERASMUS + KA226 [2020–1-ES01-KA226-HE-095430], and research project PID2020–113453RB-I00, funded by Agencia Estatal de Investigación of Spain (AEI/10.13039/501100011033).

References

Carretero, M., Berger, S., & Grever, X. (Eds). (2017). *Palgrave handbook of research in historical culture and education* (pp. 59–72). London: Palgrave McMillan

Clark, A., & Grever, M. (2018). Historical consciousness: Conceptualizations and educational applications. In S. A. Meltzer & L. M. Harris (Eds.), *The Wiley international handbook of history teaching and learning* (pp. 177–201). Arizona: Wiley.

Colomer, J. C., Sáiz, J., & Bel, J. C. (2018). Competencia digital en futuros docentes de Ciencias Sociales en Educación Primaria: Análisis desde el modelo TPACK. *Educatio Siglo XXI, 36*(1), 107–128. https://doi.org/10.6018/j/324191

Counsell, C., Burn, K., & Chapman, A. (2016). *MasterClass in history education. Transforming teaching and learning.* London: Bloomsbury.

Cózar, R., & Sáez, J. M. (2016). Game-based learning and gamification in initial teacher training in the social sciences: An experiment with MinecraftEdu. *International Journal of Educational Technology in Higher Education, 13*(2), 1–11. https://doi.org/10.1186/s41239-016-0003-4

Epstein, T., & Salinas, C. S. (2018). Research methodologies in history education. In S. A. Metzger & L. M. Harris (Eds.), *The Wiley international handbook of history teaching and learning* (pp. 61–92). Arizona: Wiley.

Fogo, B., Reisman, A., & Breakstone, J. (2019). Teacher adaptation of document-based history curricula: Results of the reading like a historian curriculum-use survey. *Journal of Curriculum Studies*, 51(1), 62–83. https://doi.org/10.1080/00220272.2018.1550586.

Fontana, J. (2013). *Europa ante el espejo*. Madrid: Planeta.

Gómez, C. J., & Miralles, P. (2016). Historical skills in compulsory education: Assessment, inquiry based-strategies and students' argumentation. *Journal of New Approaches in Educational Research*, 5(2), 139–146. https://doi.org/10.7821/naer.2016.7.172.

Gómez, C. J., Monteagudo, J., Moreno, J. R., & Sainz, M. (2020). Evaluation of a gamification and flipped-classroom program used in teacher training: Perception of learning and outcome. *PLoS One*, 15(7), e0236083. https://doi.org/10.1371/journal.pone.0236083

Grever, M., Peltzer, B., & Haydn, T. (2011). High school students' views on history. *Journal of Curriculum Studies*, 43(2), 207–229.doi:10.1080/00220272.2010.542832

Lévesque, S., & Clark, P. (2018). Historical thinking: Definitions and educational applications. In S. A. Meltzer & L. M. Harris (Eds.), *The Wiley international handbook of history teaching and learning* (pp. 119–148). Arizona: Wiley.

Metzger, S. A., & Harris, L. M. (Eds.). (2018). *The Wiley international handbook of history teaching and learning*. Arizona: Wiley.

Miralles, P., Gómez, C. J., & Monteagudo, J. (2019). Perceptions on the use of ICT resources and mass-media for the teaching of History. A comparative study among future teachers of Spain-England. *Educación XX1*, 22 (2), 187–211. https:/doi.org/10.5944/educXX1.21377

Nokes, J. D. (2010). Observing literacy practices in history education classrooms. *Theory and Research in Social Education*, 38, 515, e544.

Nokes, J. D. (2017). Historical reading and writing in secondary school classrooms. In M. Carretero, S. Berger & M. Grever (Eds.), *Palgrave handbook of research in historical culture and education* (pp. 553–572). London: Palgrave.

Reisman, A. (2012). "Reading like a historian": A document-based history curriculum intervention in urban high schools. *Cognition and Instruction*, 30(1), 86–112. doi:10.1080/07370008.2011.634081

Rüsen, J. (2012). Tradition: A principle of historical sense-generation and its logic and effect in historical culture. *History and Theory*, 51(4), 45–59.doi:10.1111/j.1468-2303.2012.00646.x

Rüsen, J. (2015). *Teoria da história. Uma teoria da história como ciência*. Curitiba (Brazil): Universidade Federal do Paraná.

Sandwell, R., & Heyking, A. V. (Eds.). (2014). *Becoming a history teacher* (pp. 60–74). Toronto: University of Toronto

Seixas, P. (2017). Historical consciousness and historical thinking. In M. Carretero, M. Grever & S. Berger (Eds), *Palgrave handbook of research in historical culture and education* (pp. 59–72). London: Palgrave McMillan.

Seixas, P., & Morton, T. (2013). *The big six historical thinking concepts*. Toronto: Nelson Education.

Wilschut, A. (2011). *Images of times. The role of a historical consciousness of time in learning history*. Charlotte: IAP.

Wineburg, S. (2001). *Historical thinking and other unnatural acts: Charting the future of teaching the past*. Philadelphia, PA: Temple University Press.

Wineburg, S. (2018). *Why learn history (When it is already in your phone)*. Chicago: UCP.

PART I
Teaching approaches on history education

1
HISTORY EDUCATION AND DEMOCRACY[1]

Ramón López Facal and Daniel Schugurensky

Introduction

Since its origins, history education has been associated with the will of the elites to promote the allegiance of the population to their political project. Educational systems were established in the 19th century partly to contribute to the consolidation of the emerging nation-states that were built on the ruins of the Ancient Regime. For a long time school curricula and textbooks maintained this logic, which was also influenced by historicism and historiographical positivism. This started to change by the second half of the 20th century when these trends had already been widely questioned and replaced by academic historiography. The changes in history education in the second half of the 20th century were related to cultural and sociopolitical changes that took place after the Second World War, on the one hand, and to the new historiographic approaches that questioned historicism, on the other. Today, with the multiple challenges posed by the ascendance of autocratic regimes in many parts of the world, it is relevant to discuss the role of history education in promoting more democratic societies.

This is a timely issue. While history education can be used to reinforce divisions, it can also contribute to promoting democracy and peace. It has been argued that current threats to democracy are closely related to the distortion or negation of historical facts and events and the emphasis on one-sided national historical narratives (Bentrovato & Schulze, 2016). The Council of Europe (2021) noted that the manipulation of the past is facilitated by inadequate historical knowledge and understanding, limited ability to reflect on the production of historical knowledge, and difficulties to distinguish inaccurate accounts from research and scholarship. Teachers can play a key role in developing these capacities among students. Unfortunately, a recent Global Survey of Teachers (UNESCO, 2021) revealed that almost half of them reported difficulties to teach issues related to tolerance, human

DOI: 10.4324/9781003289470-3

rights, and cultural diversity. According to UNESCO, these challenges are often the result of lack of historical knowledge, cultural understanding, and appropriate methodologies.

This chapter is organized in four sections. It begins with an overview of some of the new perspectives in the study of history and their relationship with changes in history teaching and with other social sciences. Next, it describes the main trends in history education theory and practice during the 20th century. The third section compares two approaches to teaching education. On the one hand is the traditional model of history education based on a teacher-centered pedagogy, rote memorization, and a master narrative that emphasizes the 'official story' of nation-states. On the other hand, the democratic model is student-centered and inquiry-based, emphasizes critical reflection, includes primary source investigation, does not shy away from controversial issues, and strives to create a more democratic school climate. This model invites students to express their perspectives and rethink national narratives and helps them to recognize their contexts, attain historical consciousness and intercultural competencies, and acquire democratic values and dispositions. The last section of the chapter provides a summary and outlines the key features of a history education that nurtures the development of informed, critical, engaged, and caring citizens that understand the origins and evolution of today's problems and can apply the lessons from the past to think about the future and build a better world. In this regard, history education is inextricably linked with citizenship education.

The historical subject throughout time: from the nation-state to the common people

During the 19th century, in Europe and the United States of America, there was a spectacular growth of historical studies interested in explaining the processes by which states were consolidated as nations. The subject of historical research was the nation-state as the center of power. The past constituted a process that served to justify its existence, highlight its achievements, and describe the wrongs committed by other countries, especially those considered historical enemies. The processes of nationalization have been extensively studied. Beyond some nuances and differences between countries, there is a broad consensus about the significant impact of the expansion of schooling in the efforts towards the widespread adoption of the official language of each nation-state. Allegiance to the nation-state relied heavily on history teaching, which was complemented by the media, literature, monuments, compulsory military service, and a series of rituals and symbols like civic commemorations, flags, anthems, oaths, and loyalty songs. The effectiveness of these policies and practices was evidenced in the massive patriotic mobilization in armed conflicts at the end of the 19th century and the beginning of the 20th century. The nationalist exaltation and the warmongering enthusiasm of the civilian population had catastrophic human, material, and moral consequences.

But something had begun to change. By the early 20th century, the idea that the subjects of historical research should be extended to broader sectors of society and culture became more widespread among academics. It was also accepted that such research should incorporate empirical methods and interdisciplinary studies. The consequences of the two world wars (1914–18 and 1939–45) led to the loss of prestige of nationalist historical narratives (brought to its climax by fascism) and to the abandonment of historicism in the academic world and eventually in educational historiography. During the Cold War the geopolitical division in two opposing blocs generated changes in the identities of citizens.

Indeed, while in the 19th and early 20th centuries nation-states had constructed a narrative about the past to assert an identity against a neighboring country (conceptualized as the secular enemy that threatened the national interest), during the Cold War the old 'secular enemies' became allies. In that context, it was necessary to build a new shared identity. The nation as a historical subject was hardly operative in the new geopolitical reality, and transnational (e.g. 'common' cultural aspects in Western societies) and local (e.g. cultural identities of specific territories) historical studies emerged. At the same time, Marxism was adopted as a conceptual framework by historical studies that analyzed long-term social and economic processes, the dysfunctions of capitalism, and the obstacles to achieve social justice, equality, personal emancipation, and the enjoyment of rights and freedoms. These studies were characterized by an interpretation of history that used an evolutionary explanatory logic (progress occurring through identifiable stages), social criticism, and, along the lines of the Feuerbach thesis, the historian's commitment to contribute to social change. There was also a growing concern for disadvantaged groups, for a history made 'from below' (people's history), and for an egalitarian ethical horizon. This influence was broad, plural, and diffuse. In this tradition, grand explanatory macro-theories coexisted with postmodern studies, ethnographic approaches, and discourse analyses, to name a few. Research topics emphasized issues related to structures and dynamics of social reproduction, hegemony, power, social movements, and cultural, social, political, and economic transformation, among others. Feminism provided the analytical category of gender and contributed to a more inclusive interpretation of history. Environmentalism increased interest in the history of the relations between humans and nature and ecological issues. World History helped to overcome ethnocentric interpretations and the limitations of national histories, and post-colonialism criticized historiographical colonialism and reclaimed non-Western cultural contributions to the history of humanity.

In the 21st century the acceleration of globalization processes is affecting economic, social, and cultural relations in an unprecedented scale. The Internet, social networks, and video, podcast, and image distribution platforms are changing the way history is made, researched, and communicated. Moreover, in the last decade many countries have experienced an antidemocratic turn, a phenomenon also known as democratic erosion, democratic deconsolidation, democratic backsliding, democratic decline, democratic recession, and democratic decay. The erosion of the democratic project is related to growing inequalities, increasing polarization, corruption, the effectiveness of fake news in manipulating social behavior, and the success of authoritarian leaders in exploiting discontent, uncertainty, and anger (Csaky, 2021; Foa & Mounk, 2017; Levitsky & Ziblatt, 2018). The Covid-19 pandemic has added a spread of xenophobia, hatred, racism, and scapegoating foreigners and minorities.

In summary, during the last century historiography has evolved in parallel with changes in society and with the problems, concerns, and aspirations of each particular period. An important turning point took place in mid-20th century as the two world wars led to a rethinking of history from a more inclusive perspective, leaving nations behind as the priority historical subject. The struggles for social justice and for the extension of rights and freedoms was related to the consideration of ordinary people (who had been ignored or marginalized in prior historical accounts) as bona fide historical subjects. This and other developments have influenced changes in history education.

Educational research and history education in the 20th century

Many of the social and cultural changes discussed in the previous section have also influenced educational theories and practices. Throughout the 20th century, new pedagogical proposals based on principles of child development and experiential learning have emerged as alternatives to the traditional model based on the mere transmission of information codified by adults to be memorized by students. Most methodological innovations advocated by early progressive educators (e.g. Dewey, Montessori) promoted an active participation of students and learning opportunities based on experimentation, inquiry, dialogue, and cooperation. This was eventually complemented with the significance influence of Piaget's contributions to cognitive psychology, the international spread of Vygotsky's studies on developmental psychology, Bruner's learning theory, and Ausubel's constructivism. At the same time, there was a growth of the international movement for democratic schools and the widespread diffusion of critical pedagogy, an approach that connected broader issues of social justice and democracy with teaching-learning processes (e.g. Freire, Apple, Giroux).

In this context, new pedagogical proposals in social studies and history teaching were developed. Stenhouse (1975, 1983) attempted to respond to the low interest of working-class students in the humanities and social sciences. In doing this, instead of focusing on learning outcomes, he concentrated first on the training and engagement of teachers. His proposal materialized in the *Humanities Curriculum Project* (HCP). He stressed the right of underserved students to learn what society considers desirable, the connection between school knowledge and extracurricular experiences, and dialogue as a method to collaborate, reflect, and improve teacher education programs and student learning. His main goal was to develop civic values that help to address some of the tensions of multicultural societies.

Social studies teaching had an important development in the United States and Canada in the second half of the 20th century. Its reception in England, together with the dissemination of the *New History* that incorporated the association between history and social sciences, favored the renewal of history teaching (Domínguez, 2015). To overcome the limitations of traditional rote teaching, Jones (1973) proposed applying active educational practices so that students learn to use the skills of historians and help them think historically. At the same time, several British researchers conducted studies on history teaching to overcome the dichotomy between teaching history as a 'body' of knowledge and as a 'way' of knowledge, seeking a more balanced and integrative approach between substantive concepts (historical knowledge) and procedural skills related to the study of history. Some of these studies, making use of the contributions from cognitive psychology and philosophy of education, explored K-12 students' conceptions about evidence, causal explanations, historical empathy, and eventually added dimensions related to substantive historical knowledge. Based on those studies, by the turn of the century Shemilt (2000) considered that British schoolchildren lacked a chronological framework of historical evolution to contextualize the topics they studied and to be able to relate the present with the past and the future.

In Germany, philosophy had a greater influence than psychology on history teaching and particularly on the development of the concept of historical consciousness. One of the most influential scholars on this line of inquiry was arguably J. Rüsen, who in turn was influenced by historians of the Bielefeld school and shared the ethical concerns of the second Frankfurt school (e.g. Horkheimer, Adorno, Habermas, Benjamin). One of the most his important contributions was the distinction between historical memory and historical consciousness: The former focuses on the past, while the latter uses the past to analyze the present and interpret the future. Rüsen (2004 and 2017) argued that the main competence for the development of historical consciousness is the capacity to orient oneself in time in relation to practical life. For him, historical consciousness can be conceptualized as a synthesis of moral and temporal consciousness.

Although Rüsen's model has been criticized for not taking sufficiently into account students' ideas about history or for its four-stage model of progression in historical awareness (Lee, 2004; Grever & Adriaansen, 2019), it had a significant impact on the theory, research, and practice of history teaching. Regarding the latter, he argued that the main task of history teaching should be equipping students with historical awareness, which in turn would help them to develop useful orientations for their future. In short, Rüsen considered the relevance of acquiring historical knowledge in the context of a larger project that focused on civic values aimed at building a more robust democracy.

In North America, the concept of historical thinking had several parallels with the German idea of historical consciousness (Seixas, 2017). Historical thinking refers to the capacity to identify, analyze, and evaluate historical developments and distinguish causation and correlation and long-term and proximate causes. It is also about understanding context, identifying continuity and change, and drawing lessons from the past to better comprehend the present.

In the United States, extensive research was carried out on the practical aspects of history teaching. Many of these studies focused on methodological approaches that took into account the work of 'expert' and 'amateur' historians. Special attention has been paid to the use of sources and to the historical context and particularly to the strategies to establish meaningful relationships between the familiar present and an unfamiliar past in order to encourage students to think historically. Some of these studies (Wineburg, 2000, 2001; Wineburg et al., 2016) found that students' views of history are primarily influenced by the family and the media, while the school plays an insignificant role in the development of historical awareness. This represents a major challenge for history teaching.

Similar concerns and lines of inquiry have been developed in Canada by the Historical Thinking Project at the Center for the Study of Historical Consciousness. Led by Peter Seixas, the main goal of this project was to promote a critical historical competence for the 21st century. Within this framework, an international conference on historical consciousness was held at the dawn of the 21st century. The main insights of that symposium were published in a book edited by Seixas in 2004. This was a pivotal moment because it was the first confluence between the progressive traditions of historical thought and the pedagogical proposals to history education advanced in Germany, England, and North America. Current research in history teaching is largely build on these three pillars.

History education today: two approaches

Currently, a wide range of approaches to history education are implemented in schools. For the sake of simplicity, they could be boiled down to two main models. At one end of the spectrum is a 'traditional model' with a conservative curriculum and a teacher-centered methodology. At the other end of the spectrum is a 'progressive model' that is student-centered and has a democratic ethos. In today's history education, conservative and democratic approaches coexist with a preponderance of one or the other depending on the social, political, cultural, and educational contexts in which they operate.

Before we delve into the models, three caveats are pertinent. First, we use the term 'traditional' cautiously, as we recognize that many 'old' models (like the Socratic method) have many progressive elements. Second, we acknowledge that in between these two paradigms there are many models and variations. Third, in the real world of schools these models are not necessarily implemented in pure form, and it may be possible to observe combinations, such as a democratic content with a teacher-centered pedagogy or a conservative content with a student-centered pedagogy.

The traditional model

The traditional model cannot be isolated from the fact that schools are 19th century institutions that served the needs of dominant groups in the industrial era and in many ways resemble the world of factories. Indeed, during the last century, social, technological, cultural, and economic changes have affected most of the world's population faster than at any previous time. Institutions and habits have not changed at the same speed. If teachers or students from the late 19th century could visit our world today, they would probably be astonished by skyscrapers, self-driving cars, airplanes, space travel, computers, televisions, and cell phones. They would also be amazed by the level of globalization, advances in civil and political rights, the 8-hour day, or increases in life expectancy. Their surprise would probably be less if they walked into a classroom. From the arrangement of objects to the interactions among teachers and students, changes have paled in comparison with the previous ones.

In terms of teacher-student relations in the classroom, the traditional model is rooted in what Sartre (1947) called 'digestive' pedagogy (a metaphor to suggest that knowledge is 'fed' by the teacher to the students to "fill them out") and Freire (1970) called 'banking education' (that is, knowledge is 'deposited' in the minds of the students). In this model, the teacher takes the central role, which consists of transmitting knowledge, following the textbook, and examining students. Students are expected to take a passive role, memorizing the information provided by the teacher. The teacher seldom considers the context, experience, prior knowledge, or perspectives of the students.

In terms of curricular content, the traditional model follows a linear and teleological chronological narrative. It spreads a monolithic interpretation of the past in the form of a 'master narrative' that emphasizes the accepted canon and excludes alternative interpretations. It uses superficial criteria to assess the past: It considers in a positive light those protagonists and events that helped the growth and consolidation of the political project of the dominant groups in their own nation and in a negative light the antagonists that weakened it. It is a banal story of 'good guys' and 'bad guys' that opposes the superior interest of an abstract entity called 'the nation' (not necessarily of the people that make it up) to 'the others', be they the other nations or the so-called 'internal enemies'. It rarely contemplates – even less celebrates – the diversity of interests among citizens.

In the traditional model, the emphasis is placed on the memorization of names, dates, and battles. Textbooks describe with detail the lives and feats of certain historical actors who are exalted as heroes, while those figures who represented different perspectives are ignored or reviled. This model, quite widespread in non-democratic political regimes, uses education to justify the status quo, indoctrinate students, and thwart social change. In these conservative master narratives, history education recurringly uses basic plots (like struggles against foreign enemies) to build national identity and develop a thread to articulate a glorious past with the justification of the present. These dominant narratives, complemented by monuments, rituals, museums, and discourses are eventually naturalized and internalized by students and teachers and hence seldom examined and challenged (Wertsch, 2002; Brescó de Luna & van Alphen, 2022; Guerrero-Romera et al., 2022). To minimize the probabilities that educators question the 'official story', in many jurisdictions the dominant groups restrict the autonomy of teachers through different mechanisms like imposing a rigid curriculum, emphasizing the weight of standardized tests, and micromanaging what teachers can say in the classroom. Beyond the school curriculum, conservative discourses are also present in a myriad of messages that endorse projects of cultural homogenization and exclusion, using xenophobic frames to recover a uniform ethnic identity that never existed.

The democratic model

The democratic model aims at nurturing knowledgeable and competent citizens who can address current issues, anticipate future problems, and partake in an inclusive society. It also aims at promoting more democratic classrooms, schools, and communities. The model incorporates relevant contributions from other social sciences and draws on constructivist approaches that understand learning as an active process. It builds on a long tradition of democratic schools, which includes experiences such as Yasnaya Polyana in Russia, Summerhill in England, Hull House and Sudbury Valley Schools in the United States, Modern School in Spain and the United States, Dom Sierot in Poland, Tolstoy Farm in South Africa, Hermitage School and Cooperative School in France, Colonia Gorky in the Soviet Union, and Escola Ciudadana in Brazil. These and other schools were promoted by many progressive educators like Tolstoy, Neill, Addams, Ferrer i Guardia, Goldman, Gandhi, Dewey, Decroly, Korczak, Makarenko, Freinet, and Freire.

In the democratic model of history teaching, students learn to think historically using the skills of historical knowledge like use of sources, causal analysis, contextualized explanations, capacity to make inferences, and ability to discriminate what is relevant from what is accessory. However, this model is not limited to the acquisition of technical knowledge. It also includes an ethical horizon that focuses on developing a historical consciousness that relates the problems of the present with the past to extract lessons for building a desirable future. The democratic model of history teaching of the 21st century is not indifferent to social dynamics like globalization, interculturality, plurality of identities, migration, and the like, and to enduring social problems such as inequality, poverty, global warming, violence, racism, sexism, homophobia, pandemics, and authoritarianism, *inter alia*. An analysis of the historical evolution of these phenomena is crucial to a better understanding of the problems and possible solutions. A democratic approach to history education acknowledges that a plurality of identities has always existed in all societies and cultures. It also recognizes that contemporary societies are the result of complex historical transformations that included oppression, conquest, and colonization. In short, the democratic approach to history education can be summarized in ten principles:

1 History teaching has an ethical dimension. It is part of an educational project aimed at building fairer and more sustainable societies. It assumes that democratic societies require informed, responsible, critical, engaged, and caring

citizens. Hence, history teaching is oriented towards developing citizens who espouse democratic values and principles.

2 History education includes historical knowledge (memory of the past) and historical consciousness (ability to analyze and interpret ruptures and continuities of the past to think and act about the future). The analysis of the past can provide insights to understand current problems and conflicts. The historical analysis of past changes (including causes, mechanisms, and consequences) is relevant for prospective studies and helps to consider different scenarios and alternatives for action. Of course, this does not preclude curiosity-driven learning.

3 History education is student-centered and emphasizes pedagogical strategies like problem-posing education, project-based learning, cooperative learning, oral histories, and visits to museums and other locations to conduct research. Other strategies like simulations, role-playing, and mock trials help students recreate and 'relive' historical episodes through experiential learning and make personal connections. Lectures are not excluded but should be used when appropriate.

4 The pedagogical strategy does not rely on a linear and decontextualized chronological narrative from the past to the present but connects the past to current social, environmental, economic, political, and cultural problems and its implications for the future. This strategy considers local, national, and global history and establishes relations between spatial and temporal dimensions and between microhistory and macrohistory.

5 Recognizing that societies are increasingly multicultural, diverse, and globalized, history education considers different perspectives, memories, and identities.

6 History education does not shy away from controversial topics, but the pedagogical approach should consider the age of the students and the context. Work on controversial topics can promote deliberative and investigative skills, improve historical knowledge and its relationship with the present and the future, and motivate students to learn more.

7 History education is inclusive and contemplates rational and emotional dimensions in the learning process. While students have different abilities, needs, and interests, everyone can be motivated and can increase their historical knowledge and historical consciousness.

8 History education nurtures the development of critical literacy to help students distinguish between facts and opinions; analyze the veracity and reliability of information; uncover ideologies, propaganda, and manipulation behind narratives; and identify agendas and silences of different sources.

9 History education uses the concepts and tools of the discipline but also relies on interdisciplinary and transdisciplinary approaches. It also nurtures connections with citizenship education.

10 The main subject of history education is not the providential heroic leader but ordinary people, power relations, and injustice. Special attention is paid to

historical events and issues omitted in traditional narratives, including groups that suffered oppression, colonial domination, dictatorships, and genocides.

Summary and conclusions

History is not just a simple chronological account of what happened in the past. It also involves critical analyses of what happened based on credible sources and data to build up interpretations. These interpretations communicate explanations that contribute to the understanding of society and can be revised if new evidence is found. The past is not a distant planet. It interwoven with our present. History provides valuable information about changes and continuities through time, the rhythm and intensity of past changes, the mutual influences between different societies, and the relationship between economic, social, political, and cultural factors. Hence, the study of history can provide verified and contextualized stories that can help make more informed, responsible, and conscious decisions today. It can also bring more appreciation for democratic gains of the past and raise concerns about current trends of democratic backsliding.

Democracy is premised on principles of equality, freedom, and participation. It implies the same rights and duties for everyone and assumes the dignity of each person. In some frameworks, this respect should extend to non-human animals and nature. In theory, democratic societies should be incompatible with privileges and exclusion. The democratic project consists of bridging the gap between aspirations and reality. In democratic countries, a tension exists between legal and real democracy and between those who struggle to expand rights and freedoms and those who want to restrict them. Educational systems are not immune to these tensions, and this is reflected in the curriculum, in teaching-learning processes, and in school governance. The emphases and silences of textbooks, the roles of teachers and students in the classroom, or the degree of participation of the educational community in decision-making can vary significantly.

In this context, history education goes hand in hand with citizenship education and with the larger project of building more democratic societies and nurturing human flourishing. This is a process that focuses on the present, draws on the past, and is future-oriented (Guldi & Armitage, 2014; McMahon, 2021). History education helps to understand relationships between causes and consequences and assess to what extent different situations of the present are the outcome of past decisions. Indeed, history education can help to identify which human actions have generated suffering and oppression or promoted well-being and happiness, and this can facilitate the analysis of the potential future impact of current decisions. In this regard, history education facilitates discernment and the ability to create narratives that can be shared with other people. History education can also help students to develop skills to understand which aspects of the past are more relevant than others, considering the depth and breadth of their impact.

To motivate students and increase relevance, history education should start – whenever possible – from situations and problems of the present that directly or indirectly affect the students and their communities. Students can investigate the origins and evolution of these problems over time and reflect together on the lessons for the future. Knowledge of history provides interpretations of the past that are useful to understand the present and, therefore, to guide the decisions of citizens in the future. In short, history education is not only concerned about the past but also with the future. Learning to question the sources of information and to inquire about the ways in which the past is known contributes to developing critical thinking skills that in turn help to understand the impact of current decisions on the future. For history education to help students understand the past and provide them with tools to think the future, it can be more effective when complemented with other areas of knowledge. Humans have formalized knowledge through academic disciplines like history, geography, economics, sociology, political science, and anthropology (just to mention some social sciences), but this structure does not need to be mechanically transferred to schools in the form of isolated subjects. At the end of the day, what matters is to nurture citizens who have a better understanding of the world and engage in nonviolent actions to create more democratic, sustainable, and happier societies.

Note

1 This chapter is a result of project PID2020–113453RB-I00, funded by Agencia Estatal de Investigación of Spain (AEI/10.13039/501100011033).

References

Bentrovato, D., & Schulze, M. (2016). Teaching about a violent past: Revisiting the role of history education in conflict and peace. In D. Bentrovato, V. Korostelina & M. Schulze (Eds.), *History can bite. History education in divided and postwar societies* (pp. 15–30). Göttingen: V&R unipress GmbH.

Brescó de Luna, I., & van Alphen, F. (2022). *Reproducing, rethinking, resisting national narratives: A sociocultural approach to schematic narrative templates*. Charlotte, NC: Information Age Publishing.

Csaky, Z. (2021). *The antidemocratic turn*. London: Freedom House.

Domínguez Castillo, J. (2015). *Pensamiento histórico y evaluación de competencias*. Barcelona: Graó.

Foa, R. S., & Mounk, Y. (2017). The signs of deconsolidation. *Journal of Democracy, 28*(1), 5–15.

Grever M., & Adriaansen, R.-J. (2019). Historical consciousness: the enigma of different paradigms, *Journal of Curriculum Studies, 51*(6), 814–830 https://doi.org/10.1080/00220272.2019.1652937

Guerrero-Romera, C., Sánchez-Ibáñez, R., & Miralles-Martínez, P. (2022). Approaches to history teaching according to a structural equation model. *Frontiers in Education, 7,* 842977. doi: 10.3389/feduc.

Guldi, J., & Armitage, D. (2014). *The history Manifesto*. Cambridge: Cambridge University Press.

Jones, R. B (1973). *Practical approaches to the new history. Suggestions for the improvement of classroom method*. London: Hutchinson

Lee, P. (2004). Understanding history. In P. Seixas (Ed.), *Theorizing historical consciousness* (pp. 129–164). Toronto: University of Toronto Press.

Levitsky, S., & Ziblatt, D. (2018). *How democracies die* (pp. 76–78). British Columbia: United States: Crown.

McMahon, D. (2021). The history of the humanities and human flourishing. In L. Tay & J. Pawelski (Eds.), *The Oxford handbook of the positive humanities*. Oxford: Oxford University Press.

Rüsen, J. (2004). Historical consciousness: Narrative structure, moral function, and ontogenetic development. In P. Seixas (Ed.), *Theorizing historical consciousness* (pp. 63–85). Toronto: University of Toronto Press.

Rüsen, J. (2017). *Evidence and meaning: A theory of historical studies*. New York, NY: Berghahn Books.

Sartre, J. P. (1947). *Une idee fundamentals de la phenomenologie de Husserl: L'intentionalite*. Paris: Situations I.

Seixas, P. (Ed.). (2004). *Theorizing historical consciousness*. Toronto: University of Toronto Press.

Seixas, P. (2017). Historical consciousness and historical thinking. In M. Carretero, S. Berger & M. Grever (Eds.), *Palgrave handbook of research in historical culture and education*. London: Palgrave Macmillan.

Shemilt, D. (2000) The Caliph's coin: The currency of Narrative frameworks in history teaching. In P. N. Sterans, P. Seixas, & S. S. Wineburg (Eds.), *Knowing, teaching and learning history: National and International Perspectives* (pp. 83–101). New York, NY: New York University Press.

Stenhouse, L. (1975). *An introduction to curriculum research and development*. London: Heinemann Educational.

Stenhouse, L. (1983\1970) *The humanities curriculum project: An introduction* (revised by J. Rudduck). Norwich: School of Education, University of East Anglia, for Schools Council.

The Council of Europe (2021). *History education can put democracies back on track*. Strasbourg: Observatory of Teaching History in Europe.

UNESCO. (2021). *Teachers have their say: Motivation, skills and opportunities to teach education for sustainable development and global citizenship*. Paris: Unesco.

Wertsch, J. V. (2002). *Voices of collective remembering*. Cambridge: Cambridge University Press.

Wineburg, S. (2000). Making historical sense. In P. N. Stearns, P. Seixas, & S. S. Wineburg (Eds.) *Knowing, teaching, and learning history* (pp. 306–325). New York, NY: New York University Press.

Wineburg, S. (2001). *Historical thinking and other unnatural acts: Charting the future of teaching the past*. Philadelphia, PA: Temple University Press.

Wineburg, S., McGrew, S., Breakstone, J., & Ortega, T. (2016). *Evaluating information: The cornerstone of civic online reasoning*. Retrieved from http://purl.stanford.edu/fv751yt5934

2
THE ORIGIN AND DEVELOPMENT OF RESEARCH INTO HISTORICAL THINKING

A key concept in the renewal of history education[1]

Cosme Jesús Gómez Carrasco and Jorge Sáiz Serrano

Historical thinking and historical consciousness in the field of history education

Over the course of recent decades, theories and research on the teaching and learning of history have attributed a key role to the concepts of historical thinking and historical consciousness as two dominant paradigms, although there is not one single tradition (Gómez et al., 2022; Lévesque & Clark, 2018). The concept of historical thinking converges, albeit vaguely, with that of historical thinking (Seixas, 2016a, 2016b, 2017a, 2017b; Köber, 2021; Kölbl & Konrad, 2015). Historical thinking makes reference to the use of historical sources and to the skills employed by the historian, whereas historical consciousness is linked more to the social role of history and its public uses in relation to memory, identity and moral education. Both concepts share points in common, although they also differ in their conceptualisations from different criteria. This depends on how the role of history is approached as a form of knowledge for society as a whole and from a more cultural and philosophical perspective (historical consciousness) or for the field of education from a psychological and cognitive perspective (historical thinking). This is also the case depending on the traditions and nomenclatures employed by academics in different countries, with greater emphasis being placed on the term "historical consciousness" in the German field in comparison with "historical thinking", which is more common in the English-speaking world.

As the main point in common in the field of education, historical thinking converges with the concept of historical consciousness when what is required is an active and skills-based dimension of school history linked to real life and the community. Learning history should extend beyond the memorisation of contents and narratives of the social past with the purpose of providing an example of civic and patriotic behaviour or mere cultural education. It should also include learning about what historical knowledge is, how it is represented and given meaning and how it can be used for guidance in the present and in the future. This implies, therefore, an initiation both in the construction of historical knowledge (making history) and in its use (using history) with the aim of understanding social reality, exercising civil rights and knowing how to interpret the elements of historical culture which are present in public life. Ultimately it implies acquiring a way of thinking historically and a historical consciousness which are neither natural nor intuitive but which require a process of instruction.

However, there are also some clear elements which separate historical thinking from historical consciousness. Indeed, it could be said that one is part of the other. The theories on what historical consciousness is from the point of view of the theory or philosophy of history, according to its most widespread interpretation in the German field (that of Jorn Rüsen, 2004 and 2005), include a global sociocultural approach to the role and function of history as a form of knowledge in contemporary societies. This is an approach which takes on different forms or dimensions if the matrix designed by Rüsen, which has been improved upon and adapted by Seixas and Lévesque (Seixas, 2016b; Lévesque, 2016; Lévesque & Croteau, 2020) and commented on by Körber (Körber, 2021), is taken into account. On the one hand is its disciplinary or scientific way of gaining knowledge of the social past (historiography), while on the other hand is its educational aspect of learning in the school context (history education). Last of all is its popular or collective way of remembering or using the social past in collective memory (historical culture and public uses of history). From this global perspective, invoking historical consciousness as an objective of learning would include learning to understand the presence of the past in daily life, participating in the historical and memorial culture of present-day plural societies and knowing how to interpret the existing public uses of history. This dimension also includes the learning of the necessary thinking competencies or skills for using historical information.

Historical thinking: a confluence of traditions for the teaching and learning of history

There are different traditions in academic research when it comes to defining how historical thinking materialises within a series of methodological concepts specific to the subject of history, which can be called second-order, heuristic or meta-concepts, strategic contents, "historical skills" or "historical thinking skills". Based on recent studies of the state of the art (Seixas, 2017b; Lévesque & Clark, 2018; van Boxtel & van Drie, 2018), three broad spheres or schools of research can be differentiated in this regard.

On the one hand is the Anglo-American school, which originated from innovative practices in England which then spread to the United States and Canada. This sphere is more practical and empirical and employs the terminology of *historical thinking*. It has defined certain interrelated historical skills which are linked to the cognitive practice of the work of the historian. On the other hand, there is the

German school, which is more philosophical and theoretical and which employs the term *historical consciousness*. This sphere also defends a historical skills-based model grounded not only in specific cognitive capacities but also in the use of historical information for individual guidance in terms of the present and the future. Last of all, the Dutch sphere must be taken into account. This school advocates the concept of *historical reasoning* as an educational objective, integrating it with a set of historical skills derived from the other models. This coexistence of traditions (England-United States-Canada, Germany and the Netherlands), along with those of other countries such as Australia, Portugal, Brazil and (particularly) Spain (Gómez et al., 2022), means that there is no clear consensus on the skills profile of historical thinking. Indeed, it could even be stated that skills have progressively been defined over time, which is confirmed by an overview of the situation.

The origin of the current conceptualisations of historical thinking lies in England at the end of the 1960s through the 1970s in connection with the confluence of two empirical research approaches to the teaching of history: one in London (under P. Lee and A. Dickinson in the Institute of Education) and another in Leeds (under D. Shemilt in the Schools Council History 13–16 Project, later known as the Schools History Project or SCHP). These two approaches would converge in the 1980s in the Cambridge History Project and, in the 1990s, only in London in the Concepts of History and Teaching Approaches 7–14 (CHATA). All of these initiatives and educational research projects drew from the confluence and influx of theoretical renovations in curricular and cognitive psychology theory (Bruner's structure of academic subjects as a body of knowledge, Hirst's forms of knowledge and Bloom's and Anderson's taxonomy of learning objectives), questionning Piagetian perspectives which limited the progression of children's and adolescents' thinking in the learning of historical contents and concepts. Based on these premises, they questionned the dominant approaches to history education, which focused on the mere transmission of information and the memorisation of contents. In their place, they explicitly advocated innovative practices based on the incorporation of the method, ways of thinking and work of the historian into the everyday tasks in the classroom, confirming children's and adolescents' possibilities for progression in terms of the learning of historical skills and concepts (Lee et al., 1996; Lee & Ashby, 2000; Lee, 2005, 2011; Chapman, 2011a, 2011b).

Thus, certain second-order concepts or specific procedures (such as evidence/proof, causality, time, etc.) came to be favoured over other possible concepts (agency-structure, centre-periphery, etc.). In summary, the conceptual framework defined by English research on historical thinking (Chapman, 2021a; Lee, 2005), which distinguished between substantive or first-order historical knowledge (factual, chronological, context-based) and second-order, meta-historical or disciplinary knowledge (time, causality, change, meaning, proof or evidence and interpretation), was of great importance and opened up the path to an active and skills-based change in the teaching of history. This change was connected to the learning of the necessary intellectual skills for analysing the past and relating it with the problems of the present. History at school was defended as a subject which required understanding rather than the mere memorisation of closed narratives, demonstrating empirical possibilities for the progression of children's learning (between the ages of 7 and 14) in the use and comprehension of second-order concepts directly connected with the knowledge of substantive historical contexts and facts.

Along the same lines of cognitive research into history learning, during the 1990s in the United States, S. Wineburg (1991, 2001) and the group which grew up around him (the Stanford History Education Group), based on the examination techniques of experts and novices (historians and students or teachers), focused on the analysis of historial literacy, i.e., the skills of the reading and writing of history: the examination of historical sources (their reading and analysis, contextualisation, corroboration, cross-checking, selection of evidence) and the production of essays or narratives based thereon (Monte-Sano, 2010; Monte-Sano & De La Paz, 2012; Monte-Sano et al., 2014; Reisman, 2012; Vos & Wiley, 2000; Wineburg et al., 2013; Van Sledrigtht, 2002, 2011; VanSledright & Limón, 2006).

The research carried out by this group made clear progress towards the understanding of the ideas held by adolescents concerning historical evidence and sources, their ability to use multiple sources of information (more recently including digital information [Wineburg, 2018]), their capacity to write analytical and argumentational essays on history and the importance in teacher training of a solid epistemological foundation regarding what historical knowledge is and how it is acquired. The later research of this group is based on the idea that the capacity to find credible information online is necessary for civic commitment and that this need is particularly acute for young people, who often resort to the Internet to learn about social and political issues (Breakstone et al., 2022).

Also in the United States, from a sociocultural perspective, the importance of the historical thinking skills has been defended in terms of citizen education (Barton & Levstik, 2004). Barton and Levstik advocated the learning of historical skills (posing problems, analysing sources and obtaining evidence, building arguments based on evidence, etc.) as one of the four purposes of school history aimed at shaping future citizens for the common good (Barton & Levstik, 2004). Along with this disciplinary or skills-based purpose, they advocated others which referred to certain specific skills: The purpose of collective identification (understanding narratives of the past), the moral purpose (recognising and understanding perspectives of the past and their historicity and any kind of otherness) and, finally, the purpose of exhibition of knowing historical information or culture (understanding personal or collective interests concerning past actions).

This momentum towards the renovation of history education originating from England and the United States also caught on at the end of the 1990s in Canada with the work of P. Seixas at the University of British Columbia. It was here that the Centre for the Study of Historical Consciousness was set up in 2001, from which a key publication (Seixas, 2004) would originate with the participation of international researchers interested in historical thinking and historical consciousness. Furthermore, the Benchmarks of Historical Thinking Project (Seixas, 2006;

Peck & Seixas, 2008), which was later renamed the Historical Thinking Project in 2011, also arose from this centre. Different formulations of historical thinking and its skills came out of this project (Lévesque, 2008; Seixas & Morton, 2013; Seixas, 2017b), which, in its most widespread version, defined the six big concepts of historical thinking: "Historical relevance" (the capacity to establish the meaning and importance of the past from the present), "source and evidence" (the skill of using sources to obtain evidence), "causes and consquences" (the skill of multi-causal explanation), "historical perspective or empathy" (the skill of understanding the historicity of the past and avoiding presentism in a contextualised explanation); "change and continuity" (the understanding of historical time and flexible uses of temporal frameworks) and the "ethical dimension" (the skill of making ethical judgements on the historical past and understanding injustice).

Although the limitation implied by restricting the concept of sources and evidence to primary sources has been pointed out, stating the need to incorporate the understanding of historical interpretations, historiographic productions and secondary sources (Gibson & Peck, 2020), this is an extremely strong conceptual framework for historical thinking. However, it has not been without criticism, be it for its cognitively enlightened universalism and its limited sociocultural validity (more within the West and its specific classroom contexts), for its lack of integral and interrelated formulation of different concepts or its partial disconnection from historical contexts and contents. Such criticisms have either been partially admitted or rebutted (Lévesque & Clark, 2018; Seixas, 2017b). Nonetheless, this proposal represents a skills-based framework which is frankly solid and has great educational value. It has been incorporated into the school history curriculums of Canada's 13 states and into teacher training courses for history education, leading to a productive field of research and materials in teacher training (Sandwell & Heyking, 2014; Gibson & Peck, 2020).

In contrast with this English-speaking (England, United States and Canada) school, the perspective adopted in Germany was different, being less empirical and more theoretical in nature. In Germany, reflections did not derive from psychopedagogical perspectives but from the philosophy of history, placing emphasis on the concept of historical consciousness as the use of the historical past in the present for personal guidance. In this regard, Rüsen's (2004, 2005) conceptualisations played a pivotal role. Therefore, in German research and theorisation, historical thinking is not seen as a goal of education in itself but as one of the goals to be attained in order to achieve an appropriate level of historical consciousness. However, there is an appropriately defined skills-based historical model derived from projects such as the Historical Thinking Competencies in History (the HITCH Project) and the FUER model (the German acronym for Research in and Fostering of Historical Consciousness) developed by A. Körber and other researchers. This model clearly defines five connected "competences" (Kölbl & Konrad, 2015; Körber & Meyer-Hamme, 2015; Körber, 2019, 2021). The first three are procedural in nature: 1) the competence of formulating historical questions (the heuristic skill of questioning problems on the past to be resolved according to contemporary interests or problems or the cultural needs of the present); 2) the methodological competence of history (the capacity to analyse primary and secondary sources [narratives] in order to build and represent historical information or to deconstruct it); 3) the competence of temporal orientation (the capacity to relate information about the past with one's own life or with contemporary life). There are also two global competences: historical subject (the capacity to represent or give meaning to the historical past) and the narrative competence, taken to be the capacity to analyse, build and deconstruct narratives in which all of the previously mentioned competences are specified. This latter competence is seen to be the most important of all.

Taking this conceptual framework as a starting point, three different levels of progression in terms of competences have been defined (Körber, 2021; Körber & Meyer-Hamme, 2015) from the perspective of the construction and deconstruction of historical narratives: the declarative level (the capacity to be aware of and identify these competences), the discursive level (the skill of using them and reflecting on them in a discourse or narrative) and the operational level (the skill of applying them in a complex way and of examining them critically). There can be no doubt that this competence-based German approach has a high degree of theoretical conceptualisation and even guides and influences the curriculum and history assessment in Germany and other countries, as is the case of Sweden (Eliasson et al., 2015; Körber & Meyer-Hamme, 2015). However, it has also received criticism for not converging more clearly with other competence-based frameworks of historical thinking (Bain, 2015). Indeed, its assessment guidelines and models of progression do not make it possible to teach students how to advance in their historical consciousness via historical thinking.

Last of all, the Dutch model, which has an integral perspective, revolves around the concept of historical reasoning (van Drie & van Boxtel, 2008; van Boxtel & van Drie, 2018). This approach is a coherent and powerful conceptual and empirical model for the teaching and learning of history, the main virtue of which is that it succeeds in blending elements and proposals from the Anglo-American and German frameworks. Its starting point is the importance in educational terms of historical reasoning as a key skill in the historical education of students as it enables a personal orientation and the capacity for civic participation in contemporary societies. This model differentiates three types of historical reasoning (continuity and change, causes and competences and differences and similarities) and details six components which are involved within it, integrating both the cognitive-disciplinary route (knowing and making history, which is more characteristic of historical thinking) and the orientation and public use of history (using history, which is more inherent to historical consciousness). These components form six skills which can be described in terms of specific activities expressed orally or in writing: 1) the ability to formulate historical questions and problems (related with an interest in studying history to guide oneself in the past and the present); 2 and 3) the capacity for historical contextualisation and the use of substantive historical concepts and contents (related with historical knowledge which is factual, chronological and of specific contexts); 4) the skill of knowing and using meta-concepts or second-order concepts (related with the knowledge of procedural skills to analyse and interpret historical phenomena and sources and to build evidence-based arguments; and lastly, 5 and 6) the skill of providing arguments and using sources, argumentation and critical analysis (related with epistemological beliefs and the aptitiude to understand the constructed nature of historical knowledge).

Undoubtedly, all of these contributions to historical thinking are fundamental in the renovation of the teaching and learning process of history via a competence-based, applicative and research dimension. This is a way towards the enrichment of the practice of school history teaching; it provides an active learning dimension which is far removed from traditional practices based on memorisation and promoting intellectual skills for the improvement of students' understanding of the social problems of the present and their participation in society as active and democratic citizens. This approach should overcome the false dichotomy between teaching via historical contents (knowing history) and teaching via historical competences (making history), as the two are intrinsically linked (Lee, 2005; VanSledright, 2011). The learning of the skills of historical thinking enriches, but is not opposed to, the learning of historical contents and contexts as the historical skills and historical reasoning are only possible *from* the knowledge and use of substantive (factual, conceptual, chronological, biological, etc.) historical contents. This is demonstrated by the conceptual framework on historical reasoning put forward by van Boxtel and van Drie (2018), which is, without a doubt, one of the most complete presentations which has been presented on this topic in recent years.

Along the same lines of integrating contents and skills, the most recent proposal originating from England on historical thinking and its concepts or methodological skills advocates connecting with the pedagogical conceptualisation of M. Young's "powerful knowledge" (Chapman, 2021b). This is taken to be key school knowledge which extends beyond the traditional curriculum based on contents and the curriculum of key competencies or skills by integrating solid disciplinary knowledge in its double cognitive and epistemological-procedural dimension and in the skills required to teach it in connection with each subject.

Academic production on historical thinking on the Web of Science

In order to gain a better understanding of research trends on historical thinking, an analysis was carried out of academic production on this topic in the field of education on the Web of Science (WoS). In order to compile the dataset, the following selection criteria were established: 1) databases: main collection of the WoS; 2) years of publication: all of the years recorded on the WoS (1979–2022); 3) search field: title, abstract and keywords. Bibliographic searches were carried out on the databases of the core collection of the Web of Science: the Book Citation Index (BCI), the Science Citation Index Expanded (SCI), the Social Sciences Citation Index (SSCI), the Arts & Humanities Citation Index (AHCI) and the Emerging

Sources Citation Index (ESCI). The search words were chosen in such a way that the selection would be focused on research and reflections on historical thinking in the field of education: "Historical Thinking and Education" or "Historical Thinking and Teaching" or "Historical Thinking and Learning" or "Historical Thinking and Student". A total of 341 documents were exported which contained one or more of these words in the title, keywords or abstract.

The analysis was carried out in three phases. In the first phase, descriptive data were extracted in order to quantify the evolution of the most common publications, topics, journals, countries and authors. The R-package bibliometrix v. 1.9.4 (Aria & Cuccurullo, 2017; R version 3.6.3; R core team, 2020) was employed, making it possible to analyse the metadata of the bibliographic records. This package has previously been used in the description of knowledge-specific domains (Nafade et al., 2018).

In the second phase, distance-based maps were built using VOSviewer (Van Eck & Waltman, 2010), a tool designed specifically to build and view these types of maps in which the distance between each pair of elements reflects their strength of association. This type of analysis "can be used to construct networks of scientific publication, scientific journals, researchers, research organization, countries, keywords, or terms. Items in these networks can be connected by co-authorship, co-occurrence, citation, bibliographic coupling, or co-citation links" (Van Eck & Waltman, 2010: 3).

In the third phase, keyword co-occurrence analysis was employed (Callon et al., 1983) to identify topics and trends in the area of research. This tool has recently been applied to the study of conceptual evolution and to trends in different fields such as neuroscience (Yeung et al., 2017) and health (Gao et al., 2017).

As far as the evolution of academic production (Figure 2.1) is concerned, three phases can be found. The first, up to 2006, shows an extremely limited period of academic production. From 1979–1991, only one paper was published and from that time until 2005 there were only 1–3 papers per year. Between 2006–2015 there was a second phase of moderate growth with the publication of around 8–10 articles per year. The greatest growth in academic production on historical thinking in the field of education has taken place since 2015, growing from seven articles in 2014 to an average of 35 articles per year from then on. One reason for this growth is the Emerging Sources Citation Index (ESCI). The emergence of this database led to journals from different geographical areas such as Brazil, Spain and Russia becoming integrated into the WoS.

The three countries with (by far) the greatest academic production are the United States, Spain and Canada. As mentioned above, this production is driven by the research groups and connections established by Peter Seixas and Stéphane Lévesque in Canada; the group of Sam Wineburg, Abby Reisman and Chauncey Monte-Sano in the United States and the DICSO, RODA and SOCIAL(S) research groups in Spain. On a second level in terms of production, with more than five publications per year, are Australia, China, Germany, Sweden, Chile, the Netherlands and Japan. Somewhat surprisingly, the United Kingdom only has a total of five publications in the time period analysed.

Origin and development of research into historical thinking 33

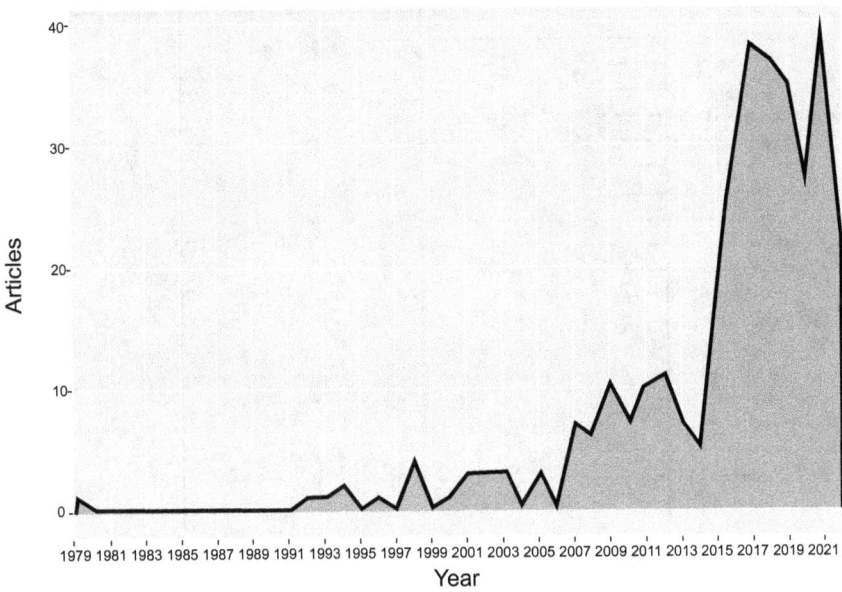

FIGURE 2.1 Annual scientific production

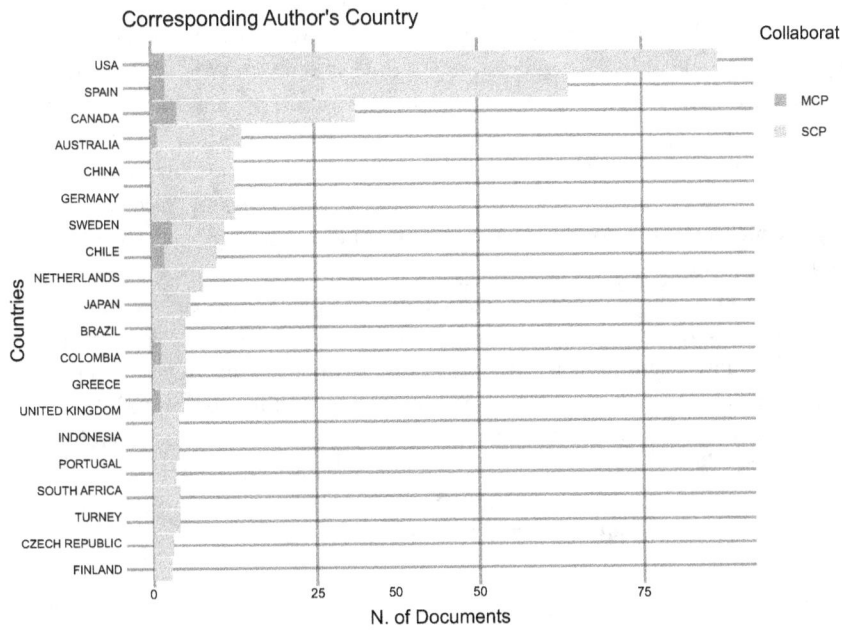

FIGURE 2.2 Corresponding author's country

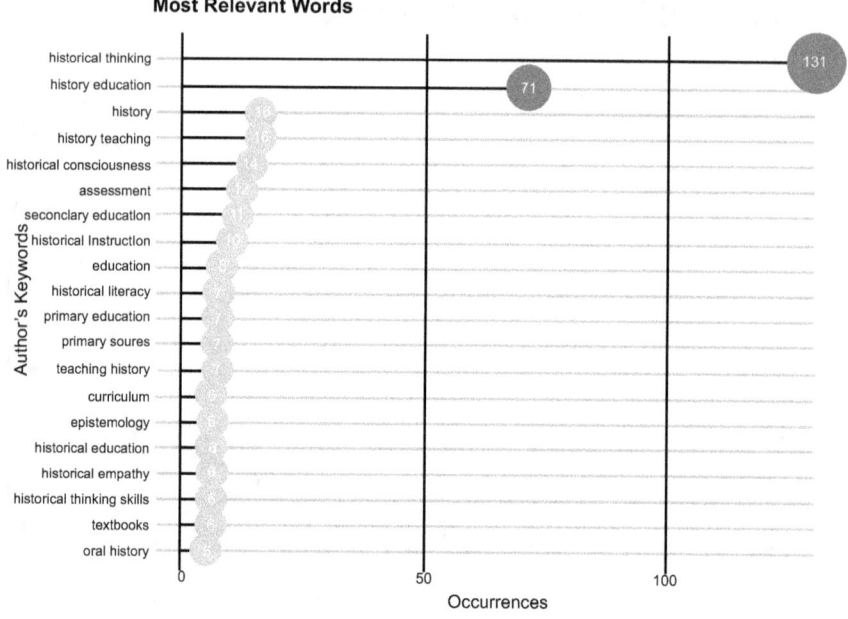

FIGURE 2.3 Most relevant words

The 20 most commonly used words in the "authors' keywords" of the publications analysed (Figure 2.3) are closely related with historical thinking and teaching. Due to their higher degree of specificity, the following words should be highlighted: "assessment", as it has been one of the key research lines (how to evaluate historical thinking among students); "primary sources", which links research on historical thinking with work on primary sources and the method of the historian; "curriculum", which is related with research on the presence of historical thinking concepts in education curriculums on an international level and "historical empathy", which makes it possible to work with students on historical understanding and contextualisation.

As can be seen in Figure 2.4, the annual trends have moved towards mainly educational issues. While in the early years the words "history" and "epistemology" were the most popular, in recent years there has been a shift towards "curriculum", "history instruction", "primary education", "history education", "secondary education" and "historical empathy". This also shows that theoretical reflection on this concept was of great importance in the early years, whereas, in the last decade empirical research in the field of education has increased in terms of both innovative proposals and research based on questionnaires, surveys and interviews (Epstein & Salinas, 2018).

As far as the main authors of the articles analysed are concerned, it can be observed that Spain (Miralles-Martínez, Gómez Carrasco and Martínez-Hita of the University of Murcia and Sáiz Serrano of the University of Valencia) and the

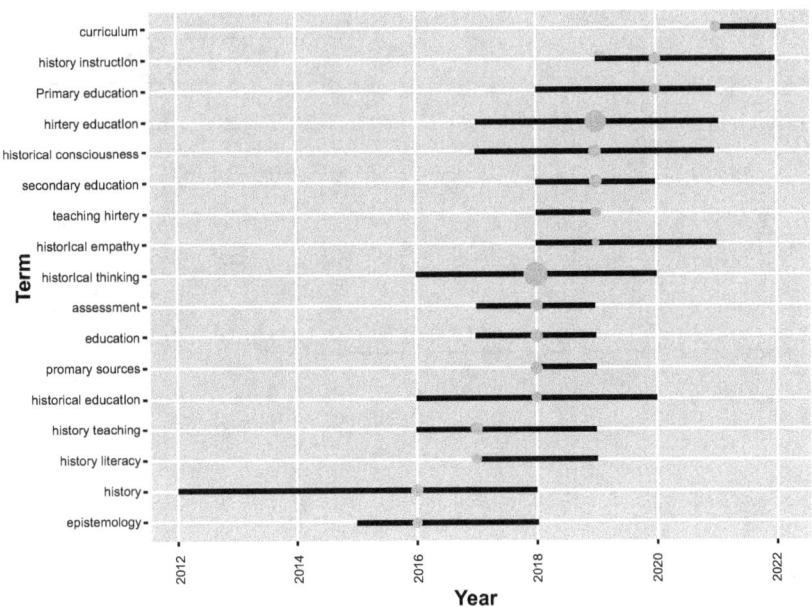

FIGURE 2.4 Trending topics

United States (Abby Reisman, Christine Baron and Chauncey Monte-Sano) lead the way. The other authors in the top ten are from Japan (Kojiri and Seta) and the Netherlands (van Boxtel). There is a certain degree of correspondence with the countries with the highest production, although there are some nuances. In Spain and Japan, production is more concentrated (particularly in Japan), whereas Canada, which has a significant position in terms of academic production, has no authors among the top ten. This demonstrates a higher degree of fragmentation of papers and a greater variety of authors.

Figure 2.6 analyses the intellectual structure of the field of knowledge (the main studies which support the research analysed). This figure shows studies which have been cited more than ten times on the WoS and their connections with other cited studies. It can be observed how this intellectual structure is connected with the points of reference provided in the first part of the chapter. There are three clusters of references whose main authors are Sam Wineburg, Peter Seixas, Stéphane Lévesque, Bruce VanSledright and Peter Lee. On the far right of the figure, interconnected references can be observed of Spanish authors, such as Gómez et al. (2014, 2015), Sáiz and López Facal (2015), López-Facal (2014) and Domínguez (2015). The main points of reference for these studies are publications by Wineburg (2001), Seixas and Morton (2013), VanSledright (2008, 2014) and Lee (2005). On the left side of the figure, the red cluster interconnects the studies (mainly

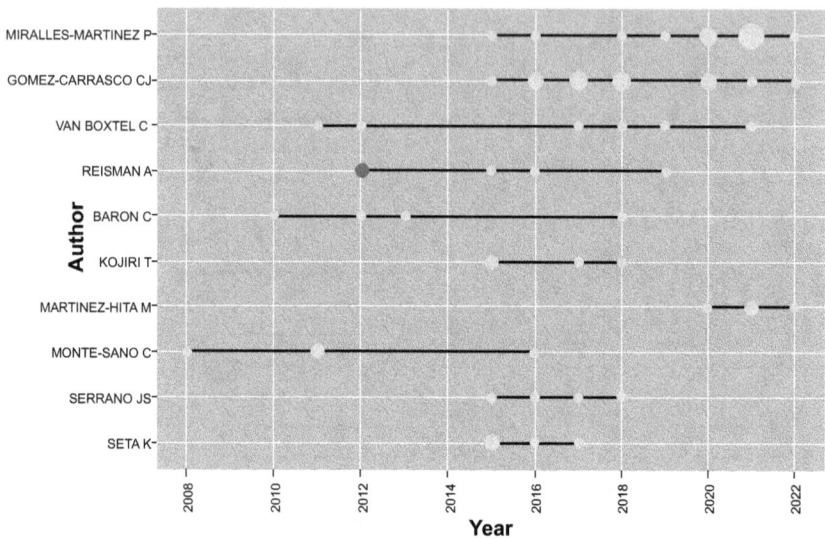

FIGURE 2.5 Top authors' production over the time

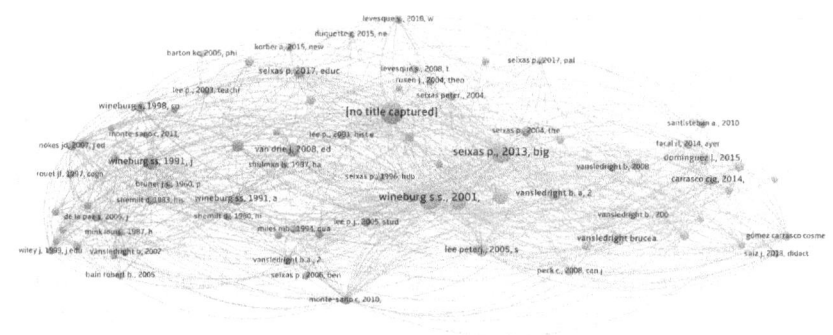

FIGURE 2.6 The intellectual structure of the field of knowledge

from the United States) on cognitive skills and historical literacy (Wineburg, 1991; Monte-Sano, 2011; De la Paz, 2005; Nokes, 2007). In this cluster, these studies are interconnected with the early research by Shemilt (1980, 1983) and Seixas (2006). The blue cluster (at the top of the figure) contains the studies which have reflected upon historical thinking and historical consciousness (Körber, 2015; Seixas, 2017b; Rüsen, 2004).

Conclusions

Historical thinking and historical consciousness are two key concepts upon which the paradigms of interpretation and research on the teaching of history have been built. The differences between the two concepts are vague. Currently, the concept of historical thinking frequently emphasises the analysis of evidence, reasoning, interpretation and argumentation. Research on historical consciousness is commonly linked to the presence of history in popular culture, narratives of the past, historical representations in the mass media and the social uses of history. However, historical thinking is not so strongly associated to the work of the historian as it once was. In recent times emphasis has been placed on the analysis of evidence, reasoning, interpretation and argumentation. Historical literacy has increased in parallel with a growing body of research on students' reading and writing skills related to the comprehension of historical concepts.

The bibliometric data show that the growth of academic production on historical thinking and history education is closely linked to the emergence of the ESCI database, which greatly increased the number of journals on the WoS. This increase has boosted the visibility of research on historical thinking carried out in countries such as Spain and Brazil. Furthermore, the results show a process of maturation of this concept is currently underway. Compared to the first period, in which theoretic research and studies on the construction of concepts were more common, the academic production of the last 5 years has been more connected to empirical research in the field of education. The main points of reference of this research are the proposals put forward by Wineburg, Seixas, Lévesque, Lee, VanSledright, Barton and the research groups which have grown up around them.

Note

1 This chapter is a result of projects "HistoryLab for European Civic Engagement: open e-Toolkit to train History Teachers on Digital Teaching and Learning", funded by SEPIE on call ERASMUS + KA226 [2020–1-ES01-KA226-HE-095430], and research project PID2020–113453RB-I00, funded by Agencia Estatal de Investigación of Spain (AEI/10.13039/501100011033).

References

Aria, M., & Cuccurullo, C. (2017). Bibliometrix: An R-tool for comprehensive science mapping analysis. *Journal of Informetrics*, *11*(4), 959–975.

Bain, R. B. (2015). Commentary: Into the swampy lowlands of important problems. In K. Ercikan & P. Seixas (Eds.), *New directions in assessing historical thinking* (pp. 64–72). New York, NY: Routledge.

Barton, K. C., & Levstik, L. (2004). *Teaching history for the common good*. New York, NY and London: Routledge.

Breakstone, J., Smith, M., Ziv, N., & Wineburg, S. (2022). Civic preparation for the digital age: How college students evaluate online sources about social and political issues. *The Journal of Higher Education*. https://doi.org/10.1080/00221546.2022.2082783

Callon, M., Courtial, J., Turner, W., & Bauin, S. (1983). From translations to problematic networks: An introduction to co-word analysis. *Social Science Information, 22*, 191–235.

Chapman, A. (2011a). Understanding historical knowing: Evidence and accounts. In L. Perikleous & D. Shemilt (Eds.), *The future of the past: Why history education matters* (pp. 169–216). Nicosia: Kailas Printers.

Chapman, A. (2011b). Historical interpretations. In I. Davies (Ed.), *Debates in history teaching*, (pp. 100–112). London: Routledge.

Chapman, A. (Ed.). (2021a). *Knowing history in schools: Powerful knowledge and the powers of knowledge*. London: UCL Press. https://doi.org/10.2307/j.ctv14t477t

Chapman, A. (2021b). Introduction. Historical knowing and the "knowledge turn". In A. Chapman (Ed.), *Knowing history in schools: Powerful knowledge and the powers of knowledge* (pp. 20–50). London: UCL Press

De La Paz, S. (2005). Effects of historical reasoning instruction and writing strategy mastery in culturally and academically diverse middle school classrooms. *Journal of Educational Psychology, 97*, 137–156.

Domínguez Castillo, J. (2015). *Pensamiento histórico y evaluación de competencias*. Barcelona: Graó.

Eliasson, P., Alvén, F., Yngvéus, C. A., & Rosenlund, D. (2015). Historical consciousness and historical thinking reflected in large-scale assessment in Sweden. In K. Ercikan & P. Seixas (Eds.), *New directions in assessing historical thinking* (pp. 171–182). New York, NY: Routledge

Epstein, T., & Salinas, C. S. (2018). Research methodologies in history education. In S. A. Metzger & L. M. Harris (Eds.), *The Wiley international handbook of history teaching and learning* (pp. 61–92). London: Wiley

Gao, Y., Wang, Y., Zhai, X., He, Y., Chen, R., Zhou, J., Li, M., & Wang, Q. (2017). Publication trends of research on diabetes mellitus and T cells (1997–2016): A 20-year bibliometric study. *PLoS ONE, 12*(9), 1–13. https://doi.org/10.1371/journal.pone.0184869

Gibson, L., & Peck, C. L. (2020). More than a methods course: Teaching preservice teachers to think historically. In C. W. Berg, & T. M. Christou (Eds.), *The Palgrave handbook of history and social studies education* (pp. 213–251). Cham: Palgrave.

Gómez, C. J., & Miralles, P. (2015). ¿Pensar históricamente o memorizar el pasado? La evaluación de los contenidos históricos en la educación obligatoria en España. *Revista de Estudios Sociales, 52*, 52–68.

Gómez, C. J., Ortuño, J., & Molina, S. (2014). Aprender a pensar históricamente. Retos para la historia en el siglo XXI. *Tempo e Argumento, 6*(11), 5–27.

Gómez, C. J., Rodríguez-Medina, J., López Facal, R., & Monteagudo-Fernández, J. (2022). A review of literature on history education: An analysis of the conceptual, intellectual and social structure of a knowledge domain (2000–2019). *European Journal of Education*, 00, 1–15. https://doi.org/10.1111/ejed.12508

Kölbl, C., & Konrad, L. (2015). Historical consciousness in Germany: Concept, implementation, assessment. In K. Ercikan & P. Seixas (Eds.), *New directions in assessing historical thinking* (pp. 17–28). New York, NY: Routledge.

Körber, A. (2015). *Historical consciousness, historical competencies – And beyond? Some conceptual development within German history didactics*. Frankfurt am Main: Deutsches Institut für Internationale Pädagogische Forschung

Körber, A. (2019). Extending historical consciousness: Past futures and future pasts. *Historical Encounters: A Journal of Historical Consciousness, Historical Cultures, and History Education, 6*(1), 29–39.

Körber, A. (2021). Historical consciousness, knowledge and competencies of historical thinking: An integrated model of historical thinking and curricular implications.

Historical Encounters: A Journal of Historical Consciousness, Historical Cultures, and History Education, 8(1), 97–119.

Körber, A., & Meyer-Hamme, J. (2015). Historical thinking, competencies, and their measurement: Challenges and approaches. In K. Ercikan & P. Seixas (Eds.), *New directions in assessing historical thinking* (pp. 89–101). London: Routledge.

Lee, P. (2005). Putting principles intro practice: Understanding history. In M. Donovan & J. Bransford (Ed.), *How students learn: History in the classroom* (pp. 31–77). Washington, DC: National Academies Press.

Lee, P. (2011). History education and historical literacy. In I. Davis (Ed.), *Debates in history teaching,* (pp. 63–72). New York, NY: Routledge.

Lee, P., & Ashby, R. (2000). Progression in historical understanding among students ages 7–14. In P. N. Stearns, P. Seixas, & S. S. Wineburg (Eds.), *Knowing, teaching, and learning history: National and international perspectives* (pp. 199–222). New York, NY: New York University Press.

Lee, P., Ashby, R., & Dickinson, A. (1996). Progression in children's ideas about history: project CHATA. In M. Hughes (Ed.), *Progression in learning* (pp. 50–81). Clevedon: Multilingual Matters

Lévesque, S. (2008). *Thinking historically. Educating students for the twenty-first century.* Toronto: University of Toronto Press.

Lévesque, S. (2016). Going beyond "narratives" vs. "competencies": A model for understanding history education. *Public History Weekly, 4,* 12, https://doi.org/dx.doi.org/10.1515/phw-2016-5918.

Lévesque, S., & Clark, P. (2018). Historical thinking. Definitions and educational applications. In S. A. Metzger & L. McArthur (Eds.), *The Wiley international handbook of history teaching and learning* (pp. 119–148). Hoboken, NJ: John Wiley and Sons.

Lévesque, S., & Croteau, J. P. (2020). *Beyond history for historical consciousness. Students, narrative and memory.* Toronto: University Toronto Press.

López Facal, R. (2014). La LOMCE y la competencia histórica. *Ayer, 94,* 273–285.

Monte-Sano, C. (2010). Disciplinary literacy in history: An exploration of the historical nature of adolescents' writing. *Journal of the Learning Sciences, 19*(4), 539–568. doi:10.1080/10508406.2010.481014.

Monte-Sano, C. (2011). Learning to open up history for students: Preservice teachers' emerging pedagogical content knowledge. *Journal of Teacher Education, 62*(3), 260–272. https://doi.org/10.1177/0022487110397842

Monte-Sano, C., & De La Paz, S. (2012). Using writing tasks to elicit adolescents' historical reasoning. *Journal of Literacy Research, 44*(3), 273–299. doi:10.1177/1086296X12450445

Monte-Sano, C., De La Paz, S., & Felton, M. K. (2014). *Reading, thinking, and writing about history: Teaching argument writing to diverse learners in the age of the Common Core* (pp. 6–12). New York, NY: Teachers College Press.

Nafade, V., Nash, M., Huddart, S., Pande, T., Gebreselassie, N., Lienhardt, C., & Pai, M. (2018). A bibliometric analysis of tuberculosis research, 2007–2016. *PLoS One, 13*(6), e0199706. https://doi.org/10.1371/journ al.pone.0199706

Nokes, J. D., Dole, J. A., & Hacker, D. J. (2007). Teaching high school students to use heuristics while reading historical texts. *Journal of Educational Psychology, 99*(3), 492–504. https://doi.org/10.1037/0022-0663.99.3.492

Peck, C., & Seixas, P. (2008). Benchmarks of historical thinking: First steps. *Canadian Journal of Education, 31*(4), 1015–1038.

Reisman, A. (2012). Reading like a historian: A document-based history curriculum intervention in urban high schools. *Cognition and Instruction, 30*(1), 86–112. https://doi.org/10.1080/07370008.2011.634081

Rüsen, J. (2004). Historical consciousness: Narrative structure, moral function and ontogenetic development. In P. Seixas (Ed.), *Theorizing historical consciousness* (pp. 63–85). Toronto: University of Toronto Press.

Rüsen, J. (2005). *History: Narration, interpretation, orientation*. New York, NY: Berghahn.

Sáiz, J., & López Facal, R. (2015). Competencias y narrativas históricas: el pensamiento histórico de estudiantes y futuros profesores españoles de Educación Secundaria. *Revista de Estudios Sociales, 52*, 87–101.

Sandwell, R., & Heyking, A. V. (Eds). (2014). *Becoming a history teacher: Sustaining practices in historical thinking and knowing*. Toronto: University of Toronto Press.

Seixas, P. (Ed.). (2004). *Theorizing historical consciousness*. Toronto: University of Toronto Press.

Seixas, P. (2006). *Benchmarks of historical thinking: A framework for assessment in Canada*. Vancouver: Centre for the study of historical consciousness, University of British Columbia.

Seixas, P. (2016a) Translation and its discontents: Key concepts in English and German history education. *Journal of Curriculum Studies, 48*(4), 427–439, https://doi.org/10.1080/00220272.2015.110161

Seixas, P. (2016b): A history/memory matrix for history education. *Public History Weekly, 4*(6). https://doi.org/dx.doi.org/10.1515/phw-2016-5370.

Seixas, P. (2017a). Historical consciousness and historical thinking. In M. Carretero, S. Berger & M. Grever (Eds.), *Palgrave handbook of research in historical culture and education* (pp. 59–72). London: Palgrave.

Seixas, P. (2017b). A model of historical thinking. *Educational Philosophy and Theory, 49*(6), 593–605. doi:10.1080/00131857.2015.1101363

Seixas, P., & Morton, T. (2013). *The big six historical thinking concepts*. Toronto: Nelson.

Shemilt, D. (1980). *History 13–16 evaluation study*. Edinburgh: Holmes McDougall.

Shemilt, D. (1983). The devil's locomotive. *History & Theory, 22*(4), 1–18.

van Boxtel, C., & van Drie, J. (2018). Historical reasoning: conceptualizations and educational applications. In S. A. Metzger & L. McArthur (eds.), *The Wiley international handbook of history teaching* (pp. 149–176). Hoboken, NJ: John Wiley & Sons.

van Drie, J., & van Boxtel, C. (2008). Historical reasoning: Towards a framework for analyzing students' reasoning about the past. *Educational Psychology Review, 20*(2), 87–110. doi:10.1007/s10648-007-9056-1

Van Eck, N. J., & Waltman, L. (2010). Software survey: VOS viewer, a computer program for bibliometric mapping. *Scientometrics, 84*(2), 523–538.

Van Sledright, B. A. (2002). Fifth graders investigating history in the classroom: Results from a researcher-practitioner design experiment. *The Elementary School Journal, 103*(2), 131–160.

Van Sledright, B. A. (2008). Narratives of nation-state, historical knowledge and school history education. *Review of Research in Education, 32*(1), 109–146. https://doi.org/10.3102/0091732X07311065.

Van Sledright, B. A. (2011). *The challenge of rethinking history education. On practice, theories, and policy*. New York, NY: Routledge.

Van Sledright, B. A. (2014). *Assessing historical thinking and understanding. Innovation design for new standards*. New York, NY: Routledge.

Van Sledright, B., & Limón, M. (2006). Learning and teaching social studies: A review of cognitive research in history and geography. In P. A. Alexander & P. H. Winne (Eds.), *Handbook of educational psychology* (pp. 545–570). Hillsdale: Lawrence Erlbaum.

Voss, J. F., & Wiley, J. (2000). A case study of developing historical understanding via instruction: The importance of integrating text components and constructing arguments. In P.

N. Stearns, P. Seixas, & S. S. Wineburg (Eds.), *Knowing, teaching, and learning history: National and international perspectives* (pp. 375–389). New York, NY: New York University Press.

Wineburg, S. S. (1991). On the reading of historical texts: Notes on the breach between school and academy. *American Educational Research Journal, 28*(3), 495–519.

Wineburg, S. S. (2001). *Historical thinking and other unnatural acts: Charting the future of teaching the past.* Philadelphia, PA: Temple University Press.

Wineburg, S. S. (2018). *Why learn history (when it's already on your phone).* Chicago, IL: Chicago University Press.

Wineburg, S. S, Martin, D., & Monte-Sano, C. (2013). *Reading like a historian. Teaching literacy in middle & high school history classrooms.* New York, NY: Teacher College Press.

Yeung, A. W. K., Goto, T. K., & Leung, W. K. (2017). The changing landscape of neuroscience research, 2006–2015: A bibliometric study. *Frontiers in Neuroscience, 11*(120). https://doi.org/10.3389/fnins.2017.00120

3
DIGITAL RESOURCES FOR RETHINKING HISTORY EDUCATION

Juan Carlos Colomer Rubio and Anaclet Pons Pons

Introduction

Athens, May 2014. While the use of digital technology in schools in the West was growing, the "European Network of Education Councils" seminar highlighted that, in this technological world, we are constantly being flooded with so-called Information and Communication Technology (ICT) and surrounded by a wide range of sources for both informal and non-formal learning. Unfortunately, in this context, learners do not question the advantages and disadvantages when accessing information. They do not read textbooks; they do not question them; they simply use technology without thinking. The current climate thus challenges the content and traditional nature of learning in school (EUNEC, 2014). Today, almost 10 years after this report, this same reflection continues to crop up, to a lesser or greater extent, in various recent pieces of research that have highlighted the inability of young people to differentiate between true information and false information or even to distinguish between digital sources that we could consider to be sponsored and those that are not (McGrew et al., 2018; Wineburg et al., 2022).

The problem seems to be clear: a large increase in online information spaces does not correspond with an improvement in the quality thereof, and this has clearly affected the educational sphere. It has affected schools as a teaching and learning environment and, in particular, subjects where media literacy work plays a significant role, as is the case of History (Haydn & Ribbens, 2017). For all these reasons, it is worth developing a slightly better understanding of what the digital challenge means. In fact, the above statement seems to offload all responsibility onto the students and their lifestyle or on the devices used rather than onto the social nature of the devices or the way in which they are to be used. Paradoxically, the 2014 Athens report seeks the solution in the same field: teachers must convert new technologies and resources into rich and innovative learning environments.

DOI: 10.4324/9781003289470-5

Rather than being mere transmitters of knowledge, they should become creators and developers of competencies. In this vein, most policies have been developed in relation to technology and have even led to the emergence of concepts such as "Digital Native" or "Digital Teaching Competence" that could be included in the same approach (Adell et al., 2019). This leads us to believe that technology is the subterfuge to the problem, the technological solution or "technological solutionism" (Morozov, 2014), the cure-all. If students are "digital natives" and speak another language, we have but to learn it and speak the same language. In short, where do we sign?

Unfortunately the solution is not that simple. Technological products are not impartial; they hide interests and settings that often prevent the critical use thereof. Beyond the impact on pedagogy, we are witnessing, as Mario Díaz (2000) points out, a dispersal of communication methods that often implies the emergence of new management practices that are simpler, more rational and more functional. In the same way that the sociology of education and critical didactics have questioned the role of traditional pedagogy in education, it is now essential to reflect on the knowledge versus power relationship of these new devices. Moreover, the same resources have been displacing the role of the teacher, who is now seen as a "mere guide" in the face of knowledge that seems to be displayed in a natural and neutral way on these same screens. Finally, this is reflected in school routines and practices themselves, which are often a far cry from the media or digital literacy needed to deal with online information.

It is for all these reasons that we have dual objectives for this chapter. On the one hand, we wish to explore the current situation of the teaching and learning of Social Sciences, specifically History, in school, paying attention to how the presence of technology has affected media literacy. On the other hand, this will translate into an analysis of how these resources are the result of that context and that only by changing the way in which they are used, in what Gardner and Davis have called "enabling meaning" (Davis & Gardner, 2013), can we help to transform that same context and improve literacy. That is to say, what matters is what we want to tell our students and how we try to do that, ensuring that the tools or resources are valid, whether good or bad, for the objective pursued, its purpose and use. This does not mean that (digital) resources are neutral but that they will not achieve a substantial improvement in historical understanding by themselves. Rather it is the use thereof that will lead to this improvement in understanding (Colomer et al., 2022).

Analysis of history teaching in the school context

This first part will focus on exploring the main features of the current school context with regard to the introduction of technology and how it has affected practices in History teaching.

The first element to consider is the abundance of information and technologies in school environments. The Clinton administration's incipient policy of providing one computer per classroom to promote "technological literacy" in the

United States in 1996 is a thing of the past (Fernández-Enguita, 2016). Today, many schools in the West have Internet connections, modern digital whiteboards, projectors and even interactive screens that allow quick access to information. However, this availability of access is ubiquitous; there are no boundaries or limits other than those imposed by the technology itself. This is the result, moreover, of its dematerialization – the fact that knowledge is no longer disseminated through print, through visual or audio media, or through fixed and specific media. Instead, it now flows in an unstable, disembodied form, waiting to be seen, read, listened to or printed. Most importantly, knowledge cannot be enclosed in a concrete medium (Pons, 2013).

Consequently, this means, among other things, that the teacher no longer has a monopolistic authority over history, nor can he or she rely on the textbook that he or she used to use to be the only reference that he or she interprets and that the students read. In other words, the cognitive landscape has changed, and paper books are competing at a clear disadvantage. The teacher cannot close the door and expect that that one place alone will give meaning to the historical past. The library is now filled with students, only now it has another name: the Internet or the web or, more particularly, Google, Wikipedia and social networks (Gamboa, 2022; Rosenzweig, 2006). This new repository is very different from the traditional library, as instead of librarians, clear rules, consultation indexes or alphabetical order it has algorithms, metadata, voluntary reviewers and interests that modify how information is shared. What is more, the content of the network is guided by multitudinous mechanisms and is not supervised by the usual renowned experts. It is the wisdom of the crowd that imposes its opinion, not a professional of the discipline (Wineburg, 2018).

Moreover, it lacks the difference of appearance. The code with which this information is written does not distinguish between text, image, sound or even books, magazines or medicinal leaflets. One thing unites it all: the screen (Sartori, 2021). It is in this context that authors such as Prensky came to affirm that we are facing a "digital native" student body because this is the ecosystem in which they have grown up. However, this does not mean that they understand it or that they know how it works. It simply exists; it is the medium they use the most. Perhaps we can say the same about teachers – whether they are "digital natives" or not – because they are not usually digitally literate either, even if they have been trained in the use of certain technological tools.

As a result of these two factors – the overabundance of technology and changes in the way historical knowledge is disseminated – certain problems have become entrenched and new ones have emerged. A recent study by Peter Burkholder and Dana Schaffer for the American Historical Association (AHA) focuses on this issue. In this study – a survey on how the American public understands history and the past – some very significant conclusions were drawn: the main sources of historical knowledge are screens (especially video sources); those surveyed consider that history can be learned anywhere, not only at school, and it's better if it is also entertaining; the most consulted sources on the past are those that are easily accessible

(Burkholder & Schaffer, 2021). Along these lines, the History Education Group at Stanford University has long affirmed that the young American population does not know how to differentiate between information with scientific authority and sponsored information (McGrew et al., 2018), which affects this limited media literacy. This is often derived from the fact that it has been subsumed under models that prioritize devices over skills, making the mistake of thinking that more devices equals greater literacy (Gutiérrez & Tyner, 2012). In fact, the situation is even more worrying if we look at teachers in training. As Santisteban et al. (2020) have pointed out, many of the students who are training to become teachers have serious problems when it comes to arguing critically about the information they find on the Internet. This means that only 19.9% of a total sample of 322 future teachers show that they understand that there are always different points of view, interests or ideologies about a social problem. Some analyses are very naïve or fail to understand the relevance of the problem or the seriousness of the approaches used in certain online sources.

This is the situation. Accustomed to dispensing meaning through the use of a school textbook in a specific place and with a fixed timetable, now school education escapes the authority and monopoly of the classroom. This means that, if there are any questions or disagreements, the student will argue in his or her favor by saying that he or she has "found it on the Internet". Moreover, it seems that intelligence now relies on devices (phones, tablets, etc.); these devices allow access to information, while teachers are just another source, although at least the only one that evaluates. This has many drawbacks, as already noted, but some advantages.

The traditional school textbook has declined as a reference not only because of its need to compete with other resources but also because it was already too rigid and uniform. What this type of textbook does is serve packaged pieces of history, full of dates and episodes, always coloring and highlighting what is considered fundamental. The student's task was and is thus to read and answer a few questions at the end of each section (Bel et al., 2019). This only works in theory. In practice, it has long since lost meaning (at least for the student). The textbook doesn't make students leave the classroom interested in what they have been told and wanting to look for additional information on the Internet. It is not even necessary; that external information is continuously chasing them and suffocating them because they are constantly connected to it (as are the teachers).

So the question is not to stop and think about what to do with the textbook but how to turn it into something else. Of course, the solution is not to digitize it. That only modifies the medium (it dematerializes it) but not what counts. In addition, it instills the naïve belief that digital in itself is good because it is new and, as such, it has to be better; it has to improve the text (Peirats et al., 2016). Sometimes we see it as a magic wand, which transforms and illuminates everything it touches, and we think that if it were not for this improvement, the advantages of new technologies would not be promoted. Nor is the solution to combine the textbook with other sources, such as Wikipedia, for example, or the websites of museums or libraries. Accumulating more information may give us the impression that we are opening the doors of the classroom, but it only creates more noise and confusion. In fact, an analysis of current Spanish textbooks has highlighted that most of the activities presented in them do not refer to external websites and when they do, they invite basic strategies of reproduction of information that do not generate new strategies or the application of what has been learned. Instead, they emphasize literally copying the text, something that is then easily forgotten after leaving school (Colomer et al., 2018).

For the same reason, it is not useful to do a similar exercise with other complementary tools, exchanging a blackboard for a projector, for example. In fact, many of these solutions do not modify but rather reinforce the pre-digital school model we described before. Something similar can happen with new digital resources, which are often seen as a solution to all problems. For example, the European Union's "Digital Education Action Plan (2021–2017)" starts with a clear finding: less than 40% of educators across the EU consider themselves to be digitally literate, and more than a third of 13–14 year olds lack basic digital skills. It always seems to be the same problem, so the solution is clear: develop a high-performing digital education ecosystem by investing in improving competences and skills, i.e. promoting the media literacy of students and teachers. This is the only way to create a European Education Area in line with the times that doesn't rely on devices as the only solution to improve education and provides teachers and students with the necessary tools to deal with this ubiquitous and changing networked information. Let's look at how this can be done.

Digital and historical literacy

So far we have seen that ending pessimism and embracing digital euphoria will not put an end to the problems we are experiencing because having new media, better infrastructure and renewed content is not enough. First, we should understand what media literacy is, as it's a key factor that affects the whole set of tools that we use today or that we can master in the future, from the simplest to the most complex.

A word processor, for example, is a powerful narrative machine with multiple possibilities, but it may generate additional problems, such as the well-known copy-and-paste feature. The same can be said of PowerPoint, designed more for the world of business and commercial presentations. It can turn a History class into a continuum of encapsulated, formatted knowledge pills, even less complex than those in a manual, thus leading to a kind of presentation culture (Haydn & Ribbens, 2017). Once we start surfing the net and searching – and we have to learn how to do that – we will come across Wikipedia as the most common result for questions about history. We should ask ourselves why this happens, what algorithms determine the search engine's answer and question ourselves about what kind of encyclopedia it is, who writes it, how opinions are arbitrated and how arguments are evidenced. In short, we need to question a place where the wisdom of the crowd reigns, and where the opinion of an expert is worth as much or as little as that of an amateur.

This is, therefore, the first step. Media literacy is not about mastering one tool but about understanding many other aspects. What problems are we trying to solve with the new media? What do we gain, and what do we lose? When, how and why should we use them? What are the dangers or unintended consequences? Is PowerPoint better than the traditional blackboard or is it a mere technical solution/illusion? Does Wikipedia surpass other content from the analogue era, or do we prefer it because it is easy to access? What values do we transmit when using these tools? What kind of product is it, who makes it, who benefits from it and how do they benefit from its use? Asking these kinds of questions when we work with technology is essential in order to make different use of it, in short, to go beyond the device or solution itself which is only a digital tool (Adell, 2018).

In addition to what was mentioned above, there are several other aspects to take into consideration. One is that relying on digital tools is a form of discrimination since not all students, families or teachers have the same means or the same skills. The so-called digital divide is not only of knowledge but also of access. This has been exacerbated by the COVID-19 pandemic as many studies have pointed out (Negueruela & Torres, 2021). Another aspect that we usually lose sight of is the connection between a certain tool and the final product of the pedagogical act: teaching. That is to say, the useful tool dazzles politicians, teachers and students all too often, who believe they have found a formula to undo the educational spell, so that we may be more involved – and entertained – by the software rather than by what it could contribute to our learning about the past.

This has been one of the most obvious dangers in the introduction of new digital tools for teaching history, such as gamification (Martínez-Hita et al., 2021) or teaching using videos on platforms such as YouTube (Colomer et al., 2022). These are often used uncritically as the only teaching material rather than as a complement to the class. These digital processes and tools shape a certain way of perceiving, experiencing and thinking about past events or processes, as well as directing our perceptions and shaping current appropriations, practices and uses. Reflecting on all this is what literacy is all about, and it comes at a significant cost, just as teaching us to write (which is also a technology) or to decipher a book, bookshop or library has been. These acts also involve greater effort because they involve sacrificing order and routine to enter a totally different world.

Once we understand the digital language, we can decide if we want to use the new resources and what for. This may include those already mentioned or others such as gamification, the "flipped classroom", strategy games, Geographic Information System (GIS) for geolocation, augmented reality, video games, Twitter or any other social network and Mindmap or Canva for mental and concept maps. We have to admit that, from the outset, all these resources have their advantages. Most of them have the attractiveness of technology and, as they are part of the students' ecosystem, they generate expectations, allowing students to become engaged and motivated from the very beginning. For this very reason, due to the initial enthusiasm they provide compared to classic practices, they can foster a relaxed atmosphere which favors participation, collaboration and ultimately, with the right strategy, meaningful learning.

Finally, as well as providing good starting questions, we must not forget that what we teach in schools is history. This discipline has methods but also a social and educational function. Any innovative approach has to think about giving meaning to historical work at a time when the discipline itself is being disputed by many others, be that the media, enthusiasts, writers, judges or legislators. If the interpretation of the past is not based on the historical method, then any outside information can compete with that of the historian and teacher of history. The easier the information is to access, the more competition it will provide regardless of whether it is false or manipulated or not.

How do we make sense of this work? Of course, we should improve the quality of the practices and the learning outcomes they offer, but above all we should share the working method, showing how historical knowledge is constructed, providing tools to show how the complexity of the past is investigated and recounted. We are sure that this implies abandoning the order and routine associated with the memorization of historical facts or characters, with chronology as the central axis, as a conveyor belt that takes us from one time to another. It is necessary to go beyond what a textbook dictates because its vast contents, however condensed they may be, generate anxiety due to the difficulty of covering them all in the weeks or months envisaged. As Stéphane Lévesque, among others, has pointed out, it is necessary to let students inquire, question and dig deeper and to find defensible answers to significant questions just as academics do when they study and discover a given problem (Lévesque, 2008). "Students cannot understand the 'game' of history if they never get to practice and play it themselves".

This dynamic involves showing students what "thinking historically" consists of. In this way students will work on strategies to analyze and contrast information that will enable them to understand the main foundations on which history is built (cause versus consequence, inference, ethics, empathy, power versus marginalization, men, women, etc.). This in turn will give them the tools to apply this thinking in other contexts and practices. It would be an illusion to think that this would imply abandoning the textbook and what it contains, but it means that today, when the whole ecosystem is digital, it is necessary to go further. A textbook contains facts, places, chronologies, concepts and certain explanations. All this must be known, but it is a closed text in an open world with an omniscient narrator who sets the course of the events described, sprinkling it with some minimal documentary references. In contrast, the digital world exposes us to sources and interpretations of all kinds. This is where the questioning of authority comes from, either because history is manipulated for political purposes in one way or another or because anyone can make their voice heard. The Internet has democratized access to and the dissemination of information. With Wikipedia, for example, you don't need a title to talk about history or any other subject, and anyone, if they receive the blessing of Internet users, can become an authority with thousands or millions of followers. Facts, places, chronologies and concepts are also shared in other digital places and in a more attractive way. As Sam Wineburg would say, we live in a time when the tools we have invented are driving us and not the other way around (Wineburg, 2018).

Therefore, teaching students to memorize a list of things or facts no longer distinguishes or serves us as teachers and, in any case, that is not historical thinking. It is not history but the past. What is it that differentiates us and gives us the authority to teach this? It's the way in which the historical discipline establishes the certainty of something, the procedures we follow and, in short, how we use documents critically and question them. That is to say, since the digital environment competes with us while also putting sources at our fingertips, it offers us an opportunity to show the game to students and claim the relevance of our craft. Moreover, by helping them to think like historians in this way, we can equip them to handle the flood of information that surrounds them. This is what Hangen has called the "digital literacy of history" (Hangen, 2015).

All this requires effort for a critical attitude to information does not come naturally. As Charles Seignobos pointed out more than a century ago:

> The spontaneous reaction of a man who falls into the water is to do anything to drown; to learn to swim is to acquire the habit of slowing down one's spontaneous movements and to make unnatural ones. The spontaneous reaction of a man reading a paper is to believe everything he reads; to learn criticism is to acquire the habit of resisting natural credulity and examining what one reads. Criticism, like swimming, must become organic through exercise.
>
> *Seignobos (1901: 33)*

Consequently, we need to work with this accessible information by showing how we approach it and the sources thereof. This type of information comes in many forms: a news item, a tweet, a post or a video that we can ask the same questions as a source. Where did it come from? How was it transmitted? Who did it and when? Is there a motive to manipulate or falsify? What does it say and how? Can it be corroborated? These and other questions must be asked. We can even, as Wineburg has repeatedly pointed out, use the web to read it as a whole, skim-reading what we find and checking it against other sources within the web. No search engine or social network will separate what is true from what is not. No one will do it for us. An old encyclopedia had editors who took professional care of its content, but Wikipedia is not an encyclopedia in that sense. The most interesting aspect of all of this is that historians, because of their constant work with sources, are equipped, prepared and trained to assist with the necessary training.

Showing what it means to think historically has other advantages in a world full of opinions and interpretations about history and about everything in general. It is important to teach people that not all opinions are equally valid because not all of them are supported by the sources, even if there are different interpretations. Along these lines, teaching and learning involves showing that these interpretations vary, because they do, as do the perspectives of historians and the time in which they live. Of course, this also means that history is controversial, and it must be so. Demonstrating this reality also serves to make students search, question and reflect, which means not only doing the historian's job but also being an active citizen. That is to say, to train in historical thinking is to train critical people who are curious and rigorous. What are we waiting for?

Teachers and historians in the face of the digital challenge: some proposals

In order to accomplish this task – of thinking historically and at the same time becoming digitally literate – there is no need for large technological investments or sophisticated software because everything is out there waiting for us. There is no lack of information to deal with. We can do exercises of all kinds. We can understand how the passage of time changes the questions and the history that results from it by analyzing and comparing a school textbook from the 21st century, another from 40 years ago and another from 70 years ago, for example. We can also study a disputed event to see how it is represented in the various countries concerned. We can, for example, look at what the wave of tearing down or questioning of certain statues like that of Fray Junipero Serra in San Francisco in June 2020 means. We can investigate who they represent, why and when they were erected, what they meant then and what they mean now, and so on.

As we have mentioned in other publications (Colomer, 2016), we currently have very interesting tools at our disposal that can facilitate the digital handling of historical sources. This is the case of Historypin, a collaborative online database that comprises historical sources, mostly photographs or small-format videos, represented in the urban space in which they were taken or created. In this way, students can describe, date, contextualize and complete the information provided by an image and give it more content. This will ultimately allow them to answer important questions and generate a new discourse that allows them to contextualize the historical reality studied in the classroom. In addition, new materials and formats have appeared that allow people to work directly on historical sources, such as the one developed by C. Gatell, R. de Miguel and D. Sobrino with the Vicens Vives publishing house for the first year of the baccalaureate in Spain and encompassed under the title "Comunidad en red" ["Networked community"] for the 2022–2023 academic year. This material, set around topics of interest, presents a large selection of primary sources and a clear and simple working method that allows students to contrast information with other online sources and generate critical and complete knowledge.

On the other hand, we also have interesting tools we can use to work on multiple perspectives and different epistemological approaches to history. In 2022, Professor Kathleen Belew (Belew, 2022) did something very simple when she decided to write a short thread on Twitter with an idea for an exercise for her students. She used the famous "Why did the chicken cross the road?" joke to ask how a social or cultural or intellectual historian, among others, would respond, and asked if anyone could help her in that regard. What the thread came up with doesn't matter as much as what the initial proposals were. Social historians would not ask about the chicken that crossed the road but about the avian community that gave rise to that chicken's decision to do so, in order to understand that crossing as a collective action. Perhaps military historians would question how it crossed, the obstacles it encountered and whether it succeeded. Intellectual historians might ask about the idea of the road, what it means, its limits and boundaries and whether it was actually crossed. Cultural historians, on the other hand, would look at the set of materials that represent chickens, crossings, roads and other things to understand why we tell that joke over and over again. Old political historians would biograph the chicken, but new political historians would be interested in its authority to cross the road and whether it was allowed to and also in the relationship of the state of both the chicken and the road. Finally, diplomatic historians would ask where the road ran and who lived on the other side. The fact itself doesn't change but the questions do and, as such, the answers are enriched.

Finally, we must emphasize that a good education is about more than just memorizing. It has to provide the ability or capacity to find relevant information (sources and evidence) and analyze it. This is the educational task that we must undertake. It has always been relevant, but it is now urgent, given the digital ecosystem which overwhelms us with a plethora of information and, at the same time, allows us to access it easily. There are few teachers who are better prepared than those knowledgeable in the historical discipline to teach those skills that bring us closer to the information and help us to interpret the sources of historical knowledge.

References

Adell, J. (2018). Más allá del instrumentalismo en tecnología educativa. In J. Gimeno (Coord.), *Cambiar los contenidos, cambiar la educación* (pp. 117–132). Madrid: Morata.

Adell, J., Llopis, M. A., Esteve, F., & Valdeolivas, M. G. (2019). El debate sobre el pensamiento computacional en educación. *RIED. Revista Iberoamericana de Educación a Distancia*, 22(1), 171–186. https://doi.org/10.5944/ried.22.1.22303

Bel, J. C., Colomer, J. C., & Valls, R. (2019). Alfabetización visual y desarrollo del pensamiento histórico: actividades con imágenes en manuales escolares. *Educación XX1*, 22(1), 353–374. https://doi.org/10.5944/EDUCXX1.20008

Belew, K. [@kathleen_belew]. (2022, January 18). Hey #twitterstorians, want to help me with a thought exercise for students? [Tweet]. *Twitter*. https://twitter.com/kathleen_belew/status/1483559598317518848

Burkholder, P., & Schaffer, D. (2021). *A snapshot of the public's views on history*. www.historians.org/publications-and-directories/perspectives-on-history/september-2021/a-snapshot-of-the-publics-views-on-history-national-poll-offers-valuable-insights-for-historians-and-advocates

Colomer, J. C. (2016). Historypin: una app para el trabajo del pensamiento histórico en Didáctica de las Ciencias Sociales. In AA VV (Ed.), *Libro de Actas. IV Congreso Internacional de Investigación en Innovación Educativa* (pp. 171–176). Murcia: Editum.

Colomer, J. C., Fuertes, C., & Parra, D. (2022). Tecnología educativa y enfoque sociocrítico en enseñanza de la Historia. ¿Dónde estamos? ¿Hacia dónde vamos? *Con-Ciencia Social*, 5, 143–160. https://doi.org/10.7203/CON-CIENCIASOCIAL.5.24271

Colomer, J. C., Sáiz, J., & Valls, R. (2018). Competencias históricas y actividades con recursos tecnológicos en libros de texto de Historia: nuevos materiales y viejas rutinas. *ENSAYOS, Revista de La Facultad de Educación de Albacete*, 33(1), 53–64.

Davis, K., & Gardner, H. (2013). *The app generation*. New Haven: Yale University Press.
Díaz, M. (2000). Foucault, maestros y discursos pedagógicos. In T. Tadeu da Silva (Ed.), *Las pedagogías psicológicas y el gobierno del yo en tiempos liberales* (pp. 29–42). Sevilla: MCEP.
EUNEC (2014). *Learning in the digital age. Report of the seminar of the European network of education councils, Athens, 5–6 May 2014*. www.eunec.eu/sites/www.eunec.eu/files/event/attachments/report.pdf
Fernández-Enguita, M. (2016). *La educación en la encrucijada*. Madrid: Santillana.
Gamboa Fallas, M. (2022). Enseñar historia mediante las redes sociales y enseñar sobre redes sociales mediante la historia: los alcances de las redes sociales en la enseñanza de la historia. *Perspectivas, 24*, 1–20. https://doi.org/10.15359/rp.24.3
Gutiérrez, A., & Tyner, K. (2012). Educación para los medios, alfabetización mediática y competencia digital. *Comunicar, 19*(38), 31–39. https://doi.org/10.3916/C38-2012-02-03
Hangen, T. (2015). Historical digital literacy, one classroom at a time. *The Journal of American History, 101*(4), 1192–1203. https://doi.org/10.1093/jahist/jav062
Haydn, T., & Ribbens, K. (2017). Social media, new technologies and history education. In M. Carretero, S. Berger & M. Grever (Eds.), *Palgrave handbook of research in historical culture and education* (pp. 735–753). London: Palgrave Macmillan. https://doi.org/10.1057/978-1-137-52908-4_38
Lévesque, S. (2008). The impact of digital technologies and the need for technological pedagogical content knowledge. In T. Di Petta (Ed.), *The Emperor's new computer: ICT, teachers and teaching* (pp. 17–28). London: Sense Publishers.
Martínez-Hita, M., Gómez Carrasco, C. J., & Miralles-Martínez, P. (2021). The effects of a gamified project based on historical thinking on the academic performance of primary school children. *Humanities and Social Sciences Communications, 8*(1), 1–10. https://doi.org/10.1057/s41599-021-00796-9
McGrew, S., Breakstone, J., Ortega, T., Smith, M., & Wineburg, S. (2018). Can students evaluate online sources? Learning from assessments of civic online reasoning. *Theory and Research in Social Education, 46*(2), 165–193. https://doi.org/10.1080/00933104.2017.1416320
Morozov, E. (2014). *To save everything, click here: The folly of technological solutionism*. New York: PublicAffairs.
Negueruela, A., & Torres, B. (2021). *La brecha digital impacta en la educación*. www.unicef.es/educa/blog/covid-19-brecha-educativa
Peirats, J., Gallardo, I. M., San Martín, Á., & Waliño, M. J. (2016). Análisis de la industria editorial y Protocolo para la selección del libro de texto en formato digital. *Profesorado. Revista de Curriculum y Formación del Profesorado, 20*(1), 75–89.
Pons, A. (2013). *El desorden digital: guía para historiadores y humanistas*. Madrid: Siglo XXI.
Rosenzweig, R. (2006). Can history be open source? Wikipedia and the future of the past. *The Journal of American History, 93*(1), 117–146. https://doi.org/10.2307/4486062
Santisteban, A., Díez-Bedmar, M. C., & Castellví, J. (2020). Critical digital literacy of future teachers in the Twitter Age. *Cultura y Educación, 32*(2), 185–212. https://doi.org/10.1080/11356405.2020.1741875
Sartori, G. (2021). *Homo Videns: televisione e postpensiero*. Roma-Bari: Laterza.
Seignobos, C. (1901). *La méthode historique appliquée aux sciences sociales*. Paris: Alcan.
Wineburg, S. (2018). *Why learn history (When it's already on your phone)*. Chicago: The University of Chicago Press.
Wineburg, S., Breakstone, J., McGrew, S., Smith, M. D., & Ortega, T. (2022). Lateral reading on the open Internet: A district-wide field study in high school government classes. *Journal of Educational Psychology*. https://doi.org/10.1037/EDU0000740

4
NARRATIVES OF THE PAST
A tool to understand history

Stéphane Lévesque

The nature of historical narrative

What is a historical narrative? The question seems straightforward. Definitions in dictionaries typically equate "narrative" to "story." In the literature, many also refer to an "account" of the past. Narrative, story, and account are often used interchangeably in both scholarly and everyday life practice. This situation leads to more confusion than clarity on the defining features of historical narrative. The difficulty with the concept pertains to the diversity of narratives in society, varying on a number of dimensions: the purposes, the methods used, the medium and genres, and the contexts in which they are produced. Even in the history discipline, historians have debated for a long time the nature of their discipline and its product. The problem, as E.H. Carr (1962) cautiously observed, comes from the fact that the answers to the question "what is history?" invariably reflect our own frame of reference in time.

Indeed, following the European scientific revolution during the early modern period, history came to be understood in the logic of positivism and a "desire for explanations which are at once systematic and controllable by factual evidence that generates science" (Nagel in Megill, 1989: 632). Replacing Christianity as the focal point of reference and civilisation, historical narratives produced by historians were meant to present enlightened and universalizable explanations of the past based on the new scientific method. During the 19th century, scientific history received serious attention in European and American scholarly circles. As French historian Fustel de Coulanges declared in 1862: "History is and should be a science" (in Lévesque, 2008: 22).

But following World War I, vocal critics – notably in France, Italy, and England – questioned the scientific approach to the past and its inability to account for the nature of culture, race, and multiperspectivity. "The moment historical facts are

DOI: 10.4324/9781003289470-6

regarded as instances of general laws," Michael Oakeshott declared in 1933, "history is dismissed" (Oakeshott, 1933: 154). Italian philosopher Benedetto Croce (1941) and his English counterpart R.G. Collingwood (1956) made it clear that historians are guided in their judgments by the sources they select as well as the interests, assumptions, and perspectives they bring to the task of interpreting the past. Pushing these ideas further, others such as Carl Becker, Arthur Danto, Paul Ricoeur (1983), and David Carr have focused more explicitly on narrativism as a method and the complex relation between the "historian and his facts," as Carr (1962) put it.

Indeed, unlike a mere chronicle, the narrative by virtue of its retrospective view "picks out the most important events, traces the causal and motivational connections among them, and give us an organized, coherent account" (Carr, 1986: 59). No historical narrative can offer an integrative interpretation of the past that would cover all aspects for all periods. Furthermore, narratives, as novelists know well, can be either real or imaginary without losing their structure and power. Yet the narrative in history, narrativist historians claim, would form a distinct literary genre. As George Macauley Trevelyan argued: "the appeal of history to us all is in the last analysis poetic. But the poetry of history does not consist of imagination roaming at large, but imagination pursuing the fact and fastening upon it" (in Evans, 1997: 250).

With the recent postmodernist critique of historical knowledge production, the connection between history and narration has been the subject of lively debates. Is history inevitably narrative in form? Are historical narratives truthful representations of the past? Hayden White (1973) compellingly argued that the historical narrative is nothing more than the historian's attempt to mediate between "the historical field, the unprocessed historical record, other historical accounts, and an audience" (p. 5). For White, when historians start to write a narrative, "they are predisposed to organise their insights into specific modes, derived from and limited in choice by what he believed to be the tropic deep structure of historical consciousness" (Parkes, 2018, para. 2). Jörn Rüsen (2005), among others, has responded by arguing that White's argument was nothing new. "No historian," he observed, "could deny the fact that there is a creative activity of the human mind working in the process of historical thinking and recognition" (p. 9). Narration is the way this creative activity is being performed.

It is not necessary here to follow all these debates, except perhaps to note that members of the discipline by and large agree with three general principles as presented by Peter Seixas (2017). First, *narrative representations and the past are conceptually and ontologically different*. The historical narrative is a construct that provides the past with a sense of coherence and direction. It does not simply show what actually happened, as Leopold von Ranke once proclaimed. Most historians now accept that their narratives are not direct, truthful copies of the past but rather "representations" of it (Rüsen, 2005: 4). As such, they cannot be cross-referenced with the past itself but only with other representations of it.

Second, *there can be more than one historical narrative for any given set of events*, centring on different questions, perspectives, ethical choices, and focalisation. There is no such thing as a complete grand narrative of the past. For Ricoeur, narratives must necessarily come to an end; they never "fully exhaust time or the possible long-term meaning of action" (Pellauer & Dauenhauer, 2021, para. 22). Through their orderly arrangements they offer a distinctive synthesis into a kind of "concordant discordance," a sort of "tensive unity which functions as a redescription of a situation in which the internal coherence of the constitutive elements endows them with an explanatory role" (Atkins, 2022, para. 10). In addition, narratives set out to answer particular questions about the past, and these questions are vast besides being informed by our own contemporary realities. "The past," as Arthur Chapman (2016a) puts it, "has a future and the future keeps rewriting the past" (p. 4).

Finally, *all historical narratives can be critiqued for their plausibility*. As I have argued, historians produce narratives that aim at representing a coherent reality that convey verifiable statements. But since history is mode of narrative representation, it has no absolutist epistemological meaning in itself, only a sense of correspondence as "plausibility" defined in terms of principles of narrative construction (Körber, 2015: 17).

History, from this view, is a complex activity that demands strategies for explaining argumentation and for justifying narrative arrangement, and these strategies differentiate narratives produced within the discipline from stories of practical life. For Allan Megill (1989, 2007), historical narratives invariably involve the blending of various tasks, including: recounting/description, explanation, justification, and interpretation.

First, a narrative aims to recount (from the French *raconter*) what the case was (what was it?). Like the telling of a tale, a narrative offers an orderly arrangement of historical actions, happenings, characters, and settings. The interaction of these four elements produces the story. Aristotle called the distinctive arrangement of events (actions and happenings) and existents (characters and settings) the plot of the story. For Louis Mink (1996), the historian's ability to produce this orderly arrangement is made possible through "synoptic judgment," the capacity to see things together and understand the intrinsic relations of prior and later events (p. 42).[1]

But for Allan Megill (1989), the historical narrative often comprises other central tasks, including "argument or justification" (p. 647). Indeed, the purpose of the historian's narrative often goes beyond a descriptive story of what happened to offer an explanation of why a past event or phenomenon came to be (explain why these events happened or why this pattern has arisen). The historian can also aim to interpret or evaluate aspects of the past (to attribute particular meaning and value) or even to justify a particular representation of the past against other

TABLE 4.1 Megill's narrative tasks

Tasks	Description
Recounting	Describing or telling what was the case
Explanation	Explaining why a past event/case came to be
Interpretation	Attributing a particular value and significance to the case
Justification	Justifying a particular representation of the case

possible representations (why this particular narrative?). This justification is based on the historian's appreciation of the past, perspective, and positionality. For Megill (1989), this whole narrating process is circular:

> As part of this recounting, explanations of historical existents and events will be offered. The explanations, once accepted by an audience as persuasive, will become part of its image of what was the case, that is, of what we might call a "representation" of the past. But images of what was the case always make possible further explanation-seeking questions. The further explanations, if accepted as persuasive, will enter into the image of what was the case and will make possible still more explanation-seeking questions
>
> Megill, 1989: 648.

Narrative and narration in history

In his *Narrative and history*, Alun Munslow (2007) presents a simplified yet powerful model of narration, based on the seminal works of literary theorists Gérard Genette and Roland Barthes, that characterises the construction of historical narratives. This model considers three elements interacting in the form of a triangle: *narrating* (the authorial function), *content/story* (the story arrangement), and *expression* (mode of representation/discourse). For Munslow, content/story and narrating exist only by means of the intermediary of the discourse (mode of expression). Reciprocally, the narrative discourse can only be such to the extent that it tells a story.

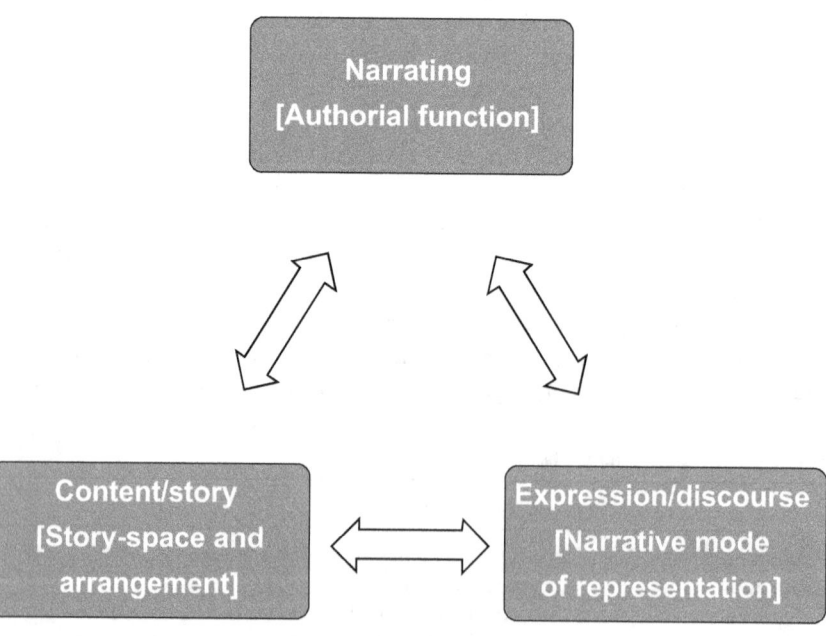

FIGURE 4.1 Munslow's act of narration

First, the past has to be organised into story-form (content/story). As noted earlier, the past is not a grand narrative to be recovered. Historical agents had stories of their own, but these are contextually situated in the past and created for purposes of their own time. The content/story is where the narrator (historian) creates the story-space, which delimits the beginning and the end, as well as the arrangement of events and existents.[2] The story-space implies that the narrator purposely selects through synoptic judgment a limited set of events that belong together. This selection is not accidental or purely time related. A story aims at causal explanation – it attempts "to lay out how one event caused another, as well as the factors that could influence those links" (Barton & Levstik, 2004: 131). The principle of narrativity, as Rüsen (2005) sums it up, "leads to a distinct strategy of explanation that underlies the peculiarity of historical thinking" (p. 60).

Second, narrating requires for Munslow a distinctive mode of representation, that of the discourse. Narrative is not merely a medium of report. It uses various aesthetic and argumentative principles to turn the past into "the past-as-history" (Munslow, 2007: 28). This crucial aspect is often neglected by historians themselves, rendering narrative discourse almost invisible to the audience (Megill & McCloskey, 1987). But as Michael Standford (1994) has argued, historical narratives invariably imply the concept of communication. "Theorists of narrative," he contended, "distinguish between 'story' – that which is to be conveyed, and 'discourse' – the process of conveying it" (p. 108).

For Munslow (2007), historians' authorial decisions centre on a number of narrative representation elements, including voice, focalisation, tense/timing, and intentionality and agency. Voice is concerned with the audibility of the author as the one who tells the story. A historical agent may tell the story in the first person (homodiegetic narrator) or as an observer of the events (first person homodiegetic observer). The author can also choose to tell the story without giving voice to past agents or witnesses by offering an explanation/interpretation/justification as an omniscient narrator who is external to the story (heterodiegetic narrator). Focalisation is concerned with the perspective or who sees within the story. Again, the focalisation can vary according to the purpose set by the author, from internal to external, to zero. In other words, the author can focalise on the internal events themselves (as in an autobiography) or decide to choose a point of view that is external to the events through the perspective of a historical observer (who knows less than the focalised agent). Finally, zero focalisation refers to the heterodiegetic narrator who is not limited by the internal events (at the time) and who knows more than the agents themselves (omniscient). In conventional history, historians tend to adopt this omniscient point of view as heterodiegetic narrators.

But historians also organise the temporal locations of the situations presented in the story. There is thus a fundamental difference between "real time" as experienced by the historical agents and "narrated time" which is "manufactured for purposes of explanation and meaning creation" (Munslow, 2007: 51). Through the narrated time, historians can use figures of analepsis (flashback) or prolepsis (flashforward) and also ellipsis (omission of time periods), pauses (to offer a reflection or recapitulation), or stretch (to expand on a real-time event) to create a diegetic universe that is both meaningful and intelligible and contributes to followability for the audience.

All of these authorial decisions would not be complete without intentionality and agency. Every historian, Munslow (2007) contends, "possesses a philosophy of action" (p. 60). This "theory of agency" makes it possible to decide who is given a perspective and/or voice in the narrative. The historian also controls how to describe the historical agents, their characters and intentions, and how to present their actions through distinctive rhetorical strategies. These authorial decisions in terms of the significance of action and agency are contextually situated. They result from the "historian's belief in the extent to which action and agency contribute to cause and effect in human affairs" (Munslow, 2007: 60).

The educational context: England, Germany, and Canada

In Europe and around the western world, history education, as conceptualised in educational research and programs of teacher education, has gradually moved away from the teaching and learning of master narratives of the collective past (the so-called romantic approach) to the development of historical thinking (Carretero et al., 2012). As Stéphane Lévesque and Penney Clark (2018) observe, the concept has literally become a "standard" in the theory and practice of history education (p. 119).

Yet this educational development has taken a variety of forms depending on culture and research traditions. In the last decades, at least three major traditions have developed in the Western world that offer useful insight for our understanding of narrative competence. In England, where the works on historical thinking have a long research tradition going back to the School Council History Project, the focus has been placed on history as a disciplinary inquiry intended at making true statements and valid claims about the past. Moving away from first-order knowledge acquisition (know that), English history educators conceptualised the notion of "second-order concepts" (know how), concepts that provide our understanding of history as a form of knowledge (Lee, 2004). These include evidence, explanation, causation, significance, and change. For Peter Lee and Rosalyn Ashby (2000), this important change in education could be described as a shift from the assumption that school history was only a matter of teaching narrative knowledge to "a concern with second-order ideas" (p. 199). For Chapman (2016b), this influential tradition "as a form of knowledge or discipline" was inspired by scholars like Jerome Bruner (1985) who claimed that it was possible for school subjects to express the epistemological structure and logic of the academic disciplines on which they were modelled in authentic ways and at age-appropriate level of presentation and complexity (p. 227).

Much of the rich literature in the English tradition has centred around students' progression in their development of history as evidenced by their mastering of second-order concepts. These studies have offered the educational community useful, evidence-based results on students' (mis)conceptions and historical ideas, at different age levels, and didactical ways to develop more sophisticated or "powerful" ideas (Chapman, 2021). Recently, some researchers have also explored the notion of historical interpretation – the ability to understand and develop a historical argument. These studies provide new empirical data on learners' understandings of argumentation but with limited consideration for the elaboration of narratives among learners (Chapman, 2011; Fordham, 2007; Kemp, 2011; Magnoff, 2016; Worth, 2013).

To know more about narrative in history and education, we need to turn to the German tradition which has relied more broadly on the philosophical notion of historical consciousness – the awareness that human beings and their cultures exist in time and need to be analysed as such. For German scholars, history is not principally a discipline to emulate. Rather, it is an essential cultural factor in everyone's life (Rüsen, 2005). People interpret past actualities in order to make sense of the world and act in the present with a view to the future. Disciplinary history, in this perspective, is a systematic way of performing this function. For Rüsen (2004), this understanding of history can be expressed in a "matrix of historiography" that offers a conceptual basis for representing, in the form of a wheel, the ongoing relationship between the discipline of history and the larger cultural circumstances (*lebenspraxis*) within which the discipline is practiced. The matrix consists of a dynamic connection among five key principles: the cognitive interest (people need temporal orientation for guidance); the theory and views that historians have concerning the past; the methods of empirical research (the rules and principles of history); the forms of historical representations (the narratives); and the functions of orientation (narratives contribute to life-practice, identity formation, and guidance for actions).

Learning to think historically in the German tradition was not initially conceptualised as an educational objective but rather as a cognitive tool for advancing historical consciousness (Körber, 2015). As Rüsen (2005) contends, the goal was to elaborate "an ontogenetic development of historical consciousness" by investigating its cognitive competencies (p. 34). At the core of these competencies lies historical narration.

Indeed, in the German tradition, narrative competence is understood as the ability to narrate a story by means of which practical life is given an orientation in the course of time. Narrativity is considered "a structural principle" of historical thinking and learning (Waldis et al., 2015: 117). The discipline of history becomes relevant to this competence insofar as it offers theories and methodological rules to articulate narratives that are theoretically guided. Through the articulation of its research and forms of representations, history responds to the general functions of life orientation through a "critical stance" (Stanford, 1994: 51).

Following this conception of historical consciousness, a number of European studies have ventured into the distinctive operations of narrative competence and reported on how students perform, notably in the context of evidence-based assessments of historical thinking. For example, the German FUER model has emphasised the dimensions of narrative construction (how to synthetically construct historical arguments from sources) and deconstruction (how to analytically evaluate and reflect on historical arguments) as well as associated progression models (see Hasberg & Körber, 2003; Körber & Meyer-Hamme, 2015). Other studies have also highlighted the nature as well as the educational challenge of evaluating narrative competence considering "there is a lack of empirically valid criteria by which narrative performance can be assessed" (Waldis et al., 2015: 117).

In Canada, a confluence of scholarly initiatives around the turn of the 21st century resulted in combination of these two European traditions into distinctive models of historical thinking. In English Canada, Peter Seixas' scholarship was an impetus for an upsurge of interest in history in the schools as "an exercise in disciplined knowledge" (Seixas, 2000: 24). Influenced by the English tradition, Seixas and his collaborators laid out a set of six historical thinking concepts functioning as problems or issues that demand comprehension and "productive solutions to them" (Seixas, 2017: 5). While these concepts (historical significance, continuity and change, evidence, cause and causation, perspective-taking, and ethical dimension) find their realisation in making sense of historical narratives (O'Neill et al., 2022), the narrative competence has yet to be explicitly addressed in curricula and educational research which, thus far, has looked predominantly at the distinctive concepts and their application in school history (Anderson, 2017). Recently studies have nonetheless ventured into students' narrative ideas in relation to historical thinking (see den Heyer, 2018; Gibson, 2017; Peck, 2010).

Interestingly, it is in French Canada that issues of historical consciousness, identity, and narration have more successfully been transposed into educational research. Under the influence of scholars such as Jocelyn Létourneau (2006) there has been a strong push in the last decade to move away from knowledge acquisition to students' narrative understandings. Starting from the constructivist belief that students are active learners who always approach formal learning with some prior-narrative knowledge, a significant body of the research in French Canada has focused on how students' narrative constructions align (or not) with official narratives of the collective past (Cardin, 2015; Duquette, 2015; Moisan et al., 2020; Robichaud, 2011). Results from these studies have offered varied and stimulating evidence of the link between students' identity and cultural belonging and their narratives and counter-narratives of the past – notably in the context of French-speaking minoritised groups within Canada.

The Québec history curriculum has recently been revised to include more directly the narrative, as recommended by the provincial report *The Meaning of History: Toward a Rethinking of the History and Citizenship Education Program in the Secondary III and IV* (Beauchemin & Fahmy-Eid, 2014). As of now, it is still unclear how Québec teachers understand, teach, and evaluate students' narratives in class (Éthier et al., 2017; Russell, 2018; Zanazanian, 2015). Interestingly, empirical works conducted in French Canada have been considered or transposed to various international studies using a similar narrative methodology to probe students' historical thinking (Calder, 2013; Carrier, 2016; Gonzalez-Monfort et al., 2016; Lantheaume & Létourneau, 2016; Reich et al., 2015; Wineburg et al., 2007).

But as Monika Waldis and her colleagues have argued, the conceptualisation of narrative competence remains vague in the educational literature, even in countries where educators have ventured into the field. Part the problem arises from the difficulty among educators at arriving at a clear understanding of what historical narratives are and how to go about teaching it.

Teaching the narrative competence

"The chief advantage of using narrative [in history education]," as Keith Barton and Linda Levstik (2004) contend, "is its familiarity" (p. 136). Children are exposed to narratives very early in life and through various family and cultural tools. Children and historians, they note, use narrative "in fundamentally similar ways": to make sense of the complexity of the past. Narrative is thus, from this view, a relevant "linguistic form" within which history realises its function of representation and interpretation (Rüsen, 2005: 26).

This is not to say, however, that students have developed sophisticated understandings of historical narratives beyond the needs of practical life. Various studies have reported on students' naïve (realistic) epistemological beliefs, often equating history with a single, authoritative narrative or "window" to the past (Lee & Ashby, 2000; Maggioni et al., 2009; Shemilt, 2000). Other studies have discussed students' narrative oversimplifications, their tendencies to reduce the complexity of the past to a set of characters and events of limited proportion and often arranged with a teleological perspective as if historical change was inevitably a rational process, usually in terms of progress (Barton, 2008; Létourneau, 2014; Shemilt, 2000; Lévesque & Croteau, 2020).

Equally interesting are studies looking at the sociocultural context of students' narratives (see Peck, 2018). Students' historical ideas do not always emanate from formal learning and often conflict with what they learn in school. Identity and ethnocultural background are two factors that seriously affect the ways in which students accept, modify, or reject new knowledge from school history (Barton & McCully, 2012; Epstein, 2009; Peck, 2010). In fact, students' adherence to particular historical narratives leads them to "discount or transform the content of the curriculum" (Barton, 2008: 247). Studies with Francophone students in Canada have revealed that the more students identify strongly with their community or "nation," the more their narratives of the collective past offer militant, politically-oriented views (Lévesque et al., 2015).

Faced with these results, how can we teach the narrative competence? There is clearly no simple answer, and responses are likely to vary from one educational context to another. Yet the previous presentation of the different traditions offers useful advice for orienting our practice as history educators. Taken together, these traditions help situate history learning both in the formal and informal sociocultural contexts in which young people live their practical life (Ahonen, 2017). As such, I believe that history educators no less than researchers need to (re)conceptualise the development of students' historical narratives as the effective result of the interplay among historical culture, practical life, schooling, and the practice of history (Grever & Adriaansen, 2017). How we conceptualise the rationale for teaching narrative competence should thus be informed by the study, influence, and interplay of these forces.

Conclusion: deconstruction and reconstruction of narratives

In conclusion, I present some pedagogical reflections on how to better integrate students' engagement with conflicting stories of the past so they can learn to (1) deconstruct their personal and community narratives and (2) generate more powerful and usable historical narratives that serve to orient their life. These reflections are also inspired by the recent works of German, Dutch, and Swiss scholars in the field (van Boxtel & van Drie, 2018; Körber & Meyer-Hamme, 2015; Körber, 2021; Waldis et al., 2015).

Our empirical works in Canada suggest that students are more likely to revise their misconceptions and learn new knowledge when they have access to relevant evidence from their own learning experience. Learners do not acquire knowledge as if it were being imprinted on some sort of mental hard drive. They learn additional information based on what know – or think they know. Educators should thus adopt a constructivist view of history learning and teach in reference to students' narrative ideas. They should use this personal connection to explore students' prior knowledge, identity, and conception of history. As Bruce VanSledright (2014) has argued, students' epistemic beliefs greatly affect how they make sense of history. The case of the "truth-lie" narrative dichotomy, he argues, makes successful investigation of the past virtually impossible (VanSledright, 2014: 71). Cultivating narrative competence thus requires the ability to deconstruct representations of the past circulating in historical culture and expressed by students. This deconstruction process makes it possible to understand the value, limit, and constructedness of narratives as defined in the previous section on the nature of historical narrative. Many narratives are told in society that may contradict, compete with, or complement one another, and this means students should be equipped with the intellectual tools, such as the ones devised by the English and Canadian scholars (e.g., causation and perspective-taking), to unpack these representations of the past. Deconstruction empowers learners; it changes the initial power relation between the narrator and the narratees who gradually learn to become more critical of the arguments presented and the narrative choices made by the narrator.

Given the performative nature of narrative, it is also necessary for students to have the opportunity to reconstruct more powerful narrative representations as a result of their critical analysis. Like Létourneau (2017), I believe that the current curricular emphasis on historical thinking inquiry does not empower students to become active historical narrators, that is, to relate learned information from various perspectives into a coherent, plausible picture of the past that makes sense to them. As he puts it, such a revised curriculum would have two complementary purposes:

Over all, reconciling the complex and the meaningful for the purpose of helping the youth understand the national past would be a two-step process: first, a methodical examination of acquired knowledge (deconstruction of national visions held by the youth, which are often closed and categorical and enshrined in established mythistory); then, a methodical development of alternative knowledge (reconstruction of compound and open representations of the collective past). (Létourneau, 2017: 236)

Recently, Andreas Körber (2021) has further elaborated this learning process in the form of a multidimensional progression model of historical thinking. While this conceptual model is still highly theoretical, it offers useful guidance on how to develop the narrative competence in ways that empower learners to apply key concepts and intellectual operations in authentic, real-life situations so they become "aware of different, more complex and powerful relations, and to reflect and to develop them" (Körber, 2021: 15). Clearly, more pedagogical work is needed to transpose such a conceptualisation to distinctive educational cultures and contexts.

In the end, I believe that history education urgently needs new approaches that aim to empower students as historical narrators who can construct more valid and usable historical narratives. These narratives should not aim to be universal or absolute truths about the past but always provisional representations open to deconstruction and reconstruction based on new questions and lived experiences useful to orient their 21st century life.

Notes

1 To know more about synoptic judgment and the process of arranging events into narrative, see my section "Understanding the sequence of events" in Lévesque (2008).
2 Historical narratives do not always explicitly present the distinctive categories of beginning, orderly arrangement, and conclusion. Following Megill, I believe that whether these are explicitly present or not, we (as narratees) can project each of these elements from what is present in the story. Accordingly, we may still consider an abbreviated or fragmented narrative as a proto-narrative. Jürgen Staub (2005) refers to this as narrative abbreviation because it contains a story or suggests other stories without being a complete narrative. These narrative abbreviations, he argues, "can be hermeneutically explicated only by recourse to the stories that they contain or suggest" (p. 62).

References

Ahonen, S. (2017). The lure of grand narratives: A dilemma for history teachers. In H. A. Elmersjö, A. Clark, & M. Vinterek (Eds.), *International perspectives on teaching rival histories* (pp. 41–62). Hoboken, NJ: Palgrave Macmillan.

Anderson, S. (2017). The stories nations tell: Sites of pedagogy, historical consciousness, and national narratives. *Canadian Journal of Education, 40*(1), 1–38.

Atkins, K. (2022). Paul Ricoeur. *Internet Encyclopedia of Philosophy.* https://iep.utm.edu/ricoeur/

Barton, K. C. (2008). Narrative simplifications in elementary students' historical thinking.". In L. S. Levstik & K. C. Barton (Eds.), *Researching history education: Theory, method, and context* (pp. 51–83). London: Routledge.

Barton, K. C., & Levstik, L. S. (2004). *Teaching history for the common good*. Hoboken, NJ: Lawrence Erlbaum Associates.

Barton, K. C., & McCully, A. (2012). Trying to "see things differently": Northern Ireland students' struggle to understand alternative historical perspectives. *Theory & Research in Social Education*, *40*(4), 371–408. https://doi.org/10.1080/00933104.2012.710928

Beauchemin, J., & Fahmy-Eid, N. (2014). *The sense of history: Towards a rethinking of the history and citizenship education program in secondary III and IV*. Quebec: Government of Quebec.

Bruner, J. (1985). Narrative and paradigmatic modes of thought. In E. Eisner (Ed.), *Learning and teaching the ways of knowing* (pp. 97–115). Chicago: University of Chicago Press.

Calder, L. (2013). The stories we tell. *OAH Magazine of History*, *27*(3), 5–8.

Cardin, J. F. (2015). La place du récit dans l'apprentissage de l'histoire. *A l'école de Clio: Histoire et didactique de l'histoire*, *1*. https://ecoleclio.hypotheses.org/275

Carr, D. (1986). *Time, narrative, and history*. Bloomington, IN: Indiana University Press.

Carr, E. H. (1962). *What is history?* Hoboken, NJ: Macmillan.

Carretero, M., Asensio, M., & Rodríguez-Moneo, M. (Eds.). (2012). *History education and the construction of national identities*. London: Information Age.

Carrier, P. (2016). L'Allemagne : un récit sans narrateur. In F. Lantheaume & J. Létourneau (Eds.), *Le récit du commun : L'histoire nationale racontée par les élèves* (pp. 179–188). Lyon: Presses de l'Université de Lyon.

Chapman, A. (2011). Historical interpretation. In I. Davies (Ed.), *Debates in history teaching* (pp. 96–108). Abingdon: Routledge.

Chapman, A. (2016a). *Developing students' understanding of historical interpretation*. London: Edxecel/Pearson.

Chapman, A. (2016b). Historical thinking/historical knowing: On the content of the form of history education. In C. Counsell, K. Burn & A. Chapman (Eds.), *MasterClass in history education: Transforming teaching and learning* (pp. 225–232). London: Bloomsbury.

Chapman, A. (Ed.). (2021). *Knowing history in schools: Powerful knowledge and the powers of knowledge*. London: UCL Press.

Collingwood, R. G. (1956). *The idea of history*. Oxford: Oxford University Press.

Croce, B. (1941). *History as the story of liberty*. London: Allen and Unwin Ltd.

den Heyer, K. (2018). Historical agency: Stories of choice, action, and social change. In S. A. Metzger & L. M. Harris (Eds.), *Wiley international handbook of history teaching and learning* (pp. 227–252). New York, NY: Wiley-Blackwell.

Duquette, C. (2015). Relating historical consciousness to historical thinking through assessment. In K. Ercikan & P. Seixas (Eds.), *New directions in assessing historical thinking* (pp. 51–63). New York, NY: Routledge.

Epstein, T. (2009). *Interpreting national history: Race, identity, and pedagogy in classrooms and communities*. New York, NY: Routledge.

Éthier, M. A., Boutonnet, V., Demers, S., & Lefrançois, D. (2017). *Quel sens pour l'histoire? Analyse critique du nouveau programme d'histoire du Québec et du Canada*. Québec: M Editeur.

Evans, R. (1997). *In defence of history*. New York, NY: Granta Books.

Fordham, M. (2007). Slaying dragons and sorcerers in year 12: In search of historical argument. *Teaching History*, *129*, 31–38.

Gibson, L. (2017, April 27–30). *Constructing students' historical reference frameworks in Canadian history using visual source-based timelines* [Paper Presentation]. American Educational Research Association Annual Meeting, San Antonio, TX.

Gonzalez-Monfort, N., Santisteban-Fernandez, A., Pagès-Blanch, J., & Sant-Obiols, E. (2016). La Catalogue : entre mémoire collective, mythes populaires et projections politiques. In F. Lantheaume & J. Létourneau (Eds.), *Le récit du commun : L'histoire nationale racontée par les élèves* (pp. 191–204). Lyon: Presses de l'Université de Lyon.

Grever, M., & Adriaansen, R. J. (2017). Historical culture: A concept revisited. In M. Carretero, S. Berger, & M. Grever (Eds.), *Palgrave handbook of research in historical culture and education* (pp. 73–89). London: Palgrave-Macmillan.

Hasberg, W., & Körber, A. (2003). Geschichtsbewusstsein dynamisch. In A. Körber (Ed.), *Geschichte – Leben – Lernen. Bodo von Borries zum 60. Geburtstag. Schwal-50/56* (pp. 177–200). New York, NY: Wochenschau-Verlag (Forum Historisches Lernen).

Kemp, R. (2011). Thematic or sequential analysis in causal explanations? Investigating the kinds of historical understanding that year 8 and year 10 demonstrate in the efforts to construct narratives. *Teaching History, 145*, 32–43.

Körber, A. (2015). *Historical consciousness, historical competencies – And beyond? Some conceptual development within German history didactics.* Frankfurt: Deutsches Institut für Internationale Pädagogische Forschung.

Körber, A. (2021). Historical consciousness, knowledge, and competencies of historical thinking: An integrated model of historical thinking and curricular implications. *Historical Encounters, 8*(1), 97–119. doi.org/10.52289/hej8.107

Körber, A., & Meyer-Hamme, J. (2015). Historical thinking, competencies, and their measurements: Challenges and approaches. In K. Ercikan & P. Seixas (Eds.), *New directions in assessing historical thinking* (pp. 89–101). New York, NY: Routledge.

Lantheaume, F., & Létourneau, J. (Eds.). (2016). *Le récit du commun: L'histoire nationale racontée par les élèves.* Lyon: Presses universitaires de Lyon.

Lee, P. (2004). Understanding history. In P. Seixas (Ed.), *Theorizing historical consciousness* (pp. 129–164). Toronto: University of Toronto Press.

Lee, P., & Ashby, R. (2000). Progression in historical understanding among students ages 7–14. In P. Stearns, P. Seixas & S. Wineburg (Eds.), *Knowing, teaching, and learning history: National and international perspectives* (pp. 199–222). New York, NY: New York University Press.

Létourneau, J. (2006). Remembering our past: An examination of the historical memory of young Québécois. In R. Sandwell (Ed.), *To the past: History education, public memory and citizenship education* (pp. 70–87). Toronto: University of Toronto Press.

Létourneau, J. (2014). *Je me souviens? Le passé du Québec dans la conscience de sa jeunesse.* Zürich: Fides.

Létourneau, J. (2017). Teaching national history to young people today. In M. Carretero, S. Berger, Stefan & M. Grever (Eds.), *Palgrave handbook of research in historical culture and education* (pp. 227–242). Palgrave-Macmillan. doi:10.1057/978-1-137-52908-4_12

Lévesque, S. (2008). *Thinking historically: Educating students for the 21st Century.* Toronto: University of Toronto Press.

Lévesque, S., & Clark, P. (2018). Historical thinking: Definitions and educational applications. In S. A. Metzger & L. M. Harris (Eds.), *Wiley international handbook of history teaching and learning* (pp. 119–148). New York, NY: Wiley-Blackwell.

Lévesque, S., & Croteau, J. P. (2020). *Beyond history for historical consciousness: Students, narratives, and memory.* Toronto: University of Toronto Press.

Lévesque, S., Gani, R., & Croteau, J. P. (2015). La conscience historique de jeunes Franco-Ontariens d'Ottawa: Histoire et sentiment d'appartenance. *Revue d'histoire de l'éducation, 27*(2), 21–47. https://doi.org/10.32316/hse/rhe.v27i2.4393

Maggioni, L., VanSledright, B., & Alexander, P. A. (2009). Walking on the borders: A measure of epistemic cognition in history. *Journal of Experimental Education, 77*(3), 187–213. https://doi.org/10.3200/JEXE.77.3.187-214

Magnoff, D. (2016). Historical interpretation: Using online discussion. In C. Counsell, K. Burn & A. Chapman (Eds.), *MasterClass in history education: Transforming teaching and learning* (pp. 2105–120). London: Bloomsbury.

Megill, A. (1989). Recounting the past: Description, explanation, and narrative in historiography. *The American Historical Review, 94*(3), 627–653.

Megill, A. (2007). *Historical knowledge, historical error: A contemporary guide to practice*. Chicago, IL: University of Chicago Press.

Megill, A., & McCloskey, D. (1987). The rhetoric of history. In J. Nelson, A. Megill, & D. McCloskey (Eds.), *The rhetoric of the human sciences* (pp. 221–238). Madison, WI: University of Wisconsin Press.

Mink, L. (1996). The autonomy of historical understanding. *History and Theory, 5*(1), 24–27.

Moisan, S., Warren, J. P., Zanazanian, P., Hirsch, S, & Maltais-Landry, A. (2020). La pluralité des expériences historiques dans le passé du Québec et du Canada. Points de vue des historiennes et historiens universitaires. *Revue d'histoire de l'Amérique française, 1–2*(74), 103–127.

Munslow, A. (2007). *Narrative and history*. Hoboken, NJ: Palgrave-Macmillan.

Oakeshott, M. (1933). *Experience and its modes*. Cambridge: Cambridge University Press.

O'Neill, K., Guloy, S., MacKellar, F., & Martelli, D. (2022). Development and validation of a practical classroom assessment of students' conceptions about differing historical accounts. *Historical Encounters, 9*(1). https://www.hej-hermes.net/9-104

Parkes, R. (2018). The practical legacy of Hayden White. *Public History Weekly, 6*(17). https://public-history-weekly.degruyter.com/6-2018-17/the-practical-legacy-of-hayden-white/

Peck, C. (2010). "It's not like [I'm] Chinese and Canadian. I am in between": Ethnicity and students' conceptions of historical significance. *Theory & Research in Social Education, 38*(4), 574–617. https://doi.org/10.1080/00933104.2010.10473440

Peck, C. (2018). National, ethnic, and Indigenous identities and perspectives. In S. A. Metzger & L. M. Harris (Eds.), *Wiley international handbook of history teaching and learning* (pp. 311–334). London: Wiley-Blackwell.

Pellauer, D., & Dauenhauer, B. (2021). Paul Ricoeur. *The Stanford Encyclopaedia of Philosophy*. Spring. https://plato.stanford.edu/archives/spr2021/entries/ricoeur/

Reich, G. A., Buffington, M., & Muth, W. R. (2015). (Dis)Union at 150: Collective memories of Secession. *Theory & Research in Social Education, 43*(4), 499–527. https://doi.org/10.1080/00933104.2015.1100151

Ricoeur, P. (1983). *Temps et récit*. Vol. 1. Paris: Seuil.

Robichaud, M. (2011). L'histoire de l'Acadie telle que racontée par les jeunes francophones du Nouveau-Brunswick. *Acadiensis, 40*(2), 33–69.

Rüsen, J. (2004). Historical consciousness: Narrative structure, moral function, and ontogenetic development. In P. Seixas (Ed.), *Theorizing historical consciousness* (pp. 63–85). Toronto: University of Toronto Press.

Rüsen, J. (2005). *History: Narration, interpretation, orientation*. New York, NY: Berghahn Books.

Russell, M. (2018). *An analysis of the Quebec history examination: Validity and historical thinking*. [Unpublished master's thesis]. Ottawa: University of Ottawa.

Seixas, P. (2000). Schweigen! die kinder! Or, does postmodern history have a place in the schools? In P. Stearns, P. Seixas & S. Wineburg (Eds.), *Knowing, teaching, and learning history: National and international perspectives* (pp. 19–37). New York, NY: New York University Press.

Seixas, P. (2017). Teaching rival histories: In search of narrative plausibility. In H. A. Elmersjö, A. Clark, & M. Vinterek (Eds.), *International perspectives on teaching rival histories* (pp. 253–268). Hoboken, NJ: Palgrave-Macmillan.

Shemilt, D. (2000). The caliph's coin: The currency of narrative frameworks in history teaching. In P. Stearns, P. Seixas & S. Wineburg (Eds.), *Knowing, teaching, and learning history: National and international perspectives* (pp. 83–101). New York, NY: New York University Press.

Stanford, M. (1994). *A companion to the study of history*. London: Blackwell.

Straub, J. (2005). *Narration, identity, and historical consciousness*. London: Berghan Books.

van Boxtel, C., & van Drie, J. (2018). Historical reasoning: Conceptualizations and educational applications. In S. A. Metzger & L. M. Harris (Eds.), *Wiley international handbook of history teaching and learning* (pp. 149–176). New York, NY: Wiley-Blackwell.

Van Sledright, B. (2014). *Assessing historical thinking and understanding: Innovative designs for new standards*. New York, NY: Routledge.

Waldis, M., Hodel, J., Thünemann, H., Zülsdorf-Kerstin, M., & Zeigler, B. (2015). Material-based and open-ended writing tasks for assessing narrative competence among students. In K. Ercikan & P. Seixas (Eds.), *New directions in assessing historical thinking* (pp. 117–131). New York, NY: Routledge.

White, H. (1973). *Metahistory*. Hoboken, NJ: Johns Hopkins University Press.

Wineburg, S., Mosborg, S., & Porat, D. (2007). Forrest Gump and the future of teaching the past. *Phi Delta Kappan, 89*(3), 168–177. https://doi.org/10.1177/003172170708900305

Worth, P. (2013). "English kind Frederick I won at Arsuf, then took Acre, then they all went home": Exploring the challenges involved in reading and writing historical narratives. *Teaching History, 156*, 9–19.

Zanazanian, P. (2015). Historical consciousness and being Québécois: Exploring young English- speaking students' interactions with Quebec's master historical narrative. *Canadian Ethnic Studies, 47*(2), 113–135. https://doi.org/10.1353/ces.2015.0013

5
CONTROVERSIAL HERITAGE FOR ECO-CITIZENSHIP EDUCATION IN SOCIAL SCIENCE DIDACTICS

Implications for initial teacher education[1]

Sergio Sampedro-Martín Elisa Arroyo-Mora José María Cuenca-López Myriam J. Martín-Cáceres

Controversial issues and eco-citizenship education

Education, understood as a driver of socio-environmental change in a complex, shifting and uncertain reality, must guarantee the training of citizens committed to their community and heritage, resilient and participatory in their immediate context. Today, therefore, it is an educational requirement to implement proposals in the area of Social Sciences that encourage students to make decisions and get involved in social and community actions under the civic principles that underpin democracy, such as equality, dignity, social cohesion and justice (Lucas & Delgado-Algarra, 2018).

However, although one of the main functions of the education system is to prepare students to learn to live and coexist in society acting as critical and active citizens, it is still common to find training deficiencies in teachers who implement teaching and learning processes in the Social Sciences. And, more specifically, in teachers of History, which consists of the transmission of theoretical and rote learning contents (Prats et al., 2021) based on a collective identity project which, as posited by Ibagón and Miralles (2021), continues to reinforce the negative and stereotyped image of the other and whose naturalisation of the victimisation of certain groups is uncritically received by students.

To provide a solution to this uncritical transmission and reception of memorised and partial contents, the introduction of controversial issues in the teaching and learning processes has been attempted in discrete contexts and at different times over the last century with the aim of promoting the reflective and critical spirit of the students. Santisteban (2019) provides a historical and conceptual review of the different ways of including theoretical or ideological conflict in the classroom, starting from the problematisation of the curricular contents as a methodological strategy and the problem-situations originating from the French-speaking context.

DOI: 10.4324/9781003289470-7

Another possible alternative to this approach is, according to these authors, to make social questions the backbone of the curriculum based on controversial issues, a concept typical of critical theory and the English-speaking world, or on current social issues, characteristic of the French-speaking context of the 1990s.

In this line, the Council of Europe recommends "addressing controversial issues for the education of a critical citizenship, which develops a socially transforming democratic commitment" (Estepa et al., 2021: 484) while stressing, through the principles established in the 2005 Faro Convention,[2] that heritage is articulated as an element for development and social participation and transformation. Thus, in the Spanish context, through the results of the EPITEC project[3] (Estepa, 2013), it became clear that heritage education, based on the analysis of relevant socio-environmental problems, is the link between emotional and territorial intelligence, leading to the forming of a critical, participatory and democratic citizenship.

Relevant socio-environmental issues addressed through direct contact with the heritage elements of the surrounding context (Estepa, 2001) allow students to relate school to life and reflect on possible alternatives to the conflicts that take place in their environment (Santisteban, 2019). Therefore, to fill the void that exists in schools regarding the controversies that revolve around heritage as a vector of identity, it is essential to equip future teachers with competencies and skills that will enable them to critically analyse the relationships established between history, heritage elements and the current socio-political model (Berríos et al., 2021). This way it will be possible to achieve a heritage education that will enable the acquisition of a greater commitment to their community, the understanding of past-present connections and the reflection on possible consequences of their actions in the present and in future (Arroyo & Cuenca, 2021; Ibagón & Miralles, 2021) in order to understand and assess them from a critical and constructive perspective, favouring the development of territorial and emotional intelligence competences (Trabajo & Cuenca, 2017).

Setting out from these premises, the EPITEC 2[4] project advocates working on the basis of controversial heritages (Estepa et al., 2021), defined as perspectives of those heritage elements that are didactically selected for various reasons that give rise to or generate conflict, controversy, dilemma or debate, whether ideological, political, economic, social, cultural or environmental, due to interaction between them or which involve some type of discrimination or hegemonic dominance of one element over another, causing the latter to be forgotten or silenced, although not always consciously.

The educational aim of addressing the controversies generated around heritage is for students in initial teacher training to analyse hegemonic history critically, along with the hierarchisation of relationships, human domination over bodies and territories and the discrimination, marginalisation and/or oppression of certain social groups and be able to take individual and collective action to build a more just, peaceful, egalitarian and sustainable society. Through this approach, the ecological advocacy that working with controversial heritages should foster in future teachers goes beyond the forming of a global or planetary citizenship, (García-Pérez et al.,

2015), through the anthropocentrism implicit in this concept, in order to achieve a new eco-citizen model (Pabón-Figueras & Pino-Mejías, 2019) in which humans have a harmonious relationship with nature with the awareness of being one more species that inhabits the planet (De la Rasilla, 2008).

For eco-citizenship training it is necessary to leverage heritage education from an ecosocial perspective so that teachers and students become protagonists of a social, political, economic and cultural shift that allows societies to live sustainably on the planet (Assadourian, 2017). Ecosocial education is focused on achieving common welfare through a civilisational change in which all individual, collective and institutional actions are based on the cornerstones that sustain human and non-human life.

From this ecosocial standpoint, it is essential, as González-Reyes (2018) states, to "educate from a dual perspective" (p. 12): one that analyses the past and present and the demands of today's society and another that projects into the future, providing students with the skills they will need throughout their lives. The surrounding context, heritage and urban landscapes are ideal for analysing and linking the past and the present, as they "help us to think about ourselves" (Díez-Bedmar, 2018: 69), to know who we are, what our community is like, the reason for our traditions and how we shape ourselves as a society. Likewise, our daily life in cities encourages us to create the spaces we want, the heritages we identify with and social transformation in pursuit of social and environmental justice. Thus, the natural, social and cultural environment is inescapable in the process of education for a critical citizenship committed to the democratic memory of its past, the problems of the present and the construction of its future (Estepa, 2019).

This past-present-future interconnection in ecosocial citizenship training aims to equip students with a set of skills that will enable them to develop in their context in a coherent, conscious, sustainable and global manner – global thinking, local action – (Delgado-Algarra, 2015). To this end, Assadourian (2017) describes ecosocial education on the basis of six principles that should be included in its implementation at all educational stages: dependence on the Earth, interdependence, creativity, deep learning, Earth-centred leadership and life skills training.

The principles of dependence on the Earth and interdependence are correlated in the basis of the ethics of care, since, as Herrero (2015) states, human beings are eco-dependent beings; we depend on nature to sustain life, as does any species that inhabits the planet, and interdependent beings, as we need the physical and emotional care that other people dedicate to us throughout our lives. It is therefore essential to promote co-responsibility in caring for people and heritage, undertaking actions that ensure the sustainability of life and security for all forms of life that coexist and live together on our planet because, in the words of Tardón (2011), "caring for life means caring for others; the fate of nature depends on human action" (p. 541).

The ethics of care in ecosocial education, in relation to the interdependence it highlights, requires educational processes to include the development of emotional competencies that complement cognitive skills and are basic for life (Bisquerra & Pérez-Escoda, 2012). In this sense, heritage education is configured as the perfect framework for this purpose, as the heritage of the immediate context is inserted into the life experiences of the students and its identitarian potential presents a great capacity for the mobilisation of emotions and values such as solidarity, understanding, commitment, joy, motivation, care, affection, accompaniment, creativity, empathy, etc. (Estepa et al., 2021). Moreover, heritage is an educational resource that arouses students' motivation, provides useful school content for the socio-environmental transformation of their surroundings and thus promotes meaningful or, in the words of Assadourian (2017), deep learning.

Ecosocial education promotes the training of eco-citizens aware that their territory is the basis on which life is built and the epicentre of social, cultural and natural development (Trabajo, 2020: 99) and who are committed to safeguarding its heritage for the socio-ecological balance and preservation of the identity of peoples. This understanding of territory as a collaborative and participatory space for societies is known as territorial intelligence (Perea-Medina et al., 2018).

Fostering the development of students' territorial intelligence is essential to encourage shared reflection and broaden the understanding of the interaction between different human agents, cultural artifacts and landscapes (Miedes & Martín-Cáceres, 2021) in order to boost the capacity for action and transformation on the environment, a concept that Giddens (2006) calls agency and which corresponds in part to the life skills training that Assadourian (2017) includes among the principles of social education for social justice and ecojustice.

In this way, the territory, relevant socio-environmental issues and controversial heritages appear as suitable elements for work in the initial training of Social Science teachers from an ecosocial perspective, either as teaching content or as resources for the development of aspiring student teachers, building an eco-citizenship that seeks social transformation under the principles of justice, ecojustice, empathy, equity and equality.

Controversial heritages for history teaching

Once we have defined what we call controversial heritages and highlighted their potential for dealing with controversial issues for educational purposes, below we present a classification of the different perspectives from which these heritages could be analysed, divided into three main blocks. We also highlight their usefulness for teaching through historical examples of each of the perspectives present in our classification.

Block 1: Heritage in conflict

In this block we will address examples of heritage elements that include perspectives that in themselves generate controversy or conflict and involve political, economic, cultural, religious or environmental positioning, as well as ethical problems through which the relevance of working with Human Rights and the Sustainable Development Goals of the 2030 Agenda becomes evident.

Anti-heritage

Anti-heritages can be used to educate in a non-violent, critical and democratic citizenship and to establish emotional bonds with the victims. This involves teaching history with memory to make students aware of the consequences (Estepa & Martín-Cáceres, 2018) as they represent counter-values such as examples of atrocities committed in wars and violent conflict. This way, history teaching can forge emotional links with the victims of the barbarities committed at different times, based on historical elements such as the Nazi concentration and extermination camps, like Dachau, Mauthausen and Auschwitz (Estepa, 2019). Focusing on the forgotten or defeated and on places of memory means another way of teaching historical facts, fostering historical empathy, emotional intelligence and critical thinking. From our position, we advocate that these spaces should help citizens reflect on these actions against human beings, even if a conflict of memories is originated by not being a vision shared by the entire population (Estepa & Martín-Cáceres, 2022).

In line with Feliú and Hernàndez-Cardona (2020), who identify the material aftermath of the Spanish Civil War as a conflictive heritage, we can highlight the Valley of the Fallen as another example of anti-heritage to work on in History. This building should be reconverted into a memorial for the victims, not only of the Civil War, but mainly of the subsequent repression, so that it can be considered as a heritage element based on the emotional links that can be established with the victims, in this case, of Franco's regime (Delgado-Algarra & Estepa, 2014; Estepa, 2019). According to Estepa and Martín-Cáceres (2018), teachers can take advantage of this heritage element as a powerful didactic resource to facilitate analysis of the plurality of perspectives and the political and ideological interests implicit therein to educate a critical and democratic citizenry, in the teaching of Social Sciences and, in particular, of History.

Heritage of cruelty

The concept of cruelty heritage refers to those customs that are part of the cultural tradition of peoples and which involve the exercise of some kind of physical violence against people or animals. We highlight bullfights as an example of cruelty heritage, declared by some autonomous communities in Spain as a heritage element to be protected, as opposed to the positions of other communities that prohibit bullfighting and similar events. On the other hand, at the state level, it is claimed that bullfighting belongs to the common cultural heritage and that it has an unquestionable relevance in the social reality of Spain (Martín-Cáceres et al., 2021). However, the rejection, animosity and the fight against those festivals that perpetuate animal torture rituals make this element a heritage which, although protected by the State, is quite controversial and therefore of great use for the teaching of history and traditions.

On the other hand, in the international context, from this perspective we can tackle socially relevant problems such as slavery in the teaching of history through heritage elements such as the Slave Monument in Stonetown (Zanzibar, Tanzania), where the mistreatment and subhuman conditions of servitude suffered by people just for being of different ethnicities are represented, to raise awareness among students about issues such as racism or xenophobia and promote a critical conscience focused on social justice and aligned against any violation of human rights.

Interested heritage

Interested heritages – as examples of heritage management and conservation that allow the analysis of conflicts between political, ideological, cultural, economic, environmental and social logic that come into play in heritage selection and activation processes – serve to promote student reflection and debate about conservation, use and enjoyment, the limits of economic development and their own responsibility for heritage as citizens. At this point, we propose historical examples of citizen mobilisations in defence of the territory, which gave rise to conflict in an attempt to stop the modification or destruction of the heritage of their locality, caused by urban speculation or other projects of political and economic interest.

We can cite the *Cabezos de Huelva* as an example of a geographical feature with a fundamental role in the origin and configuration of the city and whose archaeological sites provide us with valuable information on the human activity of past civilisations and on current lifestyles, which have been endangered for several years by urban speculation, representing an economic, environmental and identity conflict (Arroyo & Cuenca, 2021). This way, we can work on the historical aspects related to the natural environment and the ethics of care from an ecosocial standpoint for the forming of a critical, empathetic and reflective citizenry that looks after its heritage (Estepa & Martín-Cáceres, 2020).

In addition, we highlight the Iberian settlement of *Puig de Sant Andreu de Ullastret*, one of the most visited archaeological sites in Catalonia but also one of the main tourist destinations on the Costa Brava, as an example of a clash of interests between the protection of an open-air museum in a landscape environment of high cultural values and the installation of a waste plant, which generated a conflict between the public entities of the surrounding settlements and the *Generalitat de Catalunya*, as they sought to reduce the limits of protection of this historical, archaeological and natural heritage with the aim of claiming the right to continue expanding a livestock activity that they have engaged in for decades (Alcalde et al., 2012).

Both examples are indicative of situations of society's involvement in current and past heritage processes and can be treated in history teaching to work on controversy and develop critical and divergent thinking as spaces of debate for the interpretation of current and future problems.

Block 2: Silenced heritage

In this block we will discuss examples of heritage elements that include perspectives that are subjugated to dominant groups or cultures whose common nexus is subjugation, silence and oblivion.

Heritage with a gender perspective

This perspective is intended to be used to work in the classroom on the relevant social question of gender inequality, as the dominant reading in the various heritage spaces continues to be androcentric and patriarchal (Alario & Lucas, 2018; Estepa & Martín-Cáceres, 2020).

According to Bokova (2015), gender equality is crucial for a more inclusive and sustainable development. Therefore, it is necessary to review and reread the artistic heritage that has historically occupied museums and introduce works created by women co-protagonists of history, as their contributions involve different outlooks at each point in history and, despite their quality, until now their creations have remained in oblivion (Alario & Lucas, 2018). Moreover, we cannot ignore those works, traditions and customs that reproduce stereotyped sociocultural roles and patterns based on the idea of women's inferiority to men.

So, in addition to the historical treatment derived from the museum revisionism for the inclusion of these works of female authors, other examples to be worked on history may be those representations of the image of women such as that portrayed in the painting *Liberty leading the people* by Delacroix or in the sculpture *The emigrant's mother* in Gijón. In the former case, we can reassess the dimensions of the story of the French Revolution through what the author represents in the painting, which dehumanises, idealises and sexualises the image of women, not as an active agent but as an allegory of freedom, while also being an object of desire for men. In the latter, migratory issues can be addressed through the image of a mother who, on the other hand, is also known locally as *La loca del rinconín* (The madwoman of the corner) because of her unhinged expression and windblown hair, and who brings to the table issues such as the ethics of care or the marginalisation of women who do not conform to the canons and precepts of the patriarchy.

Inclusive heritage

This perspective follows the same line as the gender equity outlook. One example that we propose to work on in Social Sciences is the accessibility of the different museums or heritage interpretation centres, as well as monuments and historical constructions, as attention to the diversity and multiculturalism of people in the field of heritage must start from their communication and, therefore, whether they are sufficiently accessible to all citizens (Gómez-Hurtado et al., 2021). But the perspective of inclusion of minorities or silenced groups does not end there, as we can address values such as respect and tolerance in citizenship, highlighting heritage elements such as the sculpture *Overcoming barriers* in Burgos.

Participating in prohibiting the exclusion of the most vulnerable populations is an indispensable action towards inclusion (Ainscow et al., 2013), so we propose to address LGBT Pride Day as an inclusive heritage in history teaching. This festive event is a great example of how to work on such relevant current social issues as homophobia or transphobia by placing students in the historical origins that motivated the celebration of this international day and to enhance their empathy towards groups that have suffered, and continue to suffer, repression and subjugation.

Subjected-rescued heritage

This concept refers to heritage that is subjugated by the dominant culture, usually politically imposed, and which has been persecuted at many times in history, including that which is intended to flourish and come into play in order to break the hegemony of the strong over the weak. This perspective is worked upon setting out from the notion of social justice. As an example, we can highlight the town of Portomarín (Lugo) a place where people have been deprived of their meeting spaces, of their ways of life, of a heritage inherited over centuries by the construction of a reservoir in 1963. The town was rebuilt with heritage elements, such as churches or a medieval bridge arch, which were dismantled and relocated, and which has resulted in an unconnected relationship of the present with its past (Castro & López-Facal, 2019). Through this subjected heritage of enormous potential as a place of memory to be rescued, the teaching of history can act as a heritage resignifier, re-establishing identity links and giving people the ability to review their heritage, in addition to letting students understand that there are heritage sites, such as Portomarín, which have been subjugated by periods in history when democracy and the social action of the people were being repressed (Castro et al., 2021).

Other examples can be found in the current struggle of the Latin American people to demystify and suppress the images, monuments, toponymy, etc., linked to colonialism, which at the time meant the subjugation of the culture and traditions that existed on the American continent and which were silenced by the dominant culture that came from the European continent. In this sense, from a historical standpoint, we can approach the discovery of America as a process in which the heritage elements of the dominant culture were imposed on those identities and elements linked to other cultures, and the repercussions that this conflict has in relation to the present day. Thus, under our ideology of impartiality committed to social justice (Estepa & Martín-Cáceres, 2020), we prefer to avoid the term "discovery of America" and treat it from multiple perspectives as a process of colonialism, with its positive aspects such as the obvious development it entailed in terms of the globalisation of trade, but also negative aspects such as repression, uprooting or usurpation of the territory and its riches. Thus we can include the different views that are established taking into account the voice and stories of the defeated.

Transversal block

This block deals with heritage elements in the process of transformation towards more social positions, which allow for a double reading, that of the element in the context in which it was generated and the meaning it acquires today.

Heritage in transition

Heritage in transition refers to patrimonialisation processes of forgotten heritages adapted to today's social demands, inversely (mercantilisation of heritage) or directly (to enhance the value of heritage as an end in itself). Here we can highlight spaces that have been adapting their uses to new realities and spaces of repression transformed into spaces for peace education. In Galicia, there are two heritage elements that have undergone a modification of their original use but have been preserved: one is the *Museo do Pobo Galego*, built in the former convent of *San Domingos de Bonaval* with the aim of researching, preserving, disseminating, defending and promoting Galician culture (Braña-Rey, 2017). Another is the *San Domingos de Bonaval* park, located just behind it in the former Dominican convent estate and cemetery rehabilitated as an urban park but still preserving the burial niches (Suárez-García, 2019). These estates in transition were in a process of decay and oblivion, but now they are examples of a perfect adaptation to the topography and pre-existing elements that made up this enclave.

Another example, but this time identified as a reverse process of patrimonialisation, is the use for hotel purposes that has been given to heritage elements such as the Convent of Aracena, converted into a hotel and spa that is a tourist attraction and provides an economic return on a space that was suffering the passage of time and oblivion. As History teachers, we might ask ourselves whether or not the new use of these heritage elements is appropriate and work with the different perspectives that may arise from this dilemma.

Conclusions and educational implications

Initial teacher training, in line with the education identity and of an active and reflective citizenry committed to change and social justice (Delgado-Algarra & Cuenca, 2020), is configured as a key aspect that entails the aim that these education professionals are suitably trained to carry out the design and experimentation of teaching materials and proposals in this area (Cuenca et al., 2021).

So, starting from the premise that controversial heritage serves to address relevant socio-environmental problems in the classroom, as well as ecosocial citizenship education, and, in turn, that school research on these topics favours the development of critical thinking, we should focus on the difficulties and needs facing teachers and students regarding the teaching and learning processes, respectively (Martín-Cáceres et al., 2021).

Along these lines, Estepa et al. (2021) recommend that teachers should have the necessary skills to know how to act in this regard, as training is necessary not only for students in the teaching and learning process in the classroom from the initial educational levels but also for teachers in initial and continuing education to be able to adequately approach controversial issues for the development of critical thinking.

In short, the examples presented in this chapter are intended to establish a link between the teaching of Social Sciences, more specifically History, and the treatment of controversial issues in initial teacher training, with the aim of guiding future teachers in the use of the different perspectives of controversial heritage so that they can develop eco-citizen education in their future students.

Notes

1. This publication is part of R+D+i Project EPITEC 2: *PID2020–116662GB-I00*, financed by MCIN/AEI/10.13039/501100011033/.
2. www.coe.int/en/web/culture-and-heritage/faro-convention.
3. R+D+i project "Educación Patrimonial para la Inteligencia Territorial y Emocional de la Ciudadanía. Análisis de buenas prácticas, diseño e intervención en la enseñanza obligatoria" (EDU2015–67953-P).
4. R+D+i project "Patrimonios controversiales para la formación ecosocial de la ciudadanía. Una investigación de educación patrimonial en la enseñanza reglada" (PID2020–116662GB-I00, funded by MCIN/AEI/10.13039/501100011033/).

References

Ainscow, M., Dyson, A., Goldrick, S., & West, M. (2013). Promoting equity in education. *Revista de Investigación en Educación*, *11*(3), 32–43.

Alario, T., & Lucas, L. (2018). Nadie hablará de nosotras cuando hayamos muerto. Pérdida e invisibilidad del patrimonio artístico femenino. *Anales de Historia del Arte*, *28*, 417–430. https://doi.org/10.5209/ANHA.61623

Alcalde, G., Burch, J., Carbonell, E., & Domènech, G. (2012). Identificaciones patrimoniales en conflicto. Un análisis a partir de tres casos en Cataluña. *Revista Andaluza de Antropología*, *2*, 128–148. http://dx.doi.org/10.12795/RAA.2012.i02.07

Arroyo, E., & Cuenca, J. M. (2021). Patrimonios controversiales y educación ciudadana a través del museo en Educación Infantil. *Revista Interuniversitaria de Formación del Profesorado*, *96*(35.3), 109–128. https://doi.org/10.47553/rifop.v96i35.3.91433

Assadourian, E. (2017). Educación ecosocial: cómo educar frente a la crisis ecológica. In The Worldwatch Institute (Ed.), *Educación ecosocial: cómo educar frente a la crisis ecológica. La situación del mundo 2017* (pp. 25–47). Barcelona: Fuhem Ecosocial, Icaria.

Berríos, A., Tessada, V., & Gallegos, F. (2021). Propuestas para un modelo de educación patrimonial en la formación inicial docente de pedagogía en historia, geografía y ciencias sociales. *Revista Brasileira de Educação*, *26*. https://doi.org/10.1590/S1413-24782021260029

Bisquerra, R., & Pérez-Escoda, N. (2012). Educación emocional: Estrategias para su puesta en práctica. *Revista de la Asociación de Inspectores de Educación de España*, *16*, 1–11. https://doi.org/10.23824/ase.v0i16.502

Bokova, I. (2015). *Igualdad de género: patrimonio y creatividad*. London: UNESCO.

Braña-Rey, F. (2017). O Museo do Pobo Galego: museo integral e sintetizador. *Raigame: revista de arte, cultura e tradicións populares*, *41*, 18–29.

Castro, B., & López-Facal, R. (2019). Portomarín, la memoria herida de un desarraigo. *Revista Electrónica Interuniversitaria de Formación del Profesorado*, *22*(2), 95–110. https://doi.org/10.6018/reifop.22.2.363841

Castro, B., López Facal, R., Schugurensky, D., & Jiménez-Esquinas, G. (2021). What can be learned from decontextualised from heritage? In C. J. Gómez Carrasco, P. Miralles & R. López Facal (Eds.), *Handbook of research on teacher education in history and geography* (pp. 283–308). London: Peter Lang.

Cuenca, J. M., Martín-Cáceres, M. J., & Estepa, J. (2021). Teacher training in heritage education: Good practices for citizenship education. *Humanities and Social Sciences Communications, 8*(1). https://doi.org/10.1057/s41599-021-00745-6

De la Rasilla, L. (2008). *En la senda de la ecociudadanía. En torno al modelo asociativo-decisional de participación fraccionada en el horizonte de una ciudadanía mundial.* Informe-balance de la iniciativa INTER/SUR para la ecociudadanía 1996–2007. https://www2.world-governance.org/IMG/pdf_En_la_senda_de_la_ecociudadania.pdf

Delgado-Algarra, E. J. (2015). Conocimiento glocal y pensamiento crítico en la educación del siglo XXI. *International Journal of Educational Research and Innovation (IJERI), 4*, I–V.

Delgado-Algarra, E. J., & Cuenca, J. M. (2020). Challenges for the construction of identities with historical consciousness: Heritage education and citizenship education. In E. J. Delgado-Algarra & J. M. Cuenca-López (Eds.), *Handbook of research on citizenship and heritage education* (pp. 1–25). London: IGI Global.

Delgado-Algarra, E. J., & Estepa, J. (2014). El patrimonio como huella de la memoria histórica: análisis didáctico de dos monumentos en España y Japón. *Clio: History and History Teaching, 40*.

Díez-Bedmar, M. C. (2018). Paisajes culturales urbanos con perspectiva de género: revisión bibliográfica y repercusiones para la Didáctica de las Ciencias Sociales. *UNES. Universidad, Escuela y Sociedad, 4*, 60–77.

Estepa, J. (2001). El patrimonio en la didáctica de las Ciencias Sociales: obstáculos y propuestas para su tratamiento en el aula. *Íber. Didáctica de las Ciencias Sociales, Geografía e Historia, 30*, 93–105.

Estepa, J. (2013). *La educación patrimonial en la escuela y el museo: Investigación y experiencias.* Huelva: Universidad de Huelva

Estepa, J. (2019). Memoria, patrimonio y ciudadanía: una contribución desde una perspectiva didáctica. *Revista PH, 96*, 225–226. https://doi.org/10.33349/2019.96.4299

Estepa, J., & Martín-Cáceres, M. J. (2018). Competencia en conciencia y expresiones culturales y educación histórica. Patrimonios en conflicto y pensamiento crítico. In C. J. Gómez-Carrasco & P. Miralles (Coords.), *La educación histórica ante el reto de las competencias. Métodos, recursos y enfoques de enseñanza* (pp. 75–86). Barcelona: Octaedro.

Estepa, J., & Martín-Cáceres, M. J. (2020). Heritage in conflict: A way to educate in a critical and participative citizenship. In E. J. Delgado-Algarra & J. M. Cuenca (Eds.), *Handbook of research on citizenship and heritage education* (pp. 43–55). London: IGI Global.

Estepa, J., & Martín-Cáceres, M. J. (2022). Antipatrimonio y turismo oscuro. El público escolar. *Revista PH, 105*, 210–211. https://doi.org/10.33349/2022.105.5082

Estepa, J., Cuenca, J. M., & Martín-Cáceres, M. J. (2021). Líneas futuras de trabajo desde el proyecto Epitec: patrimonios controversiales para una educación ecosocial de la ciudadanía. In J. M. Cuenca, J. Estepa & M. J. Martín-Cáceres (Eds.), *Investigación y buenas prácticas en educación patrimonial entre la escuela y el museo. Territorio, emociones y ciudadanía* (pp. 483–492). Gijón: Trea.

Feliú, M., & Hernàndez-Cardona, F. X. (2020). The Spanish civil war in the classrooms: Working for citizenship education. In E. J. Delgado-Algarra & J. M. Cuenca (Eds.), *Handbook of research on citizenship and heritage education* (pp. 429–448). London: IGI Global.

García-Pérez, F. F., Moreno-Fernández, O., & Rodríguez-Marín, F. (2015). Problemas del mundo y educación: hacia una ciudadanía planetaria. In B. Borghi, F. F. García-Pérez & O. Moreno-Fernández (Coords.), *Novi Cives. Cittadini dall'infanzia in poi* (pp. 33–41). Bologna: Pàtron Editore.

Giddens, A. (2006). *La constitución de la sociedad: bases para la teoría de la estructuración.* Buenos Aires: Amorrortu.

Gómez-Hurtado, I., Cuenca, J. M., & Borghi, B. (2021). "Le radici per volare": una proposta di Educazione al Patrimonio inclusiva. *Didattica Della Storia*, *3*(1), 1–36. https://doi.org/10.6092/issn.2704-8217/14049

González-Reyes, L. (2018). *Educar para la transformación ecosocial. Orientaciones para la incorporación de la dimensión ecosocial al currículo*. Madrid: Fuhem Ecosocial.

Herrero, Y. (2015). Apuntes introductorios sobre el ecofeminismo. *Boletín Electrónico del Centro de Documentación Hegoa*, *43*, 1–12.

Ibagón, N. J., & Miralles, P. (2021). Temas controversiales y educación histórica. In C. J. Gómez Carrasco, X. M. Souto & P. Miralles (Eds.), *Enseñanza de las ciencias sociales para una ciudadanía democrática* (pp. 123–138). Barcelona: Octaedro.

Lucas, L., & Delgado-Algarra, E. J. (2018). Educación para una ciudadanía comprometida en la enseñanza de las Ciencias Sociales: ¿Qué piensa el alumnado de un profesor innovador sobre su aprendizaje? *Didáctica de las Ciencias Experimentales y Sociales*, *35*, 3–16. https://doi.org/10.7203/dces.35.12572

Martín-Cáceres, M. J., Estepa, J., & Cuenca, J. M. (2021). Los patrimonios controversiales en la educación patrimonial para la formación de la ciudadanía. In C. J. Gómez Carrasco, X. M. Souto & P. Miralles-Martínez (Eds.), *Enseñanza de las ciencias sociales para una ciudadanía democrática* (pp. 109–122). Barcelona: Octaedro.

Miedes, B., & Martín-Cáceres, M. J. (2021). La educación patrimonial como agente transformador. La formación de agentes de cambio en el contexto de la transición socioecológica. In J. M. Cuenca, J. Estepa & M. J. Martín-Cáceres (Eds.), *Investigación y buenas prácticas en educación patrimonial entre la escuela y el museo. Territorio, emociones y ciudadanía* (pp. 465–482). Gijón: Trea.

Pabón-Figueras, M., & Pino-Mejías, M. A. (2019). Ecociudadanía y desarrollo humano: la construcción de un modelo de turismo local sostenible. In Limón-Domínguez, D. (Dir.), *Ecociudadanía. Retos de la educación ambiental ante los objetivos de desarrollo sostenible* (pp. 85–96). Barcelona: Octaedro.

Perea-Medina, M. J., Navarro-Jurado, E., & Luque-Gil, A. M. (2018). Inteligencia territorial: conceptualización y avance en el estado de la cuestión. Vínculos posibles con los destinos turísticos. *Cuadernos de Turismo*, *41*, 535–554. https://doi.org/10.6018/turismo.41.327141

Prats, J., Alabrús, R., Fernández-Díaz, R., & García-Cárcel, R. (2021). Enseñanza de la historia científica para una educación de calidad. In C. J. Gómez Carrasco, X. M. Souto & P. Miralles (Eds.), *Enseñanza de las ciencias sociales para una ciudadanía democrática* (pp. 187–202). Barcelona: Octaedro.

Santisteban, A. (2019). La enseñanza de las ciencias sociales a partir de problemas sociales o temas controvertidos: estado de la cuestión y resultados de una investigación. *El Futuro del Pasado*, *10*, 57–79. https://doi.org/10.14516/fdp.2019.010.001.002

Suárez-García, J. M. (11–16 de noviembre de 2019). *Bonaval: el cementerio hecho parque*. [Comunicación]. XX Encuentro Iberoamericano de Valorización y Gestión de Cementerios Patrimoniales. Los cementerios como recurso cultural, educativo y turístico. Málaga, España.

Tardón, M. (2011). Ecofeminismo. Una reivindicación de la mujer y la naturaleza. *El Futuro del Pasado*, *2*, 533–542. https://doi.org/10.14201/fdp.24664

Trabajo, M. (2020). *La educación patrimonial como vínculo entre escuela y museo: un estudio de caso para la formación de la ciudadanía en Ciencias Sociales de ESO* [Tesis doctoral, Universidad de Huelva]. http://hdl.handle.net/10272/19264

Trabajo, M., & Cuenca, J. M. (2017). La educación patrimonial para la adquisición de competencias emocionales y territoriales del alumnado de enseñanza secundaria. *Pulso: Revista de Educación*, *40*, 159–174.

PART II
Cross-cutting topics on European history

6
LANDSCAPES, AGRICULTURE, PEASANTS AND ENVIRONMENT IN THE HISTORY OF EUROPE

Lourenzo Fernández Prieto

Introduction: determinism, environmentalism and landscape, an overview

In the nineteenth century, geographical determinism was strongly rooted in the study of history, coinciding with its consolidation as a modern discipline linked to the State and school systems. The German geographer Carl Ritter (1779–1859) was certainly the best-known author in this regard, and through this way of looking at the past that depended directly on territorial conditioning factors, a very geographical conception of history was established. The immense and parallel influence of Alexander von Humboldt (1769–1859) marked that period too. Such determinism was connected in part to a colonial view of the world that Europeans had developed since the beginning of their colonisation of the American and African continents, an approach that gained momentum with the development of capitalist imperialism during the nineteenth century, while at the same time it spread to other continents with the help of a scientific praxis placed at the service of States and their interests rather than the pursuit of Cartesian knowledge or Humeian empiricism. Explorations organised by geographical or scientific societies and cartography as a method of representation were fundamental in this process of forming knowledge for the exploitation of natural and environmental resources and also of human resources through slavery. The former were called raw materials and the latter, labour power. In the construction of geographical determinism applied to historical knowledge, Oswald Spengler also played an important role in interpreting the theories of Charles Darwin to make postulations about the world's biological diversity and evolution that Darwin himself had never made, as did advocates of so-called social Darwinism, with Herbert Spencer as their starting point.

In the end, during the twentieth century, the relationship between the climatic and territorial conditions in which humanity (the diverse peoples of the Earth) lived and the conditions that defined the civilisations, culture, labour and intellectual capacities of those peoples was a central and constitutive part of the historical narrative. In this context, the position of the peoples of the world with respect to Europe, taken as a model, and even more so to Northwest Atlantic Europe, and more particularly industrial and bourgeois urban Europe, became the yardstick by which to measure progress and a people's capacity for future progress. This occurred at a time when economic progress was taken as the great driver/goal of human history.

That racist and colonial historical legacy was not completely banished by later twentieth-century schools of history, no matter how much it was considered to have been overcome and repulsed. The worst derivations can be seen in interwar Europe when racism led to genocidal and criminal persecutions in Nazi Germany, Vichy France, Salò Italy, and other occupied or pro-Nazi states.

Annales, without doubt the most influential of those schools in the twentieth century, re-envisioned the role of the environment in historical knowledge, as it focussed on history as a social science in which knowledge from other social disciplines such as geography, economics, demography or sociology converged. The environment, understood from the perspective of the best regional, physical and human geography France had to offer, was the framework in which humanity developed its social relations, its different forms of labour and also its conflicts, to paraphrase Marc Bloch's (1886–1944) definition of the historian's object of study. It was one of his successors, Fernand Braudel (1902–1985), who best took up and explained Bloch's conception in his sublime 1949 work (1975) *The Mediterranean and the Mediterranean World in the Age of Philip II*. For Annales, the environment was the framework in which human action was developed, conditioning and defining peoples but not determining them. This was a broad and soft environmental vision that today can and must be reclaimed to serve as the foundation of any environmentalist vision of the past in a present where sustainability is a substantial and immediate challenge: *sustainability* as a noun rather than the *sustainable* that has often adjectivised and greenwashed any crudely productivist interpretation or approach to the past, as well as many current polluting and environmentally harmful activities.

After the 1973 oil crisis and on the basis of numerous previous studies, humanity has slowly become conscious of the planet's limits and the difficulties of sustaining forms of production and cumulative growth using finite natural resources, hitherto euphemistically referred to as raw materials. In fact, this consciousness has come about rather slowly if we consider how quickly the environmental degradation of the planet, humanity's living space, has deepened over the last 50 years. Linked to studies by authors such as James Lovelock [1979] (1989) and Lynn Margulis (1989), the forceful conclusions of the Clube de Roma, and the environmental civic awareness of the post-1968 generations, historiography has incorporated the environment and environmental conditions in more convincing and even conflicting ways into research and the historical narrative. Authors such as Alfred Crosby (who coined the term "ecological imperialism") or Donald Worster in the United

States, Piero Bevilaqua in Italy, Rolf Peter Sieferle (1949–2016) in Germany or M. González de Molina in Spain have successively, successfully and with a high degree of complexity studied the past from an environmental perspective and made it a key factor in their analyses. These and other authors have incorporated historical socio-environmental approaches that are also present in the works of K. Polanyi (1944) or in the more recent output of M. Altieri (1995, N. Koning (1994) and V. Smil (2017).

These current reformulations have been accompanied by a rereading of the idea of landscape, overcoming Renaissance elitism and also popularised nineteenth century and romantic conceptions. With authors such as A. Berque (2009) and J. Maderuelo (2005), landscape is shown as a product of transgenerational management by local communities that for exogenous reasons came to acquire a value that at times has led to a negation of the value given to it by the very people who live in, construct and support the landscape as a geomorphological space where flora and fauna are managed by men and women through complex processes of social metabolism in which a range of physical conditioners come into play. The values of tourism, leisure, environmentalism or heritage, conceived and established exogenously, are as destructive of those same values as any colonial intervention.

The other historiographical current to consider is the history from below linked to that group of British social historians spearheaded by E.P. Thompson and culminating with E. Hobsbawm that encompasses contributions by R. Samuel, R. Hilton and C. Hill, among others. This is extensive to the practice of oral history, microhistory or historical anthropology, represented by Nathalie Z. Davis, Carlo Ginzburg or Giovanni Levi, and which has begotten manifestations on every continent, including recent American researchers such as Deborah Fitzgerald and Catharine Wilson as historians of the rural world.

Through the lens of history from below, the peasantry always comes into focus, for they were the majority. Even workers and artisans were simultaneously peasants, or at least belonged to peasant households, that among other activities tilled and sowed or cared for livestock; because those who were "below" were not exceptions that heralded futures that we see present today but majorities. Across Europe, the peasantry were the majority and the workers and artisans the exception until very recently, despite some broad-brush narratives painting the latter, the proletariat, as the only true harbingers of the future. In Germany, for example, 30% of the active population was still employed in the agricultural and forestry sectors as late as 1925.

The challenge is how to formulate historical knowledge that accepts all of these changes and breaks with the racist and deterministic anchors of progress and geography as well as incorporating, in addition to the history of social majorities, the core elements of environmental history (Vanhaute, 2021; Worster, 1990).

In this sense, it should be noted that the long-term impact of agricultural activity must be considered in its organic context, in terms of the use of resources, energy and food production. The fight for the freedom to appropriate the resources they had produced was a constant in European peasant conflicts from the late Middle Ages, and the achievement of this goal was a historical milestone in some societies.

However, this conquest did not benefit all households and all groups in a peasant community equally: many single women, widows and day labourers would benefit less but would also profit somewhat thanks to the moral economy of the community for as long as contemporary capitalism did not absolutely dominate social relations in rural societies. Though far from being egalitarian or free from conflict, peasant communities deployed practices in favour of their most disadvantaged members, such as gleaning, the possibility of building some variety of precarious dwelling on common land, mutual aid between neighbours to handle the most demanding jobs or to help families that had suffered some misfortune, etc.

Avoiding presentisms, the negative impact of agricultural activity must mainly be placed in relation to the modernising green revolution after WWII. And it is in this present that it is essential to identify organic agriculture and its capacity for innovation as positive factors for a sustainable future.

Ideas about nature and the past that must be revised

The Europeans of today have an overly simple and highly idealised view of landscapes and the environmental past of the world that needs to be recalibrated. It is a deeply biological idea that autonomises nature with respect to humanity to such an extent that, though apt for our present times, does not correspond to the past, or at least to the pre-industrial past and even less so to the common European past of our ancestors over the last four millennia who were principally devoted to the management of animals and plants and secondarily of other natural resources such as water and minerals. This occurred in an increasingly intensive way, perhaps, but not always in a degrading one. Although there is a bit of everything in the past: outbreaks, famines, *ruina montium*, plagues, depletion of resources . . . the idealisation of the rural past that recreates an Arcadia that remained unchanged right up until contemporary industrialisation, essentially denies any agency on the part of the peasantry. Mutatis mutandis, it is the same mechanism that relegates pre-colonial indigenous peoples to the status of something that merely blended into a natural environment that they were incapable of modifying (when in practice they did modify it through hunting, slash-and-burn, etc.) This is by no means the only example of how, in some ideological constructs, European peasants are seen as equivalent to the natives of colonised spaces, for better or for worse.

Another idea, contradictory to the previous one but equally presentist – applied in this case in an ecological sense – is part of a teleological conception of history according to which the complete past is an accumulation of environmental degradation that led up to the present. The question is more complicated and much less linear than this.

In any case, we must begin by recognising that since the *ager* fought the *silvus* in the days of the Roman Empire, the history of Europe has been a constant struggle to create more agricultural space in order to ensure more and better nutrition for a growing population, because peasant households (including those belonging to artisans) have needed more manpower to better themselves and because simple vegetative growth has required it. Production and reproduction go hand in hand in the logic of domestic and communal life, as S. Barca (2020) explains. The whole of Europe has been directly and very intensely managed by humans since the late Middle Ages. There is no primary forest or natural space in Europe that has not been managed during the last millennium by agrarian communities, being therefore susceptible to processes of social metabolism. The statement may seem astonishing from the perspective of urban memory but not from transgenerational rural memory. In a present threatened by environmental crises and global warming, rusticity imposes itself on urbanity to the detriment of the triumphant tradition that has characterised European elites, and by extension elites worldwide, since the Renaissance and prior to decolonial criticism (Said, 1978).

The good news is that this organic relationship with the land and nature is very easy to understand with a little introspective effort (or documentary or oral family research) because even today at least three-quarters of European students are descended from great or great-great-grandparents who were peasants and emigrants, farmers or fieldhands, except in a few European regions that experienced long-term industrialisation (the English Midlands, the Ruhr, etc.)

Thus, European colonial ideas of Africa or those of white Americans regarding jungle or virgin expanses should not be confused with the history of nature in Europe and the history of its landscapes and environment. Europeans used cardinal points to get their bearings on those unknown continents and to name open spaces and even streets and neighbourhoods in the new cities they had created since the Enlightenment, a nomenclature which they did not use in their European villages and towns where everything had been renamed several times over since the days of the Roman Empire and sometimes in several different languages all at once. In fact, this idea of a primordial nature was built into the new Europes of America and Africa, colonised by Europeans and installed in Europe itself after WWII, when for example the concept of natural park was incorporated, derived from the original Yellowstone (1872). Paradoxically, a pioneer in the introduction of many environmentalist and animalist practices in Europe was Nazi Germany, although obviously in a manner distorted by its racial preconceptions (Brüggemeier, 2005): a round trip that says a lot about the diachronic circularity of intellectual and political power and how it affects our daily lives and our relationship with nature. In the same way, it had once affected the Roman, Chinese and Islamic Empires. It says a lot too about the non-linear character of history.

In relation to all the above, it is necessary to reconsider diffusionist logic in order to understand historical processes of change and transformation in relation to the rural and peasant world. The idea that there is a centre from which ideas, leaders, behaviours, cultures, technologies, etc. always emanate, and which are spread to the periphery, is almost a commonplace that serves to explain everything from hominisation to the current knowledge society revolution. However, this ahistorical present and current historiography demonstrate that the matter is much more complex. The history of science shows us how the same result can be achieved in different ways in different parts of the world and by different actors. It happened with hominisation a million years ago and again with video technology at the tail-end of the last century. Understanding that there are different paths also allows us to understand that there existed alternatives throughout the past, just as there exist alternatives in the present, without denying that there also exists inertia in any society, culture or economy, or what today is called trajectory dependency, understood as the difficulties in breaking with the past to open new and different alternatives. The interesting thing is that one can no longer fixate upon unique and dominant models that follow on from others but upon different foci and combinations that are increasingly global, even as the world seems – only seems – to be getting smaller. In addition, in the history of humanity there is an absolute globality: the planet and its environment. And there has been a strong awareness of this only in recent decades (McNeill, 2000; González de Molina & Toledo, 2014).

It would be a good idea to rethink the past using our accumulated historiographical knowledge, positioning ourselves to face the problems that the future imposes upon the present and incorporating that knowledge into history in didactic and school settings. To do this, it is necessary to redefine some concepts widely used in the historical narrative that have come down to us from the nineteenth century, which persist through inertia but have been criticised and overcome by historiography since the late twentieth century when researchers became aware of the limits of both the planet and social engineering processes designed to execute forms of forced progress.

Included in this list are terms as common as modernisation, a concept that can only be properly applied to the world after 1945 when the term begins to be used and acquired its meaning in relation to political and economic proposals for modernising those states, countries, territories or continents that remained unreached by modernity during the previous period going back to early modern times (Fernández Prieto et al., 2014); also to socioeconomic groups such as small farmers and peasants, whose way of life or forms of technology had to be modified in a productivist sense to fulfil the only function required of them in the eyes of conventional economic theory: to feed burgeoning cities and provide them with manpower (Moser & Varley, 2013). This rhetoric served the purpose of modernising European farmers (including British ones) and those of every Asian country (with the exception of Japan). To modernise those who had not reached modernity, to develop them, was a goal that gave meaning to the post-war world and that ended up acquiring, in the historiography of the second half of the twentieth century, a character that was as retrospective as it was anachronistic. To talk about the medieval modernisation of the Portuguese economy is as inappropriate as talking about the modernisation of French agriculture in the nineteenth century; it de-historicises the past and turns it into an eternal present.

Other similar terms that deserve to be redefined in the historical narrative are, as already indicated, natural or nature. And in the same sense, forest, often understood as a primitive wooded and "natural" space which has not existed in Western Europe (with the exception of Scandinavia) for a good millennium. It is also necessary to reformulate the term peasant (peasantry), carried over from anthropology, in order to understand the complexity of rural societies in which, at the same time as the peasant community with its moral economy and management of communal goods, there also exists significant differentiation between social groups related to their access to the means of production and to gender, religion, ethnicity, etc. (Vanhaute, 2021). The role of women, the concept of home and the logics of production and reproduction must be understood in the context of organic economies in a manner that is distinct from how they have been defined in the historical narrative of progress. In this way, the teleological meaning of the term is questioned, as is the idea of a history that continually advances towards an ideal present. For example, economic historians with an environmental focus have shown how, until well into the twentieth century, the achievements of industrialisation depended on the strengthening of these organic economies, in terms of fertiliser use, animal energy or wood consumption (Sieferle, 2001). If history after Auschwitz could no longer be written as a story of continuous human progress, neither can history after Hiroshima be written as a story of continuous technological progress.

Defining diverse European regional spaces

As indicated above to some extent, it is necessary to define European spaces in an aggregate and differentiated manner, in historical and historiographical terms that help to explain and compare their similarities, transnational or trans-territorial relationships and interconnections, but also different trajectories, which may be divergent or sometimes confluent. In this sense, a European regional compartmentalisation that, taking into account historical and geographical factors, differentiates between the Mediterranean, the Atlantic and the Baltic, Central and Eastern Europe, north and south in a dialectical framework may prove useful. To not define these different spaces in some way or another leads to a form of history centred on Great Britain (for economic processes) and France (for political ones), which are seen interacting with Germany and little more than North-Western Europe almost all the way back to the seventeenth century.

This compartmentalisation can help to avoid geographical and cultural determinism, to escape from the rigid framework of nineteenth-century nation-states projected back through the past down to the fall of the Roman Empire and to break free of presentism. But it must be understood and used in a historically dynamic way, to understand the Nordic military and lordly influence on early medieval Europe, combined with Christian influence from the eastern Mediterranean at the same time, to cite an example from long ago whose influence reaches into (and can be traced back from) the present. And in the same line, but looking at things the other way around, we may marvel at the unitary continental trend towards European revolts during the late Middle Ages, fought across many territories by a coalition of peasants, bourgeoisie and petty aristocrats (the third and fourth estates). These are well-studied social processes of conflict and mobilisation that somehow seem to unify the European past, from the Irmandiños who demolished stately fortresses in Fisterra on the western borders of Eurasia to the Hussites of Central-Eastern Europe.

Europe's peasant past

Europe has a peasant past that gives it a certain transnational and transhistorical unity. The great-grandparents of most of the Europeans of today were peasants: a past quickly forgotten due to a widespread scorn of agricultural labour, the will for modernity, for modernisation, rampant urbanisation throughout the twentieth century and processes of industrialisation that even extend to agriculture. Modernity is identified with cities and formal education, against which rural lifestyles and the informal learning of agricultural and artisan occupations cannot compete.

It is a past that today is remembered by grandchildren and great-grandchildren who recover family memories and almost despised genealogies, both in Europe and in America, and write novels or histories, discovering that what runs in their veins is the blood of proud labourers who came to own the land they worked or emigrants who embarked on transatlantic voyages to a newer and freer world. Authors such as Xesús Fraga (2020), John Berger (1992) and Catharine Wilson (2022), testify to this. In *Canale Mussolini*, Antonio Pennacchi (2010) recreates a family saga, his own family saga, as the story of Venetian peasants sympathetic to fascism who are transferred as settlers to the freshly drained lands of the Agro Pontino.

If we want to become familiar with the dominant social group in European history, we have to talk about the peasantry and rural society. Throughout the twentieth century, we have been more interested in the urban, commercial and industrial world, which grew little by little ahead of the large industrial cities that today make up the side of Europe in which the vast majority of us live, even if suburban developments and an apparent return to the countryside in the form of commuter towns and villages (now with the possibilities afforded by teleworking as a great source of excitement) appear to mark the decline of that image of the urban environment that was once considered liberating in the age of feudalism.

Until the middle of the twentieth century, the European peasantry occupied the most territory and carried out most of the productive activities on the continent. When it comes to the European past, the peasantry always deserves to be treated as its own topic because it included within its remit, in general terms, all the occupations of the organic rural world (usually called the pre-industrial world): fishermen, artisans, the whole range of rural trades . . . many of them part-time peasants out of necessity; at different points on the scale regarding, work, wealth and gender; with the home as the nucleus of personal life and the community (village) as a key social reference; both spaces organised for productive reproduction and leisure, as long as the lord, the king, and the State permitted it; and indeed working and improvising so that the pressures exerted by the lord, the king, the State and the Church might not prevent them from enjoying family life or celebrating carnival. Sometimes they succeeded and sometimes they did not, and this in different ways going back to the Roman Empire. Since the Great War – in fact only a century ago – the State as a nation already started to include them more effectively, willingly or unwillingly, appreciating them as in revolutionary and republican France or tyrannising them as in Spain under the thumb of dictators and aristocrats. Neither the sacks of potatoes as the workers' movement has often taken them to be, nor the embodiments of clerical ignorance perceived by liberals, European peasants have been no stranger to the politics of their time but indeed have constructed their politics in the interests of their communities, resisting with their weapons of the weak whenever it was not possible to exploit the strength of those alliances that had allowed them to tear down castle walls (fifteenth century), burn archives owned by the Church and the nobility (eighteenth century) or redistribute the land to those who work it (twentieth century) and extend their own forms of community equality to permeate new democratic States, whether in the European America of Jefferson's Republican landowners or in the Scandinavian Europe of farmers' cooperatives (Cabo et al., 2014).

The historiography of Europe must recognise the organic forms of peasant production that fed a growing population capable of sending Europeans to America as soldiers first and emigrants later and at the same time massively absorbing American plants that today seem so European like the potato, corn, tomatoes or peppers – and precisely thanks to this, continuing to grow in Italy and England – or Asian species like rice in areas such as Spain and Portugal. These plants did not displace but complemented the Mediterranean trifecta of wheat, wine and oil and linked both to the Atlantic cultivation of rye and turnips in a polyculture that would promote mixed-livestock specialisation. This was an organic form of production and a culture (illiterate, not literate) that pertained to what were in many cases the most recent ancestors of today's Europeans.

And the history of rural Europe – like urban Europe – cannot be understood if emigrants are missing. Starting in the nineteenth century, millions of European peasants moved in the direction of those new Europes, empires and the new American republics. This is an issue that deserves monographic attention because it is revealing of who we were and the best practical explanation of who we are in the world. It helps us to understand, for example, how seasonal emigration was decisive for the independence of Ireland, one of whose leaders, Éamon de Valera, avoided execution after the 1916 Rising by grace of his having been born in New York, like many children of emigrants who were saved shortly afterwards, in 1936, from the massacres following the coup d'état in Spain because they had a Cuban, Argentine or Uruguayan passport. Thus we can learn about these people, but more particularly about their parents, who travelled from the fields of Europe to the Americas, some making their way in the world through trade or industry and others even as members of the mafia. But almost all of them repatriated capital and new skills, reforming ideologies, some of which served, for example, to secure the homeland's liberation from old aristocratic traditions and anti-modern religious constraints wherever they were most felt. They fulfilled this function mainly in those territories where the small farm had been central to the organisation of production for several centuries, allowing peasants to become private owners in the framework of the liberal and democratic revolutions (Villares, 1982).

The increasing ownership of houses in contemporary times also had the effect of evicting or subordinating even further those who did not manage to accrue enough land. However, it did strengthen the community ties of the moral economy, though they have always been in conflict – even today – with the advance of possessive individualism (Congost et al., 2017). The moral economy, as defined by E.P. Thompson (1991), is the consensus within a given population concerning the moral factors that should govern the economy, obligations and reciprocal rights that explain, for example, why a large landlord would commission work that is not strictly necessary during the winter in order to provide employment to family breadwinners or would lower rents voluntarily after a plague or inclement weather or that there exists a notion of fair prices that a trader may stipulate for bread and other commodities beyond the strict laws of supply and demand.

Researching the European peasantry's past is the best way to build an agroecological future for Europe that assumes the coevolution of people and nature, in which the evolution of many European (and Asian) territories was sustained during the very long historical period that is talked about here.

In the same way, holding up a mirror to Europeans as migrants, on the one hand, and also as colonialists on the other (as discussed in other sections), allows us to focus more precisely and wisely on our role in the world of the past and the world of the future. The issue of European internal territorial diversity must also be integrated because otherwise it could well be assimilated by hegemonic histories, as we have attempted to point out here.

As Theodor Kallifatides (2021) writes, the village that lived within European peasants was placed in opposition to the physical cities that pressed in around them, in a conflict that was apparently resolved in favour of the city just a generation or two ago. Similarly, Russian historians have developed the thesis that Russian peasants during late tsarism managed to "peasantise" the very institutions that in other countries had served to assimilate them into a dominant national culture. In Russia, it was the peasants who transposed their practices and values onto the army and cities, not the other way around (Gerasimov, 2004).

Agriculture: supply, food markets and technology in Europe

In classical economic theory and in the reality of the contemporary historical evolution of central capitalist economies, the role of agriculture is perfectly defined: to supply more and more food to a growing urban population and to do so in an ever cheaper and less labour-intensive fashion, which necessarily requires significant increases in production and productivity. In all classical theoretical models, agriculture also plays an important role in the early stages of industrial development by supplying capital for industry (being one of the original areas in which capital was accumulated) and by later becoming an ambit of growing demand for industrial products in the form of input (machinery, fertilisers, pesticides, etc.). But in addition to food, agriculture (as a production sector) would also supply industry with labour power, which, bringing it all full circle, would propel an increase in the productivity of agricultural output sustained by a continuously declining labour force.

This result favours the absolute subordination of agriculture to industrial models in economic terms – and automatically assumes it to be so – but also in political and cultural terms. Rural society is subordinated to urban society or to the working class, according to the ideological model and political moment in question, whereby farmers and agricultural production are stripped of their political and cultural significance. But this has not happened in the same way in all countries, in all cases, or in all processes. In some, the transformation of agriculture and the rural world has been so traumatic that rural spaces have been abandoned, rural culture has been considered a remnant of the past, and cropping and planting systems have been so transformed as to generate chaos in the wake of the alteration of agroecosystems (wildfires) orindustrialisation (depletion of aquifers). In others, rural culture has remained a collective reference, abandonment has become less widespread, and industrial-intensive production systems have been combined with adapted extensive practices.

The most recent rural historiography debates how – going against the ideas of nineteenth and twentieth-century theorists and all their political utopias and speculations and despite the diagnoses of the social sciences and the ideas of development theorists during the second half of the twentieth century – the rural world has maintained some constants that are still appreciated today and may even be potential instruments for a sustainable future. *Rural society has survived to this day* as a singular and differentiated sphere from the urban world with problems, realities and operating guidelines that are only comprehensible within its long-term historicity.

Dependence on organic forms of production remains a global, even if not local reality, and although many of these organic forms have been on the verge of being overcome, with huge environmental costs, some remain and look set to grow in the future via organic farming. Many of these forms are now threatened by certain developments in biotechnology or the spread of GMOs.

To understand this evolution, we now offer a brief chronology of the main trends and broad processes that have defined the changes and continuities of contemporary rural societies during the last two centuries in Europe. This chronology of the rural world does vary with respect to others focussed on political evolution, for example.

Eighteenth century: the time of the English agricultural revolution

The English agricultural revolution was a dogma for historians because it was considered a prerequisite for industrialisation. What does it consist of and what characterises it? It was a stage of singular productive and technological development, framed in the first great advance of industrial capitalism.

The following took place:

- an increase in production and commercialisation.
- the commodification of the economy
- unusual population growth (new model).

Ideology: Physiocracy and Enlightenment paradigms of the individual and profitability versus *manos muertas* (idle hands) and misused wealth.

An ideal model later imitated by elites in many other countries, though paradoxically British historiography discovered that the new developments of this period took a long time to become generalised. The weight of continuity has led experts in the field to speak of the real agricultural revolution in the United Kingdom being a post-WWII phenomenon (Brassley et al., 2021). Only then did the tractor definitively triumph over the horse, artificial fertilisers over organic ones, and so on.

1800–1880: the age of great institutional reforms and the liberal agrarian revolution

This period marked a new role for the State and the market with liberalisation and the creation of national markets and the commodification of production factors (land, labour and capital). The role of the national State was decisive in breaking up feudal dependencies but also the dynamics of peasant society. The changes also begin to affect the logics of "organic production" and the social environment. There were proletarianisation advances but many peasant transformations also took place: small farms resisted and adapted to new productive and mercantile logics.

In *ideological terms:* The proposed model is that of large-scale farming (K. Kautsky, 1899), that of agriculture as manufacture. Progress is established as the dominant ideology and is considered "inevitable".

1880–1945: consolidation of smallholdings under capitalism

Within the dynamics visible in many European territories where farmers and even parties and movements become a major social and political protagonist of the period, the definitive political integration of the peasantry into the liberal state now occurred, for example with the French Third Republic, which was a pioneer of this process.

In this framework, there began the articulation of a civil society in the rural world with the emergence of new forms of organisation and agrarian associations, with an interclass orientation in some cases and the championing of smallholders' interests where that form of production was dominant (Cabo, 2022).

At this time there was also a "scramble for land" and wherever this integration process, which was also social and economic, encountered difficulties, as in the south of the Iberian Peninsula, it acquired rebellious or even revolutionary traits.

Simultaneously, some States necessarily started to acknowledge the limits that rural society imposed on the development of capitalism, for example, in relation to "property".

But the development of technological innovation in smallholdings was also experienced, even within the framework of advanced organic agriculture through the application of science (Fernández Prieto, 1992).

And the maintenance of unsalaried production relations and other features of peasant culture and forms of production was still observed.

The integration of a world market for agricultural products after the late-nineteenth-century crisis, and in the context of the second wave of industrialization, had enormous productive and social consequences throughout Europe.

In ideological term: earlier models survived but the sovereignty of the peasantry, only conquerable through the market and property, was added to the mix. Peasants were transformed into human masses and voter bases and they could no longer be repudiated by liberal politics.

1945–1973/today: the green revolution

The green revolution is an accelerated modernisation of agriculture that furthermore entails its definitive integration into the dominant economic and technological system.

The modernising ideal of maximum technologicalisation has now been fulfilled, with great environmental, social and demographic costs to which other unforeseen events have recently been added concerning food security.

Today, existing agriculture poses a major ecological problem that forces us to think about what the future can possibly hold for it.

This technologicalisation of agriculture is only possible through subsidies, but both energy and monetary accounting reflect that it is not *sustainable*.

The future must be thought in terms of sustainability, and for this, the knowledge of the sustainable forms of the past will be fundamental.

This whole schema corresponds to the European and American models, but there are large gaps between Europe and the rest of the world, as well as loose points of commonality. The modern world has experienced frequent waves of globalisation a process that we perceive in a highly accelerated form nowadays . . . but globalisation is very old. One of those common waves: during 1910–1939, the abovementioned *scramble-for-land* revolution that enveped Mexico, Russia, China and the Iberian Peninsula – with different solutions in the north and south but with the same aim for the peasants of consolidating property in terms of the dominance and control of productive and reproductive resources.

This wave persisted after WWII in the delolonising revolutions (Vietnam), which were largely peasant revolutions.

Other common waves have much to do with technological aspects and the application of innovative practices. In fact, in the European framework there are not so many differences between countries because technological packages take time to be deployed, and when they are applied, they do so with fewer differences between European countries than they are usually given credit for, although these differences do lead to varying degrees of development.

The impact of agricultural activity is historically and cumulatively negative when understood in the very presentist sense that must be associated with the post-WWII modernising green revolution. In this forward-looking present, it is essential to identify organic farming and its peasant capacity for innovation as a positive when thinking of a sustainable future.

Some educational contributions

Traditionally, history teaching, at least at pre-university stages, has not contemplated the transformation of landscapes, economic inequalities and environmental impacts in European history. The current climate emergency demands a reformulation of educational priorities by placing the understanding of the problem and the factors that have given rise to this situation at the forefront of the debate. The knowledge provided by agricultural history, from a social and environmental point of view, can be an effective tool for assessing the extent to which actions taken in the past have contributed to shaping contemporary landscapes and relationships between people and nature, their beneficial or harmful consequences, and which individuals, groups or collectives have been harmed or benefited by them. Environmental sustainability is first and foremost a political decision, as it is politics that regulates which sciences are necessary for cities and which ones citizens are required to learn "Ética a Nicómano" from Aristóteles. Knowledge of the changes in the European rural world is of special relevance if the students of today, citizens of tomorrow, are to make informed decisions and build a desirable future.

Teaching strategies for incorporating this knowledge are very varied, as indicated in the first part of this book. It is desirable that they be present in new curricula in a transversal and interdisciplinary way, rather than in the monographic form better suited to university specialisation. A suitable framework for this would be Place-Based-Education projects wherein environmental and social perspectives are systematically related, which are already being implemented in many schools. Collaborative work on school research based on the environment offers a wide variety of possibilities using local resources, such as the memory of oral and written sources, toponymy, cartography, images, etc. that allow students to become familiar with and to compare the lifestyles that have existed in a territory in the past and the present and to contrast them with other places. Education, aiming to foment historical thinking, purports to help students to develop their own discourse based on evidence and sources, rather than memorising and repeating data or narratives confected by other people. Teaching and learning to value and interpret data, to read the landscapes and memories of others and contextualise them according to the conditions of each era; discerning what is most relevant, what has affected the most people and has had a greater impact on people's lives; recognising the antecedents, even those that are remote (*longue durée*), to some situations and problems and others that have taken place in a shorter timeframe. Nonetheless, historical education for a democratic citizenship is not limited to the learning of skills and contents, though these are always necessary. It assumes an ethical perspective that provides students with an orientation for life and to learn to desire a better future. Environmental history provides the knowledge to develop an awareness of histories whose protagonists are ordinary people, often forgotten in school textbooks, until now.

References

Altieri, M. (1995). *Agroecology. The science of sustainable agriculture.* (2nd ed). CRC Press.
Aristóteles (2001). *Ética a Nicómaco.* Alianza Editorial.
Barca, S. (2020). *Forces of reproduction.* Cambridge University Press.
Berger, J. (1992). *Pig Earth.* Random House.
Berque, A. (2009). *El pensamiento paisajero.* Biblioteca Nueva.
Brassley, P. et al. (2021). *The real agricultural revolution: The transformation of English farming, 1939–1985.* Boydell Press.
Braudel, F. [1949] (1975). *The Mediterranean and the Mediterranean world in the age of Philip II.* University of California.
Brüggemeier, F.-J., Cioc, M., & Zeller, T. (Eds). (2005). *How green were the Nazis?: Nature, environment, and nation in the Third Reich.* Ohio University.
Cabo Villaverde, M. (2022). Agrarian parties in Europe prior to 1945 and beyond. In Brassart, L., Marache, C., Pan-Montojo, J., & van Molle, L. (Eds.), *Making politics in the European countryside 1780s-1930s* (pp. 313–332). Brepols.
Cabo Villaverde, M., Fernández Prieto, L., Miguez, A., Lanero, D., & Cabana, A. (2014). Conflict in the contemporary rural world. New interpretations of an old problem. *Workers of the World. International Journal on Strikes and Social Conflicts*, I (5), 7–25
Congost, R., Gelman, J., & Santos, R. (Eds.) (2017). *Property rights in Land.* Routledge
Fernández Prieto, L. (1992). *Labregos con ciencia. Estado, sociedade e innovación tecnolóxica na agricultura galega, 1850–1939.* Xerais de Galicia.
Fernández Prieto, L., Pan-Montojo, J., & Cabo, M. (2014). *Agriculture in the age of fascism. Authoritarian technocracy and rural modernization, 1922–1945.* Brepols.
Fraga, X. (2020). *Virtudes (e misterios).* Galaxia.
Gerasimov, I. V. (2004). 'Russians into peasants?' The politics of self-organisation and paradoxes of the public modernization campaign in the countryside in late imperial Russia (232-252). *Journal of Modern European History*, 2.
González de Molina, M., & Toledo, V. (2014). *Socialmetabolism. A socio-ecological theory of historical change.* Springer.
Kallifatides (2021). *The past is not a dream.* Penguin
Kautsky, K. [1899] (1974). *La cuestión agraria.* Laia.
Koning, N. (1994). *The failure of agrarian capitalism.* Routledge.
Lovelock, J. [1979] (1989). *Gaia: A new look at life on Earth.* Oxford University Press.
Maderuelo, J. (2005). *EL paisaje. Génesis de un concepto.* Abada Eds.
Margulis, L. et al. [1987] (1989). *Gaia. Implicaciones de la nueva biología.* Kairós.
McNeill, J. R. (2000). *Algo nuevo bajo el sol. Historia Medioambiental del mundo en el siglo XX.* Alianza Editorial.
Moser, P., & Varley, T. (Eds.). (2013). *Integration through subordination. The politics of agricultural modernisation in industrial Europe.* Brepols
Pennacchi, A. (2010). *Canale Mussolini.* Mondadori.
Polanyi, K. (1944). *The great transformation.* Farrar & Rinehart.
Said, E. (1978). *Orientalism.* Vintage.
Sieferle, R. (2001). Qué es la historia ecológica? In G. de Molina & M. Alier (Eds.), *Naturaleza transformada* (pp. 31–54). Icaria.

Smil, V. (2017). *Energy and civilization: A history*. MIT.
Thompson, E. P. (1991). *Customs in common*. New Press.
Vanhaute, E. (2021). *Peasants in world history*. Routledge.
Villares, R. (1982). La propiedad de la tierra en Galicia (1500–1936). Siglo XXI.
Wilson, C. (2022). *Being neighbours: Cooperative work and neighbourhood in Southern Ontario, 1830–1960*. McGill-Queen's University Press.
Worster, D. (1990). Transformations of the earth: Toward an agroecological perspective in history. *Journal of American History, 76*(4), 1087–1106.

7
SOCIAL AND ECONOMIC IMPACT OF TECHNOLOGICAL REVOLUTIONS IN EUROPE[1]

Raimundo A. Rodríguez-Pérez Pedro Miralles-Martínez Francisco Precioso-Izquierdo Pedro Miralles-Sánchez

Historiographical approach

What characterizes a *technological revolution*, that is, what allows us to speak about the emergence of a new phase in the historical development of societies is not just a confluence of a series of processes tied to technological ingenuity but also the economic, political, and cultural consequences that come about as a result of the use of new technology.

The use of the term *technological revolution* has become a category of analysis that helps us to understand the evolution of societies, particularly those that have taken shape in the West since the end of the 6th century. Although the use of this term has also been criticized for its purpose driven and vanguardist nature (Cameron & Neal, 2005), the fact remains that it has become a category of social analysis that has grown as an explanatory framework from which the economic, cultural, and political changes that affect western societies since the end of the Modern Era can be further analyzed.

The paradigm typically employed has been the British model, whose timelines, causes, and consequences have been exported as the only valid tenet to explain other European contexts. Nevertheless, while the British model stood out for its advanced nature and its characteristics of entry, development, and exit in the intense process of industrialization and modernization starting at the end of the 17th century, it can scarcely help to explain the regional and even local characteristics and variations present in other places such as France, Italy, Holland, or Spain.

Historians that have studied the development of technological revolutions normally distinguish three identifiable stages from the second half of the 18th century to the present.

The first technological revolution takes place at the end of the 18th century in the context of implementing specific technological advances such as the steam engine or the power loom in the textile and communication industries.

DOI: 10.4324/9781003289470-10

This first stage is characterized by the abundant use of coal and iron as the main sources of energy, which were key elements to sustaining the upward trend of these new systems of manufacture and communication.

In the second technological revolution the effects of the first Industrial Revolution would be felt across the entire western world throughout the first half of the 19th century. Indeed, the second major stage of the technological revolution, defined primarily by the electrification of industry, came to a close in the mid-18th century. In this new phase, other advances that stand out are the development and fine-tuning of the internal combustion engine, which would later be essential to the invention of the first automobiles, as well as the increasing importance of steel-related industries. One of the most important consequences of this second stage was the impetus to internationalize domestic economies and their increasing interconnectedness.

The third technological revolution is typically considered to start in the first third of the 20th century. Its defining characteristics are the peak of the aviation and aerospace industries, the emergence of atomic energy, and the incipient computing industry.

There are other classifications based on varied criteria that emphasize not only technological innovation but also the social and economic consequences that derive from them. Still others, in contrast, rely on much later historical periods beyond the late 18th century or the first few decades of the 19th century to date prior periods in the evolutionary development of a process that would have started practically at the time man appeared on this planet.

Salvador Salort i Vives (2012) pondered almost a decade ago, "Where are we headed?" (p. 305). He was conscious of the series of changes that western societies are undergoing on a technological level, "a swarm of discoveries and innovations that seem to attest to the coming of a new system. In this new system . . . there is a new shining star: information" (p. 306).

The truth is that the unanswered questions that Salort i Vives posed reflect a state of concern that many specialists have tried to resolve by making reference to a new stage in the technological revolution, which is taking place before our eyes. This is a reference to the Fourth Industrial Revolution, a term coined by the founder of the World Economic Forum, K. Schwab, in 2016 to refer to the new situation dominated by smart factories and online production management.

Social and economic impact

Who are the winners and losers? The effects of technological revolutions on social inequalities

One of the most important effects of technological revolutions is related to man controlling the environment. Nature is no longer an adversary for the human species due to the technological solutions that have helped it to dominate all other animal species and settle a territory that can be controlled, measured, protected, and furnished with basic necessities. Man controlling the environment thanks to technological advances (weapons, productivity, etc.) has been a constant since the development of the first recognized forms of agriculture and animal husbandry in the Neolithic period.

In this sense, it is known that the first crops cultivated appeared around 9500 B.C., thanks in part to a global warming of the Earth and also the dissemination of the most primitive tillage methods. Among others, wheat, barley, peas, and lentils were cultivated in the Levant, and rice and soy were cultivated in China between 11500 and 6200 B.C.; sugar cane and some vegetables were also cultivated in New Guinea around 7000 B.C., while remains of the primitive cultivation of cotton from around 3600 B.C. have been found in Peru.

In this sense, we consider the increase in population sedentism to be one of the most important consequences of the technological revolution linked to the appearance of the first forms of agriculture and animal husbandry. Among many other factors, the ability to provide a large group of people with a consistent, daily supply of provisions undoubtedly enabled the progressive concentration of men and women in a specific territory on an ongoing basis, which over time was essential to initiate another one of the key processes in the history of humanity: urbanization, the establishment of population centers in cities.

The process of generalizing urban environments is well-known and amply described. It can be analyzed starting with the incipient agricultural villages of the Neolithic all the way up to the most renowned urban forms of the city-states developed by the Phoenicians on the east coast of the Mediterranean, which were later continued and expanded upon by Greek cities, particularly those founded throughout the Roman Empire. According to Cameron and Neal (2005), in medieval Europe, despite the increase in urban population, especially in Italy (Venice, Genoa, Pisa, etc.) and the Netherlands (mainly in the south, in Flanders and Brabant), agricultural institutions continued to perform important functions in the identity of the economy and society. However, this trend would revert in the Modern Era, especially as a result of the increase in commerce and exploration of large areas that were inhospitable for Europeans (Africa and the Americas), as well as the growing effects of continental industrialization that began to appear around the middle of the 17th century in Great Britain, initially, and France, Germany, and the Netherlands at the turn of the century.

In the 19th century and the beginning of the 20th, one of the most significant derivatives connected to the process of urbanization was internal migration, which would cause population centers to grow even more in the majority of European countries.

A second effect of technological revolutions is the apparent differentiation between societies and how they benefit from technological advances; in other words, those that benefit from the technology developed, which can be denominated *consumer societies*, and those that are primarily involved in the production of the materials needed to build the new technology, which can be denominated *producing societies*.

This effect, which appears to be unique to the modern world, can be used to study systems of locating and transferring raw materials, used since antiquity by the Greeks and Romans – consider the numerous sites located outside the Italian Peninsula, such as those in the Iberian Peninsula (Cartagena, Mazarrón, Río Tinto, Las Médulas) or in the southeast of present day France (Collobrières, Fouillouse, Portes, St. Bresson, etc.)

However, this differentiation between societies that benefit from technological advances and those that are dedicated to producing raw materials and final products now seems more alive than ever. A recent example of this is interest in the mineral coltan, highly valued for its tantalum content, which is essential to produce the capacitors in electronic equipment such as mobile devices and laptops. Several poor countries, like the Democratic Republic of the Congo and Ethiopia, have specialized in the extraction of this raw material.

Technological revolutions and work organization: from slavery and guilds to temporary work agencies and 'false' self-employed people

By way of an introduction, Ortega y Gasset asserts there have been three key stages to the evolution of technology: "the technology of chance, the technology of craftsmen, the technology of technicians" (Ortega y Gasset, 2004). The latter began to emerge around the 16th century – around 1540 the mechanical arts (*artes mechanicae*) became popular – and indicated the emergence of technology. For other authors who follow the scientific tradition, such as Michel Serres, technology is nothing more than the sixteenth branch of 'industrial science' (Serres, 1998). Theorists of English-speaking societies, where the term *technology* has traditionally been used, include craftsmanship in technology. For example, prehistorians sometimes speak about the technology of stone polishing for one simple reason: this is the only word available to describe it (Bunge, 2006). This allows them to create their own technology time lines and transform technology into an inherent trait of human nature whose origins are inseparable from the origin of man. Another perspective asserts that technology appears when the word emerges in the English-speaking world in the 17th–18th centuries (Harvey, 2011).

Industrial and technological revolutions should be analyzed as processes rather than matching them to a specific time period. This way, at least the inequality between countries can be explained as the first Industrial Revolution did not start until late in the 20th century in less developed countries, while the second Industrial Revolution was already well underway in the United States and the most important European nations (Chaves, 2004).

Factories moved to cities, and that process of urban industrialization caused a shift of labor and resources from agriculture to industry. Cities grew, but this gave rise to problems in the new industrial city: overcrowding, poverty, poor living conditions, factory smokestacks, trash, poor health conditions, and tension between the proletariat working class and the capitalists. In England, these individuals were known as Luddites, in reference to Ned Ludd, a weaver who is credited with the first deliberate destruction of power looms (Chaves, 2004).

Moreover, a present day parallel can be seen in the dependence on machines in the case of mobile telephones, where the South Korean philosopher, Byung-Chul Han (2021a) has expressed those mobile devices are instruments of domination. Today, a *smartphone* is both a digital workplace and a digital confessional. Every device, every domination technique generates objects of worship that are used for subjugation, thus strengthening the domination. Smartphones are objects of worship for digital domination (Han, 2021b) and function as if they were rosaries.

Before the Roman Empire in the West, a personal relationship of dependence between the service provider and the object of service was subsumed into the work relationship. This concept of work is intimately related to slave labor, whereby the subject performing the activity had the exact same legal consideration as an object, of which the master was the owner. This regulation of contracting for paid work underwent no significant innovations from the fall of the Roman Empire until the late Middle Ages (around the 13th century). Towards the end of this transition, the predominant form of political organization in western Europe was feudalism, whereby complex personal relationships existed between the feudal lord and his serfs. They were recognized as subjects of rights, but they also had a status that required them to work the land owned by their feudal lords in exchange for protection. The work performed under this regime of serfdom was rendered in conditions of complete submission: serfs were prohibited from making their services available to others, and their condition of serfdom was hereditary. For these reasons, from a modern perspective, it is currently very difficult to identify substantial differences between the conditions of serfdom and slavery (Boza, 2014).

All of this is clearly visible in the organization of artisan workshops where the head of the enterprise was the master craftsman, who was responsible for organizing, directing, and perfecting the work of the employees, called journeymen. As a result, their service can be considered a pioneering form of salaried employment. Finally, artisan workshops also had apprentices, who were young workers that were interested in benefiting from the reputation of training for a profession in that workshop. They were supervised by the journeymen in the performance of their tasks (Boza, 2014).

Since workers only performed one operation continuously for extended periods of time, they developed skills and abilities that reduced the costs and time needed for production. Workers with low salaries became the new slaves of capitalism (Santiago & Silva, 2016), and workers lost control of the productive process, which they had previously maintained through artisan workshops. Protective legislation, and especially the actions of the first trade unions, were able to ensure basic rules were established that limited the abuse of employees (Boza, 2014).

Starting with the invention of the steam engine at the end of the 18th century, technological innovation has been the key driver of economic and social growth of the most developed countries. Specifically, it is how the average worker in Spain today works a third less hours and at the same time earns ten times more than at the start of the 20th century. It is for this reason that over the last two centuries all social and economic agents, institutions, businesses, and individuals have learned to coexist and take advantage of the opportunities associated with the constant and gradual pace of technological development. We are talking about phenomena ranging from rural unemployment and migration to large cities to the abandonment of coal mining. Today, once again, we are at the start of one of these waves, baptized as the Fourth Industrial Revolution or, more appropriately, the Digital Revolution, and the impact it will have on the job market must be addressed (Domenech et al., 2019).

At present, we are witnessing struggles in certain industries – characterized by extreme flexibility – that are based on online platforms to sell and deliver products and services, such as Amazon or Glovo. Businesses understand that new labor legislation, including its anti-labor provisions, offer an extraordinary opportunity to further deregulate working conditions with the goal of maximizing profits and requiring delivery men or drivers to accept becoming self-employed, a sort of ally of the company. This means they have to relinquish the minimum protection of their labor rights and enter into ruthless competition with each other to earn a pittance per unit, that is, per haul or delivery (Ntavanellos, 2021; Blanc, 2021).

Social and economic consequences of the transformation of communications

The first empires dominated the known world based on maritime expansion (Paine, 2021). They relied on commercial trading routes that allowed for exchanging products made from raw materials they lacked and were cheaper, though essential, to produce weapons, coins, or basic foodstuffs. Some examples are Mediterranean cultures such as the Phoenicians and Greeks, reaching a pinnacle with the Romans and the concept of *Mare Nostrum* as indisputable dominance.

Europeans, in search of spices and new markets explored alternative sea routes. The Portuguese and Spanish were the first to take the initiative in an age when authoritarian monarchies and the beginning of absolutism were getting underway (the end of the 15th century). The Indian Ocean and Atlantic Ocean Sea routes put the Iberian powers at the vanguard of the West (Todorov, 1987). England dominated the high seas and transoceanic routes from the 18th century, and this served as the basis for its pioneering industrial development. The United States would inherit this model starting in 1914 with its emergence as a superpower.

Those powers that have dominated technology have been the first to benefit from increasingly global power. The challenge is now to control new technologies (5G) and other systems of remote power. Not so much to control large swaths of territory but rather to get ahead of their rivals in order to control information, sources of energy – both traditional and clean – and production methods (Rifkin, 2011).

Cartography emerged to guide merchants and explorers on their journeys to far-off lands where the only means of navigation available were the observation of the stars and instrumentation such as the compass and astrolabe. This was the case of the Magellan-Elcano circumnavigation (1519–1522) or the return voyage from the Philippines to Mexico where Fray Andrés de Urdaneta (1565) discovered how to take advantage of the North Pacific current to get to Acapulco. The opening of this sea route made commercial exchange with China possible (Manila galleon) and ensured the preservation of the Spanish empire for two and a half centuries (Paine, 2021).

The first Industrial Revolution emerged in England with the invention of the Watt steam engine towards the end of the 18th century (Hobsbawm, 1998). It transformed the thermal energy of a specific quantity of water into mechanical energy, which made it possible to power vehicles, boats, and trains. This meant a qualitative leap forward in terms of reducing distances. Together with colonial and maritime dominance, it was the vertex of British power with a colonial empire spread across the Americas, Africa, Asia, and Oceania.

The West started to take interest in alternative clean energy after the oil crisis of 1973 and the staggering inflation, unemployment, and social problems caused by the increase in energy prices (Hobsbawm, 2014). This is even more relevant in Western Europe, which is dependent on the Near East, North Africa, and Russia for energy. In Europe, nuclear energy is increasingly looked upon negatively due to its danger to the environment, although it is the cheapest way of avoiding dependence on other countries for energy.

Today's hyperconnected world, with the web 3.0, has generated fear of a dystopia where large multinationals are beyond the control of governments, who had been the key actors till this point. Moreover, Chomsky (2021) plays down the importance of these changes, indicating that the arrival of the telegraph in the 19th century was much more relevant at the time than email, even though the latter is instantaneous. In perspective, he asserted that the qualitative leap forward had already occurred. In any event, the Internet has generated a fourth economic sector in addition to the three traditional ones. This also creates problems, such as fake news, and information saturation make it difficult for citizens to differentiate between real and fake information.

World powers compete to control the information flowing on the Internet. Aside from controlling the dark net and the geoposition of possible suspects, privacy and personal freedoms are restricted in pursuit of greater collective security. China is more advanced than the West in the build out of its 5G network, although the United States and Europe do not seem likely to install this technology to avoid being surveilled by the competition. However, in Europe, despite judicial sentences, we accept the hegemony of large American companies that spy on the population, businesses, and governments at the same time that they evade taxes by operating from tax havens.

The preeminence of the digital world has not come about to improve an understanding of the world but rather to facilitate the development of capitalism in a new phase. Sociologists such as Bauman (2016) and Han (2021a) have been warning of this for some time: a system of liquid societies with increasingly indistinct identities and a process that makes social and work relationships impersonal. A more connected world but with more monitoring and surveillance. A large part of the population accepts this infringement on their rights and freedoms in exchange for more leisure and free technological applications.

Technology and social improvements. Unlimited growth?

Lewis Mumford pointed out decades ago in one of his most important works, *Technics and Civilization* (1994), that every machine or technology has its root in society, that is, neither machines nor technology exist separate from the societies that produce them.

Every machine, like all literature, history, medicine, or politics, responds to the changing social needs at that juncture. Technology is developed in the heart of a society to meet distinct needs or to satisfy specific interests. In itself, there is no *good* or *bad* technology but rather uses that are more appropriate than others. The development of mobile communications technology, to give just one example, has contributed to reducing physical distances and to keeping people in contact; that is, it has solved a problem of modern society, which is increasingly willing to leave its origins behind but not to lose contact with its home environment. When this basic, primary function was largely met, problems began to arise related to excessive time spent in front of mobile device screens, the image worship we project on networks, or the need to be permanently connected while spewing personal information and data all over the Internet, which are difficult to remove later.

Another problem arising from technological development is related to the consumption of energy and natural resources. Cameron and Neal (2005), not without reason, asserted that presently:

> There is no doubt that the world – above all rich nations – is consuming resources at an unprecedented pace in history. This in itself provides a measure of its capacity to dominate the environment and solve the economic problem, but it has also given rise to the fear that resources will run out.

Recognizing the risks that every technological development may pose, in recent years an expression has come into use, 'social technology', which underscores the utility of technology to solve social problems while meeting four basic requirements or principals: simplicity, limited environmental impact, low production cost, and ease of application. According to the *Fundación Iberdrola* report, social technology "uses all of the digital knowledge and tools available to transform society".[2]

According to Peter Thomson, president of the United Nations General Assembly in 2017, as cited by Sandra Paniagua (*El Independiente*, 6/10/2018): "all over the world, smartphones are used to provide financial services to those without bank accounts, to diagnose medical conditions, and to remotely manage care for the chronically ill. The transformative power of science, innovation, and technology is abundant and obvious".[3]

Consequences of the transformation to transportation and communications

The prevalence of technology has given Europe and the West primacy in world history in terms of dominating the economy and geopolitics since the end of the Middle Ages, while seeking new markets and areas of influence. In passing, it has imposed its languages, beliefs, and forms of social organization. The test case, at the Euro-Mediterranean level, was the Roman Empire, which became the model for hegemonic political entities. In the age of discoveries, the Spanish and Portuguese established mestizo societies in America with black slave labor. As these were poor civilizations that were less technologically developed (including the Aztecs and Incas), Europeans imposed their religions, languages, and other identity traits (Todorov, 1987). This was even more the case in other areas where the indigenous peoples were more primitive, such as in North America. As for Africa, Asia, and Oceania the colonizing experience spread, notably, in the 19th century. There was not as much mixing between the colonizers and the indigenous peoples.

This white, Christian, and western hegemony is in crisis. The state of emergency of civil rights and the independence of former colonies have called into question the world system imposed by the rich north. Even after the fall of the Soviet Union, the United States cannot police the world nor spread its political system to the remaining world powers, regardless of its military dominance (Rifkin, 2011). Presently, Russia, Turkey, and China are re-emerging as world powers, having previously been dormant due to poverty, the end of their empires, or internal destabilization.

The end of the Cold War made even the most ardent liberals believe in an ideal world with a single capitalist system and western parliamentary democracies. This has been shown to be unsustainable; despite the enormous military spending of the United States, they cannot win on all fronts, not even with the best technology nor naval and military bases across the planet. After September 11th, the war on international terrorism caused priorities to change after decades battling the Soviets and their satellites (Hobsbawm, 2014). But a unipolar world does not exist. At the start of the 21st century, the world is witnessing the emergence of world powers that have been sleeping for decades (Russia) or centuries (China) and who view American hegemony negatively.

The West's reliance on cheap labor and raw materials from the southern hemisphere is evident. The well-being of the West contrasts with the misery in which a large part of the population of the world lives – a lack of rights and freedoms not to mention the growing inequalities in the heart of rich countries. Neoliberal policies and offshoring industry have caused basic sectors of the economy to be outsourced or performed with ever more modern machinery. One of the biggest challenges in the near future is reconciling those technological advances with massive job losses and social instability. We have gone from the industrial era to the collaborative stage (Rifkin, 2011). The golden age of capitalism, after World War II, ended in 1973. In the West, over the last half a century, important progress has been made in regards to the rights of women, children, religious freedom, and racial and sexual tolerance. Climate change and growing inequalities are the biggest challenges (Pardo, 2015).

Didactic objectives

- Identify and understand the economic, social, and cultural changes that resulted from technological advances throughout history.
- Analyze and assess the consequences of scientific and technological revolutions on the living conditions of different social groups.
- Examine the changes to and continuity of civil society, social and labor relations, and individual and group actions.

Topic: The social and economic impact of technological revolutions in Europe. Technological revolutions and work organization from slavery and guilds to temporary work agencies and 'false' self-employed people.
Courses: Compulsory Education and High School.

Contents

- Understand the temporary nature of explaining historical processes and its capacity to connect the past and the present. Historical awareness.
- Analysis of the establishment and consequences of capitalism: the Industrial Revolution. Compare capitalist cycles of expansion and contraction.
- Differentiate among the economic systems and regions around the world. Poverty and dependence around the world. Unequal access to resources and technology.
- Economic growth and sustainability. The challenges of globalization and the circular economy.
- Technological revolutions and work organization.

Competences – skills

Key competences:

A Mathematical competence and basic science and technology skills.

Understand how the history and evolution of science and technology help to achieve basic science and technology skills. These skills contribute to the development of scientific thought because they require the use of scientific reasoning and technology skills that lead to acquiring knowledge, comparing ideas, and applying these findings to social well-being.

Science and technology skills empower respectful and responsible citizens to critically analyze the scientific and technological events that take place over time, both past and present, as well as the consequences of these events.

These skills include attitudes and values associated with the adoption of ethical standards related to science and technology, an interest in science, support for scientific research, and the assessment of scientific knowledge; likewise, they include a sense of responsibility related to the preservation of natural resources, environmental issues, and the adoption of an appropriate attitude to achieve a healthy physical and mental lifestyle in a natural and social environment.

B   Digital literacy.

Digital literacy means the creative, critical, and safe use of information and communication technology to achieve objectives related to work, employability, learning, the use of free time, inclusion, and participation in civil society. This topic, which deals with the evolution of technology and its applications to society at large, and specifically to the world of work, clearly contributes to digital literacy as it deals with adapting to changes those new technologies bring about in people's lives.

C   Social and civic skills.

Social and civic skills involve the ability and capacity to use knowledge and attitudes about a dynamic, complex, and changing society to *interpret social problems and phenomena* in increasingly diversified contexts.

Acquiring the knowledge necessary to understand and critically analyze the codes of conduct and the uses that are generally accepted in different societies, as well as the conflicts and processes of change throughout history, is essential to fully participate in the social and interpersonal spheres of life. For this reason, it is important to understand basic concepts related to the individual, groups, *work organization, equality, and non-discrimination among men and women* and between different social and cultural groups.

People should be interested in socioeconomic and technological development and their contribution to the greater social well-being of the entire population, as well as intercultural communication, diversity of values, and respect for differences in addition to the willingness and commitment to overcome prejudice.

Historical concepts

- Acculturation: the imposition of a hegemonic culture upon others by means of political, economic, and military dominance of the western powers, which have spread their social and cultural models to their colonies in the Americas, Africa, Asia, and Oceania. They are imposed in different manners, according to the extent of cultural development and the era in which each territory is annexed to the metropole. This heritage continues to weigh on the division between rich and poor countries.
- Capitalism: a production model based on profit and private initiative. Although it emerged with European colonial expansion in the 16th century, it was

entrenched as a hegemonic system starting with the Industrial Revolution. It is based on the free market and exporting manufactured goods. It creates a poor working class (proletariat) that emigrate from rural areas and an elite bourgeoisie that are owners of factories and capital.
- Feudalism: a production method based on hierarchical relationships of dependence between lords and vassals. It arose in the European Middle Ages and was based on loyalty and a system of hierarchy including work obligations as well as obedience to and military service on behalf of a Lord (lay or religious).
- Industrial Revolution: a process of mechanization of work that increases the profits and production of capital. It started at the end of the 18th century in England and spread to Europe and the United States in the 19th century. It enabled the achievement of technological advances, putting the western capitalist powers at the vanguard of economic development and political hegemony.
- Slavery: a production model based on labor provided by bond-servants that submit to masters or slave owners who dictate their work and lives. It arose with the first civilizations in antiquity and was perpetuated in the modern contemporary periods as the basis of production in overseas colonies. It was key to the economic development of European metropoles.
- Social networks: these arose as an evolution of the web 3.0 at the start of the 21st century and allow for interaction in real time between large numbers of individuals. They are part of the so-called collaborative and horizontal Internet, communities of users that share content thanks to permanent Internet connections. They determine the means of communication, advertising, and personal and work relationships in present day societies.
- Social technology: The use of technology to solve social problems by meeting four requirements or principles: simplicity, limited environmental impact, low production costs, and ease of application.
- Technological revolution: Technological revolution can be understood as a state of common social and economic transformations for the majority of the population that result from the implementation of technological advances. What characterizes a *technological revolution* is not just a confluence of a series of processes tied to technological ingenuity but also the economic, political, and cultural consequences that come about as a result of the use of new technology.
- Urbanization: The establishment of population centers and key socioeconomic activities in cities. This process started with the first civilizations in the Middle East and Mediterranean, where writing and a governing elite also emerged, based on religious, legal, and military primacy.

Notes

1 This chapter is a result of projects "HistoryLab for European Civic Engagement: open e-Toolkit to train History Teachers on Digital Teaching and Learning", funded by SEPIE on call ERASMUS + KA226 [2020–1-ES01-KA226-HE-095430], and research project PID2020–113453RB-I00, funded by Agencia Estatal de Investigación of Spain (AEI/10.13039/501100011033).

2 (www.iberdrola.com/compromiso-social/tecnologia-social).
3 (www.elindependiente.com/desarrollo-sostenible/2018/10/06/tecnologia-social-para-mejorar-el-mundo/).

References

Bauman, Z. (2016). *Tiempos líquidos. Vivir en una época de incertidumbre*. Barcelona: Tusquets.
Boza, G. (2014). Surgimiento, evolución y consolidación del derecho del trabajo. THEMIS: *Revista de Derecho, 65*, 13–26. https://dialnet.unirioja.es/descarga/articulo/5078193.pdf
Blanc, B. (2021). Conditions de travail en Suisse: des données . . . à utiliser. *A l' encontré*. http://alencontre.org/suisse/conditions-de-travail-en-suisse-des-donnees-a-utiliser.html
Bunge, M. (2006). *Epistemología*. Barcelona: Siglo XXI.
Cameron, R., & Neal, L. (2005). *Historia económica mundial: Desde el Paleolítico hasta el presente*. Madrid: Alianza Editorial.
Chaves Palacios, J. (2004). Desarrollo tecnológico en la primera revolución industrial. *Norba: Revista de Historia, 17*, 93–109. https://dialnet.unirioja.es/descarga/articulo/1158936.pdf
Chomsky, N. (2021). *The Precipice. Neoliberalism, the Pandemic and the Urgent Need for Social Change*. London: Penguin.
Domenech, R., Neut, A., Andrés, J., & García, J. R. (2019). El impacto del cambio tecnológico y el futuro del empleo. En M. E. Casas & C. De la Torre (Dirs.), *El futuro del trabajo en España: impacto de las nuevas tendencias* (pp. 37–53). Alphen aan den Rijn: Wolters Kluwer.
Han, B.-Ch. (2021a). *No-cosas. Quiebras en el mundo de hoy*. Barcelona: Taurus.
Han, B.-Ch. (2021b, octubre 9). Byung-Chul Han: El móvil es un instrumento de dominación. Actúa como un rosario. *El País*. https://bit.ly/3nkQLeH
Harvey, C. (2011). El surgimiento histórico de la tecnología: repercusiones en los procesos de investigación. *Visión electrónica, 5*(1), 123–134. https://dialnet.unirioja.es/descarga/articulo/4016866.pdf
Hobsbawm, E. J. (1998). *La era del capital, 1848–1875*. Barcelona: Crítica.
Hobsbawm, E. J. (2014). *Historia del siglo XX: 1914–1991*. Barcelona: Crítica.
Mumford, L. (1994). *Técnica y Civilización*. Madrid: Alianza Universidad.
Ntavanellos, A. (2021). Neoliberalismo salvaje, militarismo y racismo institucional . . . y una lucha social. *Vientosur*. https://vientosur.info/neoliberalismo-salvaje-militarismo-y-racismo-institucional-y-una-lucha-social-victoriosa/
Ortega y Gasset, J. (2004). *Meditación de la técnica y otros ensayos sobre ciencia y filosofía*. Pleasant Grove, UT: Alianza.
Pardo, V. (2015). *La encrucijada de Europa. Luces y sombras para un futuro común*. Valencia: Universidad de Valencia.
Paine, L. (2021). *El mar y la civilización. Una historia marítima del mundo*. Seville: Antonio Machado.
Rifkin, J. (2011). *La Tercera Revolución Industrial. Cómo el poder lateral está transformando la energía, la economía y el mundo*. Barcelona: Paidós.
Salort i Vives, S. (2012). *Revoluciones industriales, trabajo y estado del bienestar: la gran ruptura mundial contemporánea*. Barcelon: Sílex.
Santiago, A. A., & Silva, P. (2016). El papel de la administración en la evolución humana. *Perspectivas docentes, 62*, 12–20. https://dialnet.unirioja.es/descarga/articulo/6349279.pdf
Schwab, K. (2016). *La cuarta revolución industrial*. Barcelona: Debate.
Serres, M. (1998). *Historia de las ciencias*. Barcelona: Cátedra.
Todorov, T. (1987). *La Conquista de América. El problema del otro*. Barcelona: Siglo XXI.
Web ResourcesSandra Paniagua, "Tecnología para transformar el mundo", www.elindependiente.com/desarrollo-sostenible/2018/10/06/tecnologia-social-para-mejorar-el-mundo/

8
BOURGEOISIE AND PEASANTRY

Unequal but necessary to understand European history and its identity[1]

Juan Ramón Moreno-Vera,
José Monteagudo-Fernández

Literature review

Cultural differences between rural and urban worlds are key to understand the present European identity. As Hobsbawm (1974) commented, historical discourses just pay attention to the economic urban elites that concentrate political power. Peasantry and the rural world remain "invisible" due to the economic, cultural and social inequalities (Boltvinik & Mann, 2016).

Although this situation can be tracked along all historical periods (from ancient city-kingdoms in Mesopotamia, Greek's poleis, Roman cities, Muslim *medinas*, Middle Ages trade centres – Pinon, 2001 or post-Industrial new urbanisations), the rural world has always remained important to make economy and wealth grow up (Portass, 2021).

Sadly, the hard work, the bad living conditions, the perishable products, the dependence on the weather and the control of prices by the big industrial power provoked a large rural exodus in the European 19th century to the cities.

New peripheric neighbourhoods were created for working classes in the cities. Ghettos were formed and attracted an impoverished population looking for more stable works (Leeds, 1994). The bad conditions of the new proletarian population, economic inequalities and poverty, originated the first working-class organisations as unions and political parties. During the second half of the 19th century and along the 20th century, conflicts between peasants, workers and bourgeoisie elites were frequent.

After the two world wars, the creation of the European Union and the arrival of democracy in the last decades of the 20th century and the first of the 21st century, European population identity is more related to the defense of the universal welfare state, democratic values, tolerance, world peace, religious freedom, respect for environment and the recognition of rights for social minorities.

Bourgeoisie and peasantry

What social differences exist between the urban and rural populations?

At first glance, as commented Unikel Spector "the urban population is that which lives in cities and the rural population is that which does not" (1968: 2). However, there is no single answer, and the definition of urban space implies a theoretical challenge.

Furthermore, the most commonly used administrative criterion in European countries is the number of inhabitants of each area, which varies according to the country in question. Thus, it is necessary to distinguish between urban and rural populations via new approaches which are not only based on the physical (city-nature) or administrative (inhabitants) context.

Historically, beyond the cultural (migrations, marginalisation), economic (poverty), environmental (pollution, mobility) or political (borders, pensions, etc.) implications, from the social point of view, people of working age fundamentally move towards cities, which are where economic activity is concentrated. This rural exodus began with the Industrial Revolution of the 18th century, continued in the 19th and 20th centuries and has persisted in the 21st century. The main consequence of this movement from the countryside to the city is that, in the 21st century, we live in essentially urban societies (Shatterthwaite, 2003) in which the (younger) urban population keeps on growing, whereas the (ageing) rural population decreases.

In terms of historical studies, the rural population has become increasingly "invisible" within the political, military and social processes of contemporary history. Thus, as Hobsbawm said "a rural labouring class was too unimportant" (1974: 268) and is practically ignored when learning history, as our vision of "urban aspects" corresponds to cities, which are the product of industrial expansion and the capitalist economy. However, it should be taken into account that, in other periods of history, the conception of "urban" and "rural" may have been different to our own and that urban development processes and the emergence of the first cities do not follow the same premises, not do they have the same intentionality of "modernity and development" as our cities today (Leeds, 1994: 52).

Indeed, urbanisation processes and the most ancient cities have been discovered by way of techniques of archaeological research in areas of the Near East: Bestansur (7660 B.C. in Iraqi Kurdistan), Sheik-e Abad (7560 B.C. in Iran) and Çatalhöyük (7000 B.C. in central Anatolia, Turkey). These first "modern" cities were the result of processes linked to sedentarism, the stabling of animals and the storage of products.

In fact, these cities formed the central nucleus of the populations and housed the political and religious powers of the dominant classes, as happened in Chinese empire (Wheatley, 1971) or America (Pons Carmona, 2014). Indeed, in this first great urban age, the rural environment continued to work at full capacity (agricultural and livestock production). However, the sources available make no mention of any kind of political representation in public life (Klíma, 1979).

In Europe, the first urban centres appeared somewhat later (between 6200 and 5000 B.C.) and were established in the Mediterranean area on the Aegean coast of the Anatolia peninsula (Turkey) and on the islands and mainland of present-day Greece due to the influence of other ancient civilizations in the Mediterranean.

It was not until the Metal Age (between 3000 and 2000 B.C.) that the first urban civilizations can be found on the Greek coast with the appearance of the first Mycenaean cities (the inhabitants of which Homer called Achaeans). These new cities had clear urban planning: temples (such as the one in Lerna), palaces (such as the one in Tiryns) and acropolises (such as the one in Mycenae).

The political stability of the Mediterranean area made it possible for these Greek poleis to prosper independently and to increase in size to the point of becoming great centres of population. Thus, for the design of new poleis arising due to the growth of Greek thalassocracy in the Mediterranean, the Greeks developed a model of urban planning which implied more than a mere set of buildings and designed a complete model to provide a positive response to the needs of a completely civilised community.

Therefore, the acropolis, a high city, continued to exist as a ceremonial site and a refuge (in case of attack), while the population established itself in the Asty or low city. Here, there were public places such as the Agora (an open public space which became the political, social and economic centre of the polis), the defensive walls (due to the political independence of each polis, which could result in confrontations), recreational places, such as the amphitheatre or the stadium (dedicated to sporting events). The most widespread urban planning model was the grid plan, created by the Greek mathematician Hippodamus of Miletus. Streets were designed at right angles, creating rectangular blocks of houses, and were divided in importance according to their width: streets of 5 to 10 metres in width (main streets) and those of less than 5 metres in width (secondary streets).

Roman society inherited many of the Greek traditions, including, of course, the orthogonal urban planning. Housing was divided into quadrangular blocks cutting streets at right angles. The main streets were the Cardo (north-south) and the Decumanus (east-west), at the intersection of which was located the forum, a large public space which constituted the social centre of community life (temples, palaces and administrative centres).

Before the definitive conquest of the city of Rome by the Ostrogoths (476 A.D.), a progressive ruralisation of the population was under way. In words of Baron et al. (2019) this should not be understood as a sign of social decline, as the cities did not disappear. Rural populations were strengthened as a strategy for resilience and to ensure agrarian and livestock production and the delivery of food to the population.

Late ancient ruralisation was maintained in the west of continental Europe whereas, during the Middle Ages, great urbanisation took place in the Islamic and Byzantine Empires.

As Portass (2021) indicated, contrary to popular belief, rural peasantry was fundamental in the establishment of feudal economy. Agrarian and livestock production remained stable (independently of who was in power), thus ensuring the subsistence and functioning of the system of vassalage. This economic stability and dynamism brought about the gradual growth of the urban population during the late Middle Ages (10th–15th centuries) as the towns and cities again became strategic hubs for trade and economic transactions.

The urban transition from ancient to medieval cities was not simple as, in most cases, human settlements were established in pre-existing cities. Thus, many urban elements remained and others were simply transformed (Pinon, 2001).

From the Late Modern period onwards, cities have undergone a series of morphological changes brought about by new urban needs. For instance, the Industrial Revolution led to a significant rural exodus and the massive arrival of inhabitants of working age to cities. Factories and industries were installed on the outskirts of the cities (extending beyond the old medieval walls and, in many cases, destroying them). This led to the need for new housing concentrated in the suburbs and on the outskirts of the cities. In most cases, these were working-class neighbourhoods in which high-rise buildings accumulated to make the most of the space, leading to a high degree of massification and population density with the subsequent negative effect on public services such as education, healthcare and transport. However, the main consequence was the rapid decay of these urban areas and the creation of ghettos and marginalised neighbourhoods in economic, labour, social and ethnic terms.

In the 21st century, cities and urban planning began to experience new challenges: environmental problems (Badii et al., 2017), the decentralisation of institutions, the parity of neighbourhoods and the elimination of inequalities. These are, by no means, easy problems to solve and the urban continuities of previous centuries do nothing but make the task more difficult. The concept of the 21st century city includes the creation of more pleasant outskirts, with wider avenues and the inclusion of urban transport (trams, metro, bus), the creation and promotion of cycle lanes to increase safety and the use of environmentally sustainable means of transport to help reduce pollution levels in large cities.

Peasantry and its identity: economical inequalities in a capitalist urban world

In the previous section, there has historically been a complex difference between the participation of peasantry in sociopolitical processes and that of the urban population. In fact, in words of Leeds (1994) these groups are in different positions of the "social order" within the globalised society of today, in which the bourgeois and urban social classes maintain their (fundamentally economic) control over peasants and the rural population as a whole.

Peasantry and the rural population have certain defining characteristics by which they can be identified, according to Boltvinik and Mann (2016). On the one hand, agrarian production has a discontinuous character due to the biological cycles of plants and animals and to their dependence on meteorological conditions.

In addition, in the rural environment, most of the products offered to the economic market are perishable (Boltvinik & Mann, 2016) and the great capitals which acquire them can dominate and impose the prices as, if they are not sold in time, they end up losing their usefulness. That implies the persistence of an impoverished peasantry far removed from the great centres of economic and political power in our society where there is an imbalance between the work done, the time spent, the physical effort made and the economic retribution received for their products, which often does not even cover the costs of their production.

In addition to these economic barriers, there are other obstacles by which the rural population in Europe can be identified. On the one hand, gender inequality still exists, as the work (both in agriculture and livestock rearing) is frequently carried out by women who either do not receive a salary or are very poorly paid. On the other hand, there are social and cultural obstacles due to the fact that as the work is physically hard and not well paid. It is commonly carried out by migrant populations, which settle in rural areas but which, in many cases, cannot participate actively (due to administrative and bureaucratic issues) in the political decisions of the area in which they live.

Bourgeoisie and urban boom in Europe

As Hobsbawm (1974) said, until 1830, there was really only one industrialised country in Europe: England. The rest of the continent was just setting out on the path to becoming an industrialised society and a liberal urban economy.

From the middle of the 19th century, Europe underwent a great industrial, economic, political and social revolution and experienced significant change from the countryside to the cities where great industrial capital and an impoverished working-class population originating from rural areas began to concentrate.

In truth, any urban centre, from the tribal settlements of prehistory to the great megalopolises of the present day, functions as a space for trading, transfer and communication. However, cities today also have other functions, such as being the seat of different institutions (governments, religions, education, healthcare, justice, etc.), as well as hosting a varied population dependent on different professional specialities or fields of knowledge. Therefore, in words of Leeds (1994) historical discourse has focused on the interests of the "specialised" urban classes and has repeatedly omitted the rural "subclass", which is considered to be "unspecialised".

The urban bourgeois classes of present-day Europe base their political and economic power on the liberal revolutions of the mid-19th century, in which they consolidated their quotas of representative power to the detriment of other dominant social classes: parliamentarism in order to control the nobility and the monarchy (e.g., in England and the United States) and confiscation to control ecclesiastical power (e.g., Spain).

Economically, the urban bourgeoisie, which arose in the 19th century, based its growth on industrial development with the support of the cheap extraction of raw materials (imperialism and colonialism) and the control of salaries and working conditions of the working class which emigrated from the countryside to the city in search of greater job stability, even though it was just as badly paid.

Therefore, socially, European cities are characterised by a great economic dichotomy: in the same context there are bourgeois neighbourhoods with acceptable living conditions, better buildings, larger houses, better cleaning, better communication connections, better educational and cultural services, and other (normally peripheral) neighbourhoods with worse communications, educational and healthcare services, in which a more impoverished and working-class population is concentrated.

Between these two urban realities, according to Dejung et al. (2019), there is the urban middle class, which originated from the urban growth of the 19th and 20th centuries, with citizens who, in spite of a lack of economic privilege, actively participate in the social and political life of the city, gaining access to the highest levels of education and intellect.

Social conflicts: the rural and urban world facing marginality and inequality

If we delay the analysis of social conflicts to Roman times, we can say that this civilization was extremely urban, aristocratic and unequal. In the later years of the Republic and the High Roman Empire, society was clearly stratified into two groups (Roldán, 2000). On the one hand, there was the privileged class, to which one belonged as a result of property and wealth (fundamentally agrarian). This class occupied the positions of power and prestige. Below them was a great heterogeneous mass of population, urban and rural, which was differentiated according to their economic activity, legal profile (freeborn, freed men or slaves) and their level of citizenship (Roman citizens, Latins or pilgrims).

The aforementioned inequalities in Roman society became greater in the Late Roman Empire (3rd–5th centuries), with society becoming more hierarchical and polarised. In general, Late Roman society was divided between a powerful class (potentes) and a humbler class (humiliores) (Santos, 2000). It was in this context that the armed peasant revolts, known as bagaudae, took place (Bravo, 2007). The bagaudas were not revolutionaries because they lacked an alternative social model; they were rather rebels against the power of Rome, an increasingly dictatorial and oppressive power (Romero, 2006).

The patriarchal nature of ancient Roman society meant that it was also extremely unequal between men and women, although this inequality also depended on the social class in question (Mateo & Pastor, 2020). These differences due to sex could be observed in the political and legal spheres. For example, the pater familias held power over the life of his wife in the first centuries of the Roman Republic and women were excluded from political voting. The main social role attributed to the women of the Roman oligarchy was reproduction, from which the high social status of Roman matrons was derived.

At the beginning of the Medieval Age the final disappearance of the Western Roman Empire implied the "decline" of urban life. Thus, in the middle of the 6th century, the majority of the population lived in the countryside and the cities which survived did so due to the fact that they were political capitals, episcopal sees, military fortresses of a strategic nature, places of worship guarding relics or due to the existence of small groups of merchants and craftsmen (Mazo, 1999).

In this context of a rural majority, small landowners got by on what was grown communally. This was difficult due to the system of biennial crop rotation (the most widespread system), the use of rudimentary techniques and the lack of fertiliser, all of which led to low yields. Added to this was the part which was to be kept in order to pay tribute to their masters. Thus it is not surprising that they had to seek sustenance in the forests or ask for alms.

Exercising power over this vast majority of poor people were the large landlords who owned enormous extensions of land and who had no problem feeding themselves. Their vast domains had a part reserved for them and their families and another part divided among settlers, who, in exchange for the usufruct of the land, were required to provide the lord with a series of services in kind, in money and work (Mazo, 1999).

There is not much evidence of social conflict in the Early Middle Ages (6th–10th centuries). With more than 90% of the population living in rural areas, it was relations in the countryside which led to the tensions and resistances of the time. The armed rebellions of a general nature are scarce and badly-documented, such as the Stellinga uprising in Saxony (841–842) or that of the Norman peasants (966–967) (Monsalvo, 2016).

As this occurred in Western Europe, Christides (1996) tells us that in the political system developed in Constantinople the cities became the decisive centres of economic life as powerful urban trade. However, the basis of the economy and wealth was still the land, which was essential in the power of the dominant landowning and military aristocracy.

The roles of men and women in the Byzantine Empire were clearly differentiated (Martín & Faci, 2000). Byzantine women had few rights, although some of the empresses played significant roles in State affairs. That was the case of the empress Theodora, the wife of Justinian I, who played a significant role in keeping her husband in power during the Nika riots (532 A.D.), the worst eruption of violence in Byzantium. As a result of the actions of Justinian's ministers, the people and the Senate rose up against the emperor. Half of the city was set on fire and, when the flames drew near to the palace, Theodora shouted at her husband "Royal purple is the noblest shroud" (Brown, 1971).

Compared with the ruralisation of Western Europe, Islamic lands represented a clearly urban panorama. Their importance was due to their political, administrative, religious and economic functions (López et al., 2000).

In the Islamic world, the commandments of the Quran regarding the subordination of women to men in Muslim society were clear. They were recommended to stay in the harem, which they could only leave in exceptional cases and in the company of an adult woman. Although they were not expressly prohibited from attending mosques, they were advised to pray at home. Markets, washing places and water wells were the only places in which women lived their social lives outside of male authority in rural areas. Inequality between men and women was also established on a legal level, although they were considered equal in terms of spirituality (López et al., 2000).

There were extremely diverse marginalised groups (such as astrologers, cripples, Jews and Black people) in both Byzantine and Islamic societies (Christides, 1996). These groups were considered to be strange creatures, bad omens and bearers of misfortune. In the case the Muslim world, on the other hand, was more accepting of Black people. Thousands of them were recruited into the armies and interracial marriages between Black and Caucasian people were common.

From the 11th century onwards, Europe underwent a period of economic and demographic growth which made it possible to improve communications between European regions whilst the process of work distribution accelerated, favouring the appearance or resurgence of merchant cities, and within them, a bourgeoisie of artisans and merchants. The cities filled up with peasants escaping from the dominion of the rural lords and taking up artisanal trades: cobblers, carpenters, weavers, etc. However, cities were not as numerous nor did they acquire as much importance as is normally attributed to them and neither were they ever centres of equality or oases of freedom. Although men were free and legally equal, their inhabitants were differentiated by their wealth and their politic capabilities (Martín, 2000). In the second half of the 13th century, this situation brought about the revolts of the guilds, led by the masters in the face of the abuses of the Urban Patriciate, as occurred in the merchant cities of Flanders (Bruges, Ypres, Ghent), those of the north of Italy (Bologna, Florence), France (Orleans, Rouen) and Barcelona.

Therefore, organised municipal movements, led by guild masters, coexisted with anarchic revolts that vented their hatred by burning the houses of patricians or Jews, who they blamed for the calamities afflicting the population. On other occasions, these revolts were the consequence of laws introduced to avoid raising salaries. In Portugal, Castile, France and England workers were obliged to work for a previously established salary and begging was punished, thus favouring the rich by providing them with cheap labour. The revolts only became successful when they were led by leaders of the urban bourgeoisie, as was the case of the Parisian revolts of the 14th and 15th centuries, such as the Cabochien Revolt (1413), the Ciompi Revolt in Florence and the conflict between La Busca and La Biga in Barcelona (1453).

Economic and social inequalities were also reproduced in rural areas (Martín, 2000). However, peasant uprisings against the power and abuse of the lords lacked organisation and were isolated in nature. In the case of northern Italy, the preaching of Fra Dolcino regarding the abolition of repressive hierarchies and a return to an evangelical society launched the peasantry into a revolt against the nobility which was subsequently quashed. In Flanders, the peasant uprising was a result of high county taxes and ecclesiastical tithing. English peasants rose up against the abuses of their lords who demanded more services than were due. Galicia witnessed the Irmandiño Revolts and Catalonia saw the Wars of the Remences.

Again Martín (2000) tells us that women were considered to be inferior to men in medieval times in Western Europe, often being considered to be men's property. Although they were not permitted to exercise the priesthood, convents and monasteries were created for them, in which they were encouraged to lead a pious life away from men. Reclusion in these places, although they continued to be in a position of subordination and were subjected to the designs of men, did not prevent some nuns from becoming cultured, writers and counsellors to other ecclesiastic leaders. Upper-class women were encouraged to occupy themselves in activities connected with textile production and to behave in accordance with strict rules of conduct.

In countries such as England and Castile, women were even able to reign, unlike other places such as Aragon, where their rights were passed on to male sons but were not personally exercised. On the other end of the social scale, peasant or artisan women were only given the right to work if it was an absolute necessity for them. The domestic service enjoyed by many noble houses was carried out by girls who had been kidnapped in wartime and become slaves.

Whatever the case, what is true is that throughout the early modern period, economic development led to an increase in inequality in the distribution of income due to the reduction in the real salaries of peasants, artisans and the growing industrial proletariat. Urbanisation and industrialisation led to a sharp increase in the degree of concentration of capital in cities (Van Zanden, 2005). This resulted in the increase of the poor and the beginning of uprisings and revolts, such as the Revolt of the Comuneros in Castile (1521), the uprising of Moriscos of the Alpujarras (1568), the actions of Thomas Müntzer (1524–1525), the croquants (1636–37) or Nu Pieds (1639) (Betrán & Moreno, 2000a).

In the case of revolts such as those of the Fronde in France (1648–1654), the convergence of interests of the artisans, bourgeois merchants and nobility concerning an increase in taxes gave rise to many interpretations (Tricoire, 2012).

Following Betrán and Moreno (2000b), the situation did not improve in the following century when a process that can be referred to as refeudalisation took place. Indeed, the social conflict, caused by economic aspects, became even more intense. This process of refeudalisation was stronger in Eastern Europe where the ecclesiastic and noble landlords sought to compensate the reduction in price of agricultural products exported to the West via an increase in feudal taxes imposed on peasants. In Russia, for example, peasants were no longer able to decide to leave the land after 1590 and the time period during which a landowner could pursue heads of family or any other member of the community who had escaped was extended before it was eventually abolished in 1649. Thus, Russian peasants became serfs whom the lord could sell with or without the land. The number of obligatory days of work in the lord's demesne was also increased. Taking this situation into account, it is not surprising that hatred towards landowners led to violent revolts breaking out, such as those of 1670 in the basins of the Volga and Don Rivers.

As far as the situation of women is concerned, at least in Western Europe, it was not until the 18th century that a change took place in the way they were considered. At that time, women who reigned in large and small states, such as Russia and Austria, ascended to the throne. Discourses were elaborated on the role of women, and civil rights and feminist politics began to be advocated (Martínez-Shaw & Alfonso, 2000),

As we said before, in the 19th century, the relationship between the countryside and the city experienced a turning point, which would continue and even intensify to the present day as a result of the rural exodus due to industrialisation. Indeed, the installation of factories in cities, in conjunction with the mechanisation of agricultural tasks and the end of community-owned lands forced thousands of former countryside-dwellers to seek employment in the manufacturing and tertiary sectors in cities. Initially, the mass arrival of inhabitants led to the disordered growth of cities with the appearance of insalubrious and polluted neighbourhoods crammed with workers, as described by Engels (1845). However, in the second half of the century, plans for urban organisation were implemented with the suburban development of cities such as Paris, Stockholm and Barcelona (Villares & Bahamonde, 2001).

The social conflicts of the 19th century mainly involved the industrial workers of the cities (the proletariat) and the peasants of the rural areas. They were a response to the new capitalist economic structures and the politics of liberalism, particularly on the part of the proletariat, which worked in terrible conditions in urban factories (low salaries, 12–14-hour days, lack of safety, child labour). Of particular significance in England was the Luddite movement and the followers of the "Captain Swing". It was not until the proletariat became aware of class that the first true workers' organisations, such as trade unions and political parties (the latter in the second half of the century thanks to the impetus of the scientific socialism of Marx and Engels) were created. Indeed, the participation of the industrial working classes was noteworthy in the revolutions of 1830, 1848 and in the Paris Commune of 1871 (Villares & Bahamonde, 2001).

The new industrial civilisation of the 20th century brought about a new type of social relations which lent particular importance to the collective actions of workers and peasants. This phenomenon was brought to the world's attention with the triumph of the Russian Revolution. In Western Europe, however, its impact was less intense due to the development of the welfare states and the recognition of social and collective rights (Riesco-Roche, 2001).

The last third of the 20th century witnessed the emergence of new social movements demanding, among other things, world peace, respect for the environment, the rights of minorities and the recognition of the social role of women. As far as women are concerned, it was not until World War I, due to their work in factories in the rear-guard and as nurses on the front lines, that their situation began to change, leading to their access in masse to work in the industrial sector at the end of the conflict, a situation which continued in the second post-war period. Having gained suffrage in most Western European countries following World War II, the feminist movement experienced a halt in its activity, which restarted in the 1960s and focused on new demands relating to the right to abort, divorce and birth control, as well as an improvement in the intellectual education of women with the aim of increasing their possibilities for social and labour development (Villares & Bahamonde, 2001).

Didactic objectives (D.O.) for secondary education

The main target is to make the students reflect about the inequalities between rural and urban world, explaining their evolution and their importance to understand the current European identity:

- D. O. 1 To explain the current characteristics of rural and urban societies and how they evolved from Prehistory to Contemporary ages.
- D.O. 2 To discuss what the inequalities between urban and rural worlds are and the conflicts caused.
- D.O. 3 To propose new ways to bring closer the rural and the urban world in Europe.

In terms of competencies, we could concrete the following competencies:

- To research and select information from primary and secondary resources.
- To investigate in teams to produce knowledge.
- To communicate the contents learned using different tools.
- To collaborate with local and regional governments to preserve rural and urban heritage.
- To participate as citizens to reduce the social and economic inequalities between urban and rural world.

Resources, tools and materials for the classroom

The website HistoryLab is focused on European history transversal topics. Teachers could find different resources as pictures, maps, urban plans, cadastres or documents.[2]

Conceptual concepts related to the topic

- *Urban plans and environment:* Although cities grow up by a planified concentration of houses, institutions and services, in the last decades the preoccupation for environment and climatic change allow a mix between urban and natural areas inside the city.

- *Marginalisation, poverty and minorities*: Economic inequalities appear both in the cities and in the rural world where workers, migrants and minorities live in impoverished neighbourhoods. Capitalism concentrates power and decisions in favour of economic elites.

Notes

1 This chapter is a result of projects "HistoryLab for European Civic Engagement: open e-Toolkit to train History Teachers on Digital Teaching and Learning", funded by SEPIE on call ERASMUS + KA226 [2020–1-ES01-KA226-HE-095430], and research project PID2020–113453RB-I00, funded by Agencia Estatal de Investigación of Spain (AEI/10.13039/501100011033).
2 https://historylab.es/projects-collections/3-rural-world-and-urban-world-in-the-formation-of-the-european-identity/.

References

Badii, M. H., Guillén, A., Fernández, L. G., & Abreu, J. L. (2017). La urbanización en relación con el desarrollo sustentable. *Daena, International Journal of Good Conscience*, *12*(1), 69–94.
Baron, H., Reuter, A. E., & Markovic, N. (2019). Rethinking ruralization in terms of resilience: Subsistence strategies in sixth-century Caricn Grad in the light of plant and animal bone finds. *Quaternary International*, *499*, 112–12. https://doi.org/10.1016/j.quaint.2018.02.031
Betrán, J. L., & Moreno, D. (2000a). *Renacimiento*. Madrid: Arlanza ediciones.
Betrán, J. L., & Moreno, D. (2000b). *Barroco*. Madrid: Arlanza ediciones.
Boltvinik, J., & Mann, S. A. (2016). *Peasant poverty and persistence in the 21st century. Theories, debates, realities and policies*. London: ZED Books Ltd.
Bravo, G. (2007). Ejército, agitación social y conflicto armado en occidente tardorromano: un balance. *Polis: revista de ideas y formas políticas de la antigüedad clásica*, *19*, 7–34.
Brown P. (1971). *The World of Late Antiquity*. London: Thames and Hudson.
Christides, B (1996). Marginados en el mundo bizantino y árabo-islámico: lisiados, feos y negros. *Cuadernos del CEMYR*, *4*, 101–106.
Dejung, C., Motadel, D., & Osterhammel, J. (2019). *The Global Bourgeoisie: the rise of the middle classes in the Age of Empire*. Princeton, NJ: Princeton University Press.
Engels, F. (1845). *The condition of the working class in England*. Leipzig: Ellio Bigand Ed.
Hobsbawm, E. (1974). *Las revoluciones burguesas*. Madrid: Guadarrama.
Klíma, J. (1979). *Sociedad y cultura en la antigua Mesopotamia*. Madrid: Akal.
Leeds, A. (1994). *Cities, classes and the social order*. Ithaca, NY: Cornell University Press.
López, P., Viguera, Mª J., y Vázquez, Mª C. (2000). *El islam*. Madrid: Arlanza Ediciones.
Martín, J. L. (2000). *Edad Media*. Madrid: Arlanza ediciones.
Martín, J. L., & Faci, J. (2000). *Bizancio*. Madrid: Arlanza Ediciones.
Martínez-Shaw, C., & Alfonso, M. (2000). *Ilustración*. Madrid: Arlanza Ediciones.
Mateo, C., & Pastor, Mª (2020). La desigualdad entre hombres y mujeres en la antigua Roma: un estudio sobre sus concepciones y conocimiento en el alumnado de Historia. *Cuadernos de Arqueología de la Universidad de Navarra*, *28*, 81–100. https://doi.org/10.15581/012.28.001
Mazo, F. (1999). Edad Media. Siglos V-X. En C. Gispert (Dir.), *Historia Universal*. Ciudad de Mñexico: Océano.

Monsalvo, J. Mª. (2016). *Los conflictos sociales en la Edad Media*. Madrid: Síntesis.
Pinon, P. (2001). La transición desde la ciudad antigua a la ciudad medieval: permanencia y transformación de los tejidos urbanos en el mediterráneo oriental. En P. Passini (Ed.), *La ciudad medieval: de la casa al tejido urbano* (179–214). Toledo: Universidad de Castilla-La Mancha.
Pons Carmona, Y. (2014). *De la ciudad utópica colonial al sueño americano [Trabajo Fin de Grado]*. Barcelona: Universitat Politécnica de Catalunya.
Portass, R. (2021). Peasants, Market Exchange and Economic Agency in North-western Iberia, c. 850- c. 1050. *Past & Present, 1*, 1–34. https://doi.org/10.1093/pastj/gtab001
Riesco-Roche, S. (2001). Población, ideologías y movimientos sociales. En E. González Calleja, J. Aróstegui & S. Riesco (Coords.), *El siglo XX* (pp. 105–168). Madrid: Arlanza Ediciones.
Roldán, J. M. (2000). *Historia de Roma*. Salamanca: Ediciones Universidad de Salamanca.
Romero, P. (2006). Los bagaudas: ¿los primeros revolucionarios de la historia? *Clio: History and History Teaching, 32*.
Santos, N. (2000). La decadencia de Roma. En J. Mangas, M. J. Hidalgo, M. Bendala & N. Santos (Eds.), *El ocaso de Roma* (pp. 66–89). Madrid: Arlanza Ediciones.
Shatterthwaite, D. (2003). El continente urbano. *Boletín CF+S, 23*, 1–7.
Tricoire, D. (2012). La Fronde, un soulèvement areligieux au XVIIe siècle? De l'opposition "dévote" sous Richelieu aux mazarinades de 1649. *Dix-septieme siecle, 4*, 705–717.
Unikel Spector, L. (1968). Ensayo sobre una nueva clasificación de población rural y urbana en México. *Estudios Demográficos y Urbanos, 2*(1), 1–18. https://doi.org/10.24201/edu.v2i01.59
Van Zanden, J. L. (2005). Una estimación del crecimiento económico en la Edad Moderna. *Investigaciones de historia económica, 2*, 9–38.
Villares, R., & Bahamonde, A. (2001). *Historia del mundo contemporáneo. Siglos XIX y XX*. Barcelona: Taurus.
Wheatley, P. (1971). *The origins and character of the ancient Chinese city*. Venice: Aldine.

9
FAMILY, DAILY LIFE AND SOCIAL INEQUALITY IN EUROPE[1]

Raquel Sánchez-Ibáñez and Antonio Irigoyen-López

Historiographical approach

The family is a fundamental concept in social science subjects and, in particular, in the teaching of history. It is a complex concept with many meanings. Perhaps the simplest is that which defines the family as the basic cell of social organisation (Chacón & Bestard, 2011). It is therefore the first set of people to which an individual belongs. In this definition, the term belonging is key because it identifies the existence of a strong bond of consanguinity or affection that unites people. Through the family, it is possible to study the configuration of social groups that structure a society, the domestic economy, demographic aspects, political culture, religiosity, customs, artistic manifestations, etc. Thus, from the environment closest to the individual, it is possible to analyse the behaviour of people in the natural, social and cultural environment. This fact makes the family a fundamental object of study for various social and human sciences such as anthropology, sociology, law, demography, geography, history and art history.

Topics such as the family, the life cycle and inequality has been fundamental historiographical subjects to understand the structure of present and past societies. The study of the family in Europe started in the 1950s in connection with demographic studies, and in the 1970s and 1980s it developed. The family became a relevant historical category based on the dominant historiographical school of thought, the Annals school. Interest in studying mentalities, sexuality and childhood placed daily life at the heart of research, and various studies were published by such notable authors as Le Goff (1988) and Foucault (1976, 1984a y 1984b). In the mid-1980s, the Cambridge Group for the History of Population and Social Structure, driven by the works of Peter Laslett (Laslett, 1989; Wall et al., 1983), stood out in the field of family studies. In this period, influential research was produced in the field of historical social anthropology, which focused on family models and their evolution over time.

DOI: 10.4324/9781003289470-12

This evolution of family dynamics and social relations of inequality (social groups and classes) over time has been a line of historiographical research with very outstanding works, such as the two volumes published by Burguière et al. (1988), the three-volume compendium of European Family History coordinated by Barbagli and Kertzer (2002) and the monographs on the evolution of the family in England (Abbott, 2003) and in Spain (Chacón & Bestard, 2011). These publications cover the evolution of different topics related to the family in a European framework from the 16th to the 20th century (legislation, kinship, demography, servitude, material resources, etc.). More recent is the work of Sovic et al. (2015) focusing on Northern and Eastern Europe, where the evolution of changes in these regions, from the Modern Age to the present, in relation to the life cycle, family structure (marriage and inheritance), the house (material culture) and domestic life, is collected.

A more global and longer territorial approach (from 10000 BCE to the present) is offered by the work of Maynes and Waltner (2012), which traces a journey from domestic life in the first Neolithic communities to the demographic, economic and cultural challenges facing the family in the future. In the American context, the encyclopaedia by Coleman and Ganong (2014) is of interest, which compiles a wide range of family-related terms, although most of them are focused on contemporary times. A comparison over time on family dynamics can be found in the work of Ross (2006).

Finally, from a more educational outreach approach, the work of Wall et al. (2001) is relevant, offering a collection of original essays by scholars on the historical study of the family from various parts of the world, and represents a new departure in this field. The essays cover a great variety of topics, and many countries are represented. Recently, the book published by Evans (2021) examines the practice, meanings and impact of undertaking family history research for individuals and society more broadly. In addition to McConnell's book (2022) that, assuredly, has new material for educators and leads from their research of the family's yesterdays to depictions of the family's contemporary setting.

In relation to social inequality, two reference works are the classic book by Kriesberg (1979) and the work edited by Price and Feinman (1995), which provide a broad approach to this problem and which begin in prehistory. The latter book deals with aspects such as the economy (modes of production), social marginalisation (slavery), the social reproduction strategies of the elites (nobility and Church) and the habits and customs of social groups. More recently, and with a more didactic approach, the works of Warwick-Booth (2013) and Hurst et al. (2015) stand out, they are user-friendly introductions to the study of social inequality and studies its forms, causes and consequences.

Family, daily life and social inequality

Explaining society in terms of families and individuals and not only in terms of classes and social groups allows students to understand society in its complexity and, above all, in its diversity. While elements such as family origin (consanguinity), ethnicity, economic heritage can group people into classes or social groups with defined characteristics, it is within families that all these elements are articulated. Therefore, it is through the family that people's life trajectories, the life cycle and the strategies that shape social organisation can best be explained.

In the words of Ferrer (1995), social organisation strategies are the result of historical experimentation with the variables at hand (familiar and unfamiliar). If the historical context remains stable (legal, economic, etc.), the strategies remain stable, but when the context changes, the strategies cease to serve or produce adverse results, so that a new experimentation must begin with uncertain results that can provoke profound changes in family behaviour. Thus, the age of entry into marriage, the choice of spouses, the determination of how many children marry and who they are, the distribution of inheritance, the introduction of children into the labour market, etc. are decisions that could be taken not only by the father of the family but also by the rest of the parental group and which will vary according to historical circumstances.

Thus, in the Ancien Régime, in order to maintain their patrimony, families devised strategies in which they combined marriage and celibacy for their sons and daughters. In Catholic Europe, turning daughters into nuns and sons into clerics or friars was a socially accepted way of keeping them celibate. However, it was also possible for a daughter or son to remain unmarried and live with his or her parents in order to care for them as they grew older. In any case, when two people married, it was because they had sufficient resources to settle down and start a family; not having them, according to Fauve-Chamoux (2002), prevented marriage. There were areas in Europe, such as in the Austrian Tyrol, where legislation prohibited marriages for those who did not have a certain income in order to prevent marriages between the poor (Lanzinger, 2016).

However, for other areas, historiography has maintained that couples from the working classes and day labourers married earlier precisely because they did not have this problem of access to resources. The opposite happened with people from the landowning groups, as well as the nobility and the bourgeoisie, who were forced to delay marriage until they had sufficient income of their own. The way to access them could be through inheritance, so they had to wait until the father died to access the property, although they could also achieve it through the advance of the inheritance. However, there were other ways of obtaining resources, such as working for others. In the case of women, it was common for them to work as maids in order to accumulate capital with which to build up their dowry, something that made them more attractive on the marriage market.

In any case, in the Old Regime, marriage was a tool to regulate the demographic system. In point of fact, by increasing the legal marriage age for women, the amount of time they could viably procreate was reduced and, as a result, so was the number of children they could have. On this point, there were generally differences between Western and Eastern Europe (Hajnal, 1965). In the latter, the legal age for first marriage for women was less than 22 years old, and there was a definitive female celibacy rate of less than 5%. On the other hand, in Western Europe women married for the first time between 24.5 and 26.5 years old with a definitive female celibacy rate between 10 and 20%. As a result, marriage was used as a veritable contraceptive in Western Europe that functioned to limit the birth rate and, consequently, slow demographic growth (Chaunu, 1974). By contrast, when a crisis affected mortality due to epidemics, famine, or war, the marriage rate increased, and that also increased the birth rate allowing population levels to recover.

It should be borne in mind that, around the 17th century, the world population reached 500 million people and continued to grow, doubling every 200 years. In fact, only a few years after the publication of the well-known work of Malthus (1798) on the imbalance between the rate of production of food (arithmetic progression) and the increase in population (geometric progression), this figure reached 900 million people.

The causes of this cycle of population growth were mainly the decrease in the death rate due to improved hygiene conditions and improvements in medicine and an increase in the birth rate. There were also important economic factors caused by the Industrial Revolution, which started in England in the 18th century and spread to many European countries (France, Germany, Holland, Sweden, Portugal, Spain and Italy) over the following century. In countries like France, England and Germany the economic effects of the Industrial Revolution (agglomeration of factories and a boom in the supply of raw materials and energy) caused a series of notable demographic and social changes. In the most industrialised regions and the trade hubs, the population increased rapidly, and large cities were formed. On the axis that connects England and Genoa, the biggest industrial centers grew around the coal and iron mines of the Rhine and Po rivers. This helped countries like Belgium, which had significant carbon deposits, to become one of the major powers on the European continent. However, a wealth of energy resources was also an important factor in the increase in economic and social imbalances between Northern and Southern Europe, which was more traditionally focused on agriculture and the textile industry.

As regards population, there was an inflection point in the first half of the 20th century. The disastrous consequences of the world wars together with the public health crisis caused by the Spanish flu epidemic in 1918 eroded the world population. It is estimated that approximately 70 million people died as a result of the two world wars. As for the Spanish flu epidemic, according to the latest estimates, it is believed that more than 50 million died worldwide from the illness.

Nevertheless, between 1800 and 1900 the world population nearly doubled, and halfway through the 20th century it reached 2.5 billion people. From that point forward, above all, towards the end of the 20th century, population growth stagnated. The key factor contributing to this was the fall in the birth rate, especially in countries in the northern hemisphere. At this point, a gap appeared between growth in Africa, Asia and South America, where birth rates continued to be elevated, and European countries. The population in the latter, due to low mortality rates, began to age, while the growth rate slowed (below 0.5% annually). Despite an increase of 180 million people between 1950 and 2000, at present, only one out of every ten people on the planet live in Europe. In all of Europe, demographic growth is weakening, and a majority of regions are even experiencing negative growth. This decrease has been partially mitigated by massive transoceanic emigration during the first decade of the 21st century.

According to estimates from the United Nations (2021), if migration policies and flows for European countries continue as is, the population on the continent will decrease by 91 million people by 2050. The countries who will suffer the biggest decrease in population will be Russia (20.9 million), Italy (16.2 million), Ukraine (11.5 million), Spain (9.4 million) and Germany (8.8 million). Moreover, according to predictions from Eurostat (2003), the countries that will grow 10% by 2025 are Ireland, Luxembourg, Denmark and Holland. By contrast, countries like Sweden and the United Kingdom will not experience any decrease through 2025.

Low fertility rates affect the formation of new families. In turn, the difficulties young people face in achieving stable employment and economic independence from their families also impact the formation of families. These factors, together with social and cultural factors that directly impact the structure of families, have made a wide variety of family structures more visible: single parent, extended, homosexual parents and children from adoption or artificial insemination, among others.

Currently, new concepts of family have emerged related to life cycles and the manner in which they advance that are the result of new practices: families that choose not to have children, divorces, new marriages, separations, adoptions and many other variations that have redefined the life cycle. People's aspirations to improve their social well-being and their careers have remained constant over time; by contrast, changing perspectives and economic circumstances have increased the possibility for social mobility in comparison to prior centuries. In time periods like the Old Regime, while social mobility existed, it was much reduced and depended on the ability of the person to amass economic resources through complex social and family networks. As a result, in most cases, you could predict the social and life cycle of a person at birth based on their social class. Nowadays, in developed countries this linearity regarding life cycles has become blurred as opportunities have grown.

From a cultural perspective, it is noteworthy how the prevailing patriarchal model of society has been called into question since the end of the 19th century due to the progress of democratic values. The main consequence of this fact is that women have progressively gained ground in terms of rights, which has leveled the playing field with men in many regards (the right to vote and access to university studies and jobs that were previously forbidden for women). Nevertheless, a significant salary gap still exists, and it is one of the main challenges at present. According to a report from the United Nations (2021), on average women earn 23% less than men who perform the same job. Countries where the differences are greatest are located on the Arabian Peninsula (Yemen and Saudi Arabia), in West Africa (Morocco and Mauritania) as well as India.

On the other hand, the transition from the extended family to the nuclear family has been in many territories one of the effects of industrialisation and migration from the countryside to the cities in contemporary times (Casares, 2008). As well as its survival in other regions, it is synonymous with more local economies and less populated nuclei. The comparison between different territories is interesting because, while Western Europe and England have evolved towards a nuclear model and, therefore, towards forms more centred on the cohabitation in the home of a couple and their offspring, in Ibero-America the extended family continues to be predominant in many regions. Factors explaining this difference are the sharp decline in the birth rate in Europe and the repeated economic crises, which make it difficult to maintain the welfare system, thus reducing family size. By contrast, in other regions where inter-family and intra-family solidarity replaces state services (education, health, security), women's participation in the world of work beyond the home is limited and patriarchy hampers the democratisation of family relations, traditional family models remain in place (Sarkisian & Gerstel, 2012).

The identification of roles within families also makes it possible to study fundamental aspects such as patriarchy and matriarchy, which are fundamental to understanding people's behaviour. The women's rights achieved since the end of the 18th century in countries such as the United Kingdom and the United States and which have progressively spread to other countries cannot be understood without understanding the effects of patriarchy in society. It is essential for students to understand that, through the family, practices derived from the culture of a place are internalised and, in turn, their development and transmission through the family nucleus consolidate them over time. This is why changes in customs and mentalities in a society are always slower. This circumstance is visible today, where technological, political and economic changes occur more rapidly than ideological, social and cultural changes.

In Europa the decline of the traditional family and the patriarchal model has opened up the possibility for different family structures and behaviors that go beyond traditional gender roles. Nowadays, we should speak of families, and not family, to encompass the variety visible at present: single-parent families, adoptive, without children, reconstructed, and with homosexual parents, among others. Likewise, gender identity has also gone beyond the binary man-woman concept to include a mixture of both or others (transgender, fluid, neutral, polygender) that identify the perception a person has of themselves. This has been a true challenge for family and kinship studies as well as for countries trying to update their policies to reflect this new social reality. Over the last decade, the parliaments of many countries have approved laws that recognise and ensure the equality of rights for everyone, regardless of their gender. In Latin America, Argentina (approved in 2011), Colombia (approved in 2015), Bolivia (approved in 2016), Ecuador (approved in 2016), Chile (approved in 2018), Costa Rica (approved in 2018) and Uruguay (approved in 2018) changed their laws. In North America, Canada approved a law in 2017 allowing people to legally change their gender, and although no federal law has been passed in the United States, 26 states allow a person to change their gender without having to undergo surgery. Africa is the continent with the strictest laws in the world, and only three countries have legalised sex changes (Botswana,

Namibia and South Africa). In Asia, 27 countries have legalised sex change as well as two in Oceania. Europe is the continent with the most countries where sex change is legal, and in nine of them (Belgium, Denmark, Ireland, Luxembourg, Malta, Holland, Norway, Portugal and Spain), this can be done without meeting any prior requirements.

In addition to gender inequality, social and economic inequality, which in many places leads to poverty, is also a current concern. Generally speaking, in the regions where the urbanization and economic development processes were less intense, solidarity among inhabitants helped to limit the differences related to the possession of assets. In fact, recent studies indicate that the gap between the rich and the poor is growing faster in developed countries when compared with others like China, Brazil or India. The most recent global economic crises, in 2008 and again after the COVID-19 pandemic, have caused the differences in dwellings, diet and assets among people in countries such as Spain to accelerate. A recent report produced by the Organization for Economic Cooperation and Development (Ciani et al., 2021) warns that Spain and other countries (Italy, France, Greece and Portugal) have also experienced an increase in social inequality.

Reducing inequality and ensuring that nobody is left behind are an integral part of achieving the Sustainable Development Objectives. The United Nations (2021) indicates that inequality is also increasing for the most vulnerable populations in countries with deficient health systems and those that are facing humanitarian crises. Refugees and migrants, as well as indigenous populations, the elderly, people with disabilities, and children are at particular risk of exclusion. Moreover, hate speech directed at vulnerable groups is increasing.

In recent years, social legislation has improved in various European countries with the goal of offering people at risk of social exclusion or on the brink of poverty better protection for housing, diet and basic necessities (water, electricity). On a European level, these objectives have a legal foundation that is set out in Articles 19, 145 to 150 and 151 to 161 of the Treaty on the Functioning of the European Union (TFEU). The fight against poverty and social exclusion is one of the specific objectives of the European Union in the area of social policy. Between 1975 and 1994 the European Economic Community carried out a series of pilot programs with the goal of fighting poverty and exclusion. However, given the absence of a legal foundation, the community action undertaken in this realm was constantly criticised. That is why the European projects that have been approved and the efforts made by different countries to reduce social inequality in recent years are so important. In France in 2019, a program providing support to 9 million Frenchmen living below the poverty line was approved for a value of 8 billion euros. In Italy in 2013, the *Sostegno per l'Inclusione Attiva* (SIA) was approved, which provides funds via a bank card to the most disadvantaged in order to buy basic necessities.

In the same vein, the Spanish government approved a Royal Decree in 2020 to establish a subsistence wage. This was motivated by data published by Eurostat (2018), according to which the Gini coefficient in Spain was almost three times higher than the average for the European Union. Incomes of the lowest 20% of the population in Spain represent only one sixth of the incomes of the highest 20%, while in the European Union this figure is only one fifth. Portugal is in a similar position to Spain. It is one of the most unequal countries in the European Union, and the incomes of the richest 20% of the population are 6.8% higher than the incomes of the poorest 20%. According to a recent study, the impact of social transfers (not including pensions) on reducing poverty levels is clearly lower in Portugal than in other countries, although without these policies (e.g. the subsistence wage) the intensity of poverty would be much greater.

However, the most striking case at the European level is Sweden, which has experienced a sharp increase in social inequality despite being a model welfare state since the second half of the 20th century. Nevertheless, since the start of this century the richest 0.1% have an average disposable income 38 times greater than the average wage earner. In fact, data indicate that the richest 1% of Swedes owned 18% of all assets in 2002, but this figure rose to 42% in 2017. The result is that Sweden has one of the highest levels of inequality in Europe, on par with Brazil, South Africa and the United States.

Without a doubt, reducing social inequality of the population is an urgent challenge after the recent global economic crises in 2009 and as a result of the effects of the COVID-19 pandemic. European institutions and governments should provide efficient aid programs so people in situations of poverty and at risk of exclusion can obtain basic necessities. It is also important to provide the necessary mechanisms to bolster job stability that will ensure access to housing, health and education. It is not enough that the right to decent housing or access to free education has been included in the Charter of Fundamental Rights of the European Union since 2000. Over the following decades, European citizens will need to push forward and take action. Active and democratic participation must lead to the approval and implementation of effective programs and measures to reverse the present situation of increasing social and economic inequality, both at the national level of European countries as well as across the globe.

Didactic objectives

- Know how to explain, from the analysis of different sources, that there are multiple causes that produce the cycles of growth and decline of the world and European population.
- Analyse the effects of the ageing of the world and European population.
- Understand the concept of the family as a basic cell of social organisation and a space for sociability.
- Be aware of the evolution of the concept of the family over time.
- To value family diversity in the context of democratic citizenship.
- Contextualise social inequality in terms of time and space by analysing and contrasting different sources.
- Relate the importance of economic and cultural factors for the existence of social inequalities.

- Understand the changes and permanence of social inequality in Europe.
- Analyse how the patriarchal model of society influences the social and legal inequality of women.
- To value the importance of passing laws that lead to equal rights for people.
- Identification of the multiple factors involved in the evolution of the population (multi-causality).
- Identification of the consequences of the ageing of the European population.
- Analysis of various sources to contextualise social inequality in Europe.
- Analysis of sources of various kinds to understand the cycles of growth and decline of the European population.
- Identification of elements of change and continuity in the establishment of social hierarchies.
- Assessing our responsibility as citizens in relation to inequality among the population on the basis of gender, ethnicity, culture, religion, economic level, etc.
- Adopt a historical perspective to understand the evolution of the concept of the family and the life cycle over time.

Historical concepts

- Ancien Régime: an expression for the final centuries (17th and 18th) of the Modern Age – from 1453, when Constantinople fell to the Turks, to 1789, with the French Revolution.
- Birth rate: the number of births registered per thousand inhabitants in a given time, usually one year.
- Death rate: the quantity of people that die in a specific place and time in relation to the total population.
- Fertility rate: the ratio of the number of births occurring in a certain period of time to the number of people of childbearing age in the same period.
- Infant mortality rate: number of infant and child deaths occurring during the first year of life per 1000 estimated births for a given area and period.
- Life cycle: the life process of an organism from birth to death.
- Material culture: the objects and products made by people that are used in everyday life.
- Matrimonial endogamy: union or reproduction between individuals of common ancestry, i.e. of the same family, lineage or group.
- Migration: the movement of a population from one place to another that brings about a change in habitual residence.
- Natural increase: indicates the increase or decrease in population that occurs as a result of the difference between live births and deaths only.
- Population: a group of people that live in a specific area.
- Rate of natural increase: the difference between the number of births and deaths in a population in a specific time period.
- Spanish Influenza (1918–1920): a pandemic caused by an outbreak of influenza virus type A, subtype H1N1.

- Social homogamy: the name given to a marriage where the spouses share the same social status.
- Social stratification: when people are grouped according to certain criteria or because they share certain attributes.

Note

1 This chapter is a result of projects "HistoryLab for European Civic Engagement: open e-Toolkit to train History Teachers on Digital Teaching and Learning", funded by SEPIE on call ERASMUS + KA226 [2020–1-ES01-KA226-HE-095430], and research project supported by the MICINN [PID2020-113453RB-I00 / AEI / 10.13039/501100011033].

References

Abbott, M. (2003). *Family affairs: A history of the family in 20th century England*. Routledge.
Barbagli, M., & Kertzer, D. I. (Coords.). (2002). *Historia de la familia europea*. Paidós.
Burguière, A., Klapisch-Zuber, C. K., Segalen, M., & Zonabend, F. (1988). *Historia de la familia. El impacto de la Modernidad*. Alianza Editorial.
Casares García, E. (2008). Estudios sobre el cambio en la estructura de las relaciones familiares. *Portularia*, *VIII*(1), 183–195.
Chacón, F., & Bestard, J. (Eds.). (2011). *Familias: historia de la sociedad española (del final de la Edad Media a nuestros días)*. Cátedra.
Chaunu, P. (1974). *Histoire science sociale. La durée, l'espace et l'homme à l'époque moderne*. CDU y SEDES.
Ciani, E., Fréget, L., & Manfredi, T. (2021). Learning about inequality and demand for redistribution: A meta-analysis of in-survey informational experiments, *OECD Papers on Well-being and Inequalities*, 2. https://doi.org/10.1787/8876ec48-en.
Coleman, M. J., & Ganong, L. H. (2014). *The social history of the American Family: An Encyclopedia*. SAGE.
Eurostat (2003). Trends in households in the European Union: 1995–2025. *Statistics in Focus*, *3*(24). https://bit.ly/3C0fU5G
Eurostat (2018). *Annual activity report*. European Commission. https://bit.ly/3fw6abD
Evans, T. (2021). *Family history, historical consciousness and citizenship: A new social history*. Bloomsbury.
Fauve-Chamoux, A. (2002). El matrimonio, la viudedad y el divorcio. In M. Barbagli & Kertzer, D. I. (Coords.), *Historia de la familia europea* (pp. 331–376). Paidós.
Ferrer Alòs, Ll. (1995). Notas sobre el uso de la familia y la reproducción social. *Demografía histórica*, *13*(1), 11–28.
Foucault, M. (1976). *Histoire de la sexualité, 1. La volonté de savoir*. Tel Gallimard.
Foucault, M. (1984a). *Histoire de la sexualité, 2. L'usage des plaisirs*. Tel Gallimard.
Foucault, M. (1984b). *Histoire de la sexualité, 3. Le souci de soi*. Tel Gallimard.
Hajnal, J. (1965). European marriage patterns in perspective. In D. V. Glass & D. E. C. Eversley (Eds.), *Population in history. Essays in historical demography. Volume I: General and Great Britain* (pp. 101–143). Aldine Transaction.
Hurst, Ch. E., Gibbon, M. F., & Nurse, A. M. (2015). *Social inequality: Forms, causes, and consequences*. Routledge.
Kriesberg, L. (1979). *Social inequality*. Prentice-Hall.

Lanzinger, M. (2016). Soltería: contextos, impactos y trayectorias en la Europa Central (siglos XVIII-XIX). *Revista de Historia Moderna*, 34. https://doi.org/10.14198/RHM2016.34.03

Laslett, P. (1989). *A Fresh Map of Life: the emergence of the third age*. Harvard University Press.

Le Goff, J. (1988). *La Nouvelle histoire*. Editions Complexe.

Malthus, T. (1798). *An essay on the principle of population*. Printed C. Roworth, Bell Yard, Temple Bar.

Maynes, M. J., & Waltner, A. (2012). *The Family: a world history*. Oxford Unniversity Press.

McConnell, R. C. (2022). *Tracing your family history with the whole family: A family research adventure for all ages*. Pen & Sword Books Limited.

Price, T. D., & Feinman, G. M. (Eds.). (1995). *Foundations of social inequality*. University of Wisconsin.

Ross, S. M. (2006). *American families past and present: Social perspectives on transformations*. Rutgers University Press.

Sarkisian, N., & Gerstel, N. (2012). *Nuclear family values, extended family lives. The power of race, class, and gender*. Routledge. https://doi.org/10.4324/9780203141977

Sovic, S., Thane, P., & Viazzo, P. (2015). *The history of families and households: Comparative European dimensions*. Brill Academic Publishers.

United Nations (2021). *Shaping our future together. Listening to people's priorities for the future and their ideas for action*. United Nations.

Wall, R., Hareven, T. K., & Ehmer, J. (Eds.). (2001). *Family history revisited: Comparative perspectives*. Associated University Presses.

Wall, R., Robin, J., & Laslett, P. (1983). *Family forms in historic Europe*. Cambridge University Press.

Warwick-Booth, L. (2013). *Social inequality: A student's guide*. SAGE.

Web resource

Eurostat. Trends in households in the European Union: 1995–2025. https://ec.europa.eu/eurostat/web/products-statistics-in-focus/-/ks-nk-03-024

10

POWER AND POWERS IN THE HISTORY OF EUROPE

Oligarchies, political participation and democracy[1]

María del Mar Felices de la Fuente, Ramón Cózar Gutiérrez, Álvaro Chaparro Sainz

Theoretical framework

Analyzing the historiographic production of such a prolific subject as the one focused on the study of power in Europe throughout its history is, to say the least, a complicated task. Despite the difficulty, a brief outline of the issue will be presented in the following pages from different analytical levels, indicating some referential works on this subject. Therefore, the present text aims to approach the existing scientific production around the theme of power and the powers in the European continent to develop a didactic proposal for teaching the history of Europe from this perspective in secondary education.

We thus develop a historical approach to different aspects of power in Europe, as well as the social structures associated with it, focusing mainly on studies that delve into concepts such as monarchy, church, social position, wealth, elites, aristocracy, nobility and oligarchs. Terms such as democracy, nationalism, dictatorship or nation-state, closely linked to the foundations of today's Europe, will also be addressed.

From a general perspective, it should be noted that studies on power and the different forms in which it is presented throughout history have received, from a theoretical level, the attention of numerous researchers from scientific disciplines as divergent as philosophy, psychology, or history (Russell, 1938; Mills, 1957; Cartwright, 1959; Gulick, 1967; Bachrach & Baratz, 1970; Foran, 1997). In this sense, these studies propose the craving for power as a fundamental part of human nature, which implies that the organizations that guarantee power are connected through individuals who, in turn, are responsible for constructing different forms of social power that are equally interrelated. This vision is, in our opinion, the key to understanding the scientific approaches published on the study of power in recent decades, not only at the continental level but also worldwide.

Initially, research that, with a generalist prism, addresses the study of power or the control of its structures in a broad spatial framework, in this case, European, such as the works of Blockmans (1997), Scales & Zimmer (2009) or Dardanelli (2017), should be acknowledged. Research of a more traditional nature that sometimes focuses on the study of power by applying a long-term analysis, as in the works of Gulick (1967), Bailey & Barclay (2017) or Tripp (2013); or on specific periods of history, as is the case, for example, for the Antiquity era, by Huskinson (2000) or Mennen (2011); or, for the Middle Ages, the studies by Duby (1973), Berkhofer et al. (2005), Boone & Howell (2013), Sánchez-Pardo & Shapland (2015) and Bovey (2015). In the same vein, focusing on the Modern Age we note the works of Monod (1999), Blanning (2002), Nexon (2009), Hazen (2017), Ringrose (2018), Lamal et al. (2021) and Pérez-García (2021). Finally, for the current contemporary era, we highlight the studies of Hamerow (1989), Vincent (2007), Gusejnova (2016) and Evans (2017).

Furthermore, several scientific productions have been identified that focus their interest on specific chronological and thematic contexts. In other words, they do not focus on extensive periods but more limited periods or more minor themes. It is worth noting, within this prism, the work of Richard J. Evans (2017), which reconstructs a history of power in Europe between the fall of Napoleon Bonaparte and the outbreak of World War I while interpreting the formation of the modern world through a panorama of governments, wars and revolutions that engender changes in society. Likewise, we can point to studies within a specific theme that have addressed the study of power or the consequences linked to an event in the control structures. The work of Ringrose (2018) focused on European expansion and the control of new territories routed through the Near East and Asia, as well as the maritime routes to the American continent, which is an example of this. Similarly, we found a study questioning when the concept of a nation first became a fundamental political factor, thus extrapolating the analysis to other more recent historical periods (Scales & Zimmer, 2009).

Similarly focused on a central theme, we find various studies focused, for example, on the cultural revolution that would transform the world in the Renaissance, particularly art, philosophy, science and technology. Thus, according to Blanning (2002), new social margins were generated that led to the emergence of unknown spaces, such as the public sphere. The emergence of newspapers, academies, gatherings, laboratories, lending libraries, cafeterias, voluntary associations, the printing press, etc. altered the established order. In short, a series of forces of change in early modern societies altered existing power structures (Lamal et al., 2021).

In this analysis framework, where studies focus on specific elements, we observe how power in Europe rested on two fundamental pillars of control: the Church and the Monarchy, particularly throughout the Middle Ages and the Modern Age. The relationship between the two foundations was continuously evolving, shaping, adapting and reconstructing itself (Monod, 1999; Nexon, 2009; Bovey, 2015). Some authors (Bentzen & Gokmen, 2020) question: "Why does religion continue to play a central role in some societies and institutions?" It is a question that goes hand in hand with issues such as the process of separation between church and state throughout history (Fox, 2011) or the construction of cross-cutting religious networks that undermined the ability of early modern European rulers to divide and contain local resistance to their authority.

In contrast, some research focuses on specific historical figures, analyzing power from more specific prisms or more focused visions. In this field, we find studies such as that of Beard (2021), which focused on the figure of Roman emperors; the work of James (2010) about aristocrats; the studies of Dwyer (2008) or Hazen (2017) on the figure of Napoleon Bonaparte or, finally, around dictatorial figures such as Hitler, Stalin or Mao (Larres, 2021).

However, in recent years new research perspectives have emerged that re-evaluate the conventional definition of power and have given space to the representation of women in this framework. Thus, for example, the binomial of women and power in the Middle Ages emerges in some research from the beginning of the century (Johns, 2003; Erler & Kowaleski, 2004). These studies have revealed new relationships of female power in the medieval household and community, such as the cultural power exercised by the wives of Venetian patriarchs. They also seek to transcend the polarities of public and private, that is, male and female, to offer a more realistic analysis of the functioning of power in medieval society where wives and consorts are no longer seen as decorative assistants, giving them the importance they require (Berkhofer et al., 2005).

Likewise, in recent years new visions have sprouted in the historiographical framework of power, as is the case of the emotional aspect, that is, the application of the developments of emotivity to a given historical context since emotions are considered as drivers of social change acting within the balances of power (Bailey & Barclay, 2017). Similarly, we highlight research with a strong spatial aspect, which responds to Henri Lefebvre's assertion that space is "produced" (Lefebvre, 1974) and, consequently, addresses questions related to how space is perceived and used to consolidate power structures (Boone & Howell, 2013).

In this sense, it is worth mentioning a line of study linked to geopolitics and the management of power in different geographic spaces that focus the interest of numerous specialists in balancing international forces on the European continent. Thus, the European state system that, since the Middle Ages, has guided these balances of power constitutes a critical framework of study in the understanding of power in Europe (Sheehan, 2005; Little, 2007; Dinneen, 2018; Andersen & Wohlforth, 2021).

Finally, we would like to highlight a study that, from a current perspective, invites us to reflect on Europe starting from the analysis of a multidimensional crisis that is environmental, cultural, political, social and economic that entirely affects the structure on which the idea of Europe was built and that, ultimately, forces us to rethink the very existence of the European project (Innerarity et al., 2018). In conclusion, a debate on the result of a historical construction carried out over centuries and which, at present, could be decisive for determining how Europe will be configured in the future.

Power and powers in the history of Europe

Focusing now on how power has been exercised and projected throughout history, it is clear that it has not always taken the same forms. If we go back to prehistoric times, the societies and cultures contextualized in this period progressively acquired greater complexity in their mode of organization, lacking in their initial phases what we understand today as the State. However, this does not imply that prehistoric societies had no power. Indeed, power existed and was represented symbolically, either as personal power, with one individual making decisions, or communally, through small assemblies where issues would be debated to reach consensus (Miller & Tilley, 2008; Kelly, 2015).

We have evidence of the exercise of power since the Upper Paleolithic, a period from which, for example, some stone staffs found in caves could be considered symbols of patriarchal chiefs or guides of those forms of societies (Hayden, 2018). Later, in the context of the Metal Ages, specifically in the Copper Age, in one of the most important settlements of this period in Europe, Los Millares (Almeria, Spain), grave goods, tombs and burials have been dated that show the existence of social differences and, therefore, restricted access to privileges reserved only for the power elites that controlled these territories. These elites would later emerge due to specialization in specific resources such as metallurgy, control of prestige goods and the emergence of dependent and tributary agricultural settlements (Maicas, 2019).

In the European context, along with these differentiated societies, we also have examples that lead us to rethink the forms of power in prehistoric societies. An example of this is the case of the Neolithic settlement of the Cucuteni-Trypillia culture, originating in Eastern Europe in Romania and Ukraine, where no differentiated hierarchy has been found, but rather a somewhat egalitarian society that could exercise a type of communal power (Dumitroaia, 2012).

From the Neolithic revolution and the emergence of the first states, from the Copper Age and especially in the Bronze Age, in much of Europe, walled settlements emerged where evidence of social divisions and small groups of warrior-like aristocrats who probably used violence to maintain their status and exercise power, were more evident. Ornaments and other objects, such as spatula-idols, representing symbols of difference in rank and power, have been found in some of these settlements (Fokkens & Harding, 2013). During this period, increasingly differentiated societies developed. The Germanic, Latin, Gallic, Iberian or Lusitanian peoples were consolidated. Likewise, the commercial networks that spread throughout Europe played an essential role in this process, giving rise to economic elites with social prestige, whose power was evidenced by their grave goods and the possession of weapons.

During the Early Bronze Age, civilizations with urban organization and palace states, led by kings and warrior social elites that developed hierarchical political, social and economic systems, reached their apogee. These civilizations gave rise to various cultures spread throughout several European territories, such as the Unetice culture, the Armorican burial mounds and the Argar culture, which is acknowledged as the first urban and state society in the western Mediterranean. In Iron Age

Europe, Hallstatt, La Tène and Tartessos also stand out as cultures in which power was exercised by a military elite, similar to an aristocracy, whose armament was superior due to the use of iron.

From the beginning of ancient history, society became increasingly hierarchical, giving rise to the figure of a person or groups of people who would exercise political power. In this sense, Ancient Greece was a turning point in the conception of power and the implementation of new forms of power leading to democracy. In Greek cities, the oldest political system was the monarchy, exercised by kings, but after deteriorating, power began to be held by nobles under a political system called "aristocracy". The term aristocracy means "government of the best", a concept first used by Aristotle and Plato to describe a system in which only the best citizens, chosen through a careful selection process, would become rulers. These noble citizens were privileged men, members of certain families with great wealth, who based their power on land ownership (Akrigg, 2019).

Over time, citizens, especially those who began to get rich in trade and industry, showed their discontent with this system and the arbitrariness of the nobles, demanding to participate in the exercise of power, so that soon a new form of government known as oligarchy emerged that implied that those with high incomes had greater political rights and could participate in the government of the State. This system resulted in classifying citizens by virtue of their income, generating a new form of government: timocracy. This system would be replaced by "oligarchy" and later developed further to become "democracy" (Pomeroy, 2012).

In Ancient Greece, democracy was restricted to half its population, as women and foreigners were disenfranchised from voting. The presence of slaves in these societies also means that we cannot speak of democracies as we understand them today. Nevertheless, Greek democracy remained alive until the 4th century BC.

In Ancient Rome, models were developed that are now considered the origin of Western civilization. In terms of power, it took various successive forms, a monarchy, an oligarchic republic and, later, an autocratic empire (Dunstan, 2011). At the time of the Roman Republic, power split into several powers, forging institutions such as the Senate, the various magistracies and the army. Later, during the Roman Empire, power mainly was in the hands of the emperors who consolidated unipersonal and centralized governments.

As time went on, in the Middle Ages and up to the Modern Age, the exercise of power was linked to sovereignty. However, in this period, power and powers were manifested in different spheres and were not exercised unipersonally or embodied in a specific person or institution. A multiplicity of connected powers existed in the Middle Ages, either in competition or collaboration. Consequently, we can speak of the great powers, the monarchy, the nobility and the Church regarding their jurisdictional scope and legitimization strategies. We can also recognize ascending powers that are organized and controlled from the base as members of the social group that took the form of urban power in guilds, corporations that engendered, developed and fostered a sense of identity in elites and influential and powerful groups that would crystallize in the coming centuries and be integrated into power.

In the medieval feudal system, the power of the monarchs would nevertheless be limited by the nobility and the Church. The feudal arrangement between medieval kings and their nobility was based on the monarch granting offices, honors and lands in the form of fiefs. In short, feudalism was a mutually beneficial pact. However, medieval kings had limited capacity for collecting taxes and lacked standing armies, which hinted at a latent political weakness (Bolton & Meek, 2007). Being a member of the nobility was a prerequisite for occupying positions of trust in the kingdom and promotion, especially in the army, the Court and often in the highest functions in government, the judiciary and the Church. Some nobles also acted as local rulers, whose status was based on the feudal system, so they also held a significant amount of power within a medieval society marked by a stereotyped division where the lower class was subject to the will of the upper class. Despite these privileges, throughout the Middle Ages, events such as the Black Death, which struck Europe repeatedly from the middle of the 14th century, seriously weakened the power of the nobility.

Along with the nobility, religion and the Church as a source of power played a central role in the medieval worldview, especially in remote areas, where they coexisted with pagan beliefs firmly rooted in the local ideology (Bovey, 2015). The Church justified its power by claiming that it had received it from God, represented on earth by the Pope and the Church he led. The weakness of the medieval states led to the increase of the power of the Church. Nevertheless, this power was not absolute as in the minds of most medieval Europeans there was no higher power than that of the Christian God.

The transition to modernity runs between continuity and change. The "Modern State" replaced the feudalism of the Middle Ages. This change was characterized, among other things, by strengthening the sovereignty of a central power. The great monarchies of the Renaissance were sovereigns over a complex mosaic of composite or segmented domains (Elliot, 1992), institutionally and politically, but also culturally. On the other hand, European monarchies wanted to increase their power by conquering new territories. The great expeditions of the Spanish and Portuguese first, and later of the English, Dutch and French, opened routes from west to east and from north to south, laying the foundations of the "world-economy". Likewise, meetings between Europeans and members of other societies would foster cultural exchanges that would transform both (Ringrose, 2018).

The pretension of monarchies characterized the development of power relations in the Modern Age to impose themselves on those powers that forced them to seek an equilibrium based on treaties of alliances (*Cortes* in Spain, *États Généraux* in France, *Tagsatzung* in Germany or Parliament in England). Monarchies moved towards centralism and absolutism through the development of administrative organs of government and justice (bureaucracy), the promotion of the treasury and taxation and the strengthening of diplomacy and the army. In centuries characterized by the multiplicity of situations and differences in pace, the evolution of each monarchy towards absolutism was very different. It depended on the political capacity, social composition, cultural and ideological bases and international context. The revolts and revolutions throughout Europe towards the middle of the 17th century challenged the political order, although with very different results. In France, for example, the triumph of absolute monarchy reinforced the shift toward authoritarianism and the hegemonic role of the monarchy. In England, by contrast, the revolutions of 1640 and 1688 culminated in the advent of parliamentary monarchy.

Furthermore, the medieval image of the itinerant King was abandoned. The Court became a center where diverse spaces of power converged and from where the organization of the European monarchies was articulated. A meeting place for rulers and ruled (Starkey et al., 1987) where new power structures would germinate. The monarchs used all the means at their disposal to project the Court's power to the rest of society through images of court life (Blanning, 2002; Cámara et al., 2015) through ostentatious ceremonials and celebrations, protocol, costumes, etc. Representatives of the elites came to the Court in search of royal favor in exchange for services rendered, while the monarch used this type of patronage relationship as the safest and most effective way to keep their territories united and maintain the loyalty of their subjects (Martínez, 2006). The nobility lost its warrior essence to become a *nobility of service*, in line with the new function of its members in society or administration. The monarchy stripped the nobility of effective power, configuring the Court as a field of attraction for clientelist networks around the person of the king, based, fundamentally, on the monarch's concentration of immense resources: military power, taxation, the appointment of positions and the dynamics of honors (Imízcoz, 1996). In addition, the link between monarchs and cities, where municipal oligarchies were rampant, also weakened the nobility. The heightened tensions of the mid-17th century forced the monarchs to reorganize their power relations with the different social groups. A process that had as its main consequence the ennoblement of a bourgeoisie that sought a place in the system of privilege.

Spiritual and temporal power remained, at least initially, two complementary entities. However, over time, the authority of the Papacy began to diminish, questioned by the monarchies. The first concordats on ecclesiastical affairs were signed, granting the civil authorities broad powers over the affairs of the national clergy. In addition, the Church witnessed its doctrinal and political division, imbued by new thinking and the ideals and ways of life permeating a changing world. Western Christianity split into several churches. Luther, Calvin and Zwingli, among others, called for a profound reform that would put an end to Rome's moral and ecclesial deficiencies and move toward more authentic religiosity. Concurrently, Henry VIII also broke with Rome by proposing a schism *(Acts of Supremacy)* that would establish the Anglican Church. The breakup of Christianity and the establishment of several churches altered the confessional and political bases of power relations. The Catholic Church promoted the Counter-Reformation through the Council of Trent, reaffirming the central dogmas of the Catholic faith vis-a-vis the Protestants. The rupture led to a process of confessionalization that had its political drift in the monarchies under the principle *"cuius regio, eius religio"*. In the following centuries, confessional conflicts would clash and divide society, especially within the great monarchies of France, England and Spain (Monod, 1999; Nexon, 2009).

When looking at the 18th century, it is necessary to analyze the changes brought about by the Enlightenment. Philosophers and thinkers studied the relationship between individuals and governments. Locke and Rousseau introduced ideas that gave more weight to the rights of individuals. Human rights, freedom, property and equality of men were approached from a new perspective emphasizing reason and progress (Meiksins, 2012). The elimination of privileges and secularization would radicalize Enlightenment thinking. It established that sovereignty resided in civil society as a whole, and there was talk of a "contract" whereby the will of the community grants power to the State in exchange for guaranteeing its civil rights. However, the desire to transform the social-political structure would not be implemented until the revolutionary processes at the end of the century.

The Enlightenment illuminated everything and brought into crisis the principles that sustained the darkness of the Ancien Régime society. The revolutions of the late 18th century (French, American and Industrial) led to the triumph of the new bourgeoisie as the preeminent group, ousting the nobility (Hobsbawm, 1978). Likewise, a decisive step was taken in the evolution of the European monarchies towards the liberal State, which would develop following the bourgeois revolutions of the 19th century, already in the Contemporary Age.

The concept of revolution is a response to the demand for change. Leading the way, a social class usually imposes its demands on the ruling class, aided by a mass movement. Achieving this objective does not require forms of violence, although the use of force is common. The bourgeois revolutions of the 19th century established a *New Regime* characterized by the triumph of liberalism in all its aspects: political, social, economic and cultural. Under this new regime, sovereignty now belonged to the nation. This last concept acquired a new meaning, that of the nation-state, a characteristic of contemporaneity. The liberal State was legitimized by law and not by force. Constitutionalism, the separation of powers and representation, became the main pillars on which the government of the State would be based, giving rise to new forms: Parliamentary Monarchy, Constitutional Monarchy or Assembly or Revolutionary Monarchy. Representation added value to the concept of suffrage. Most European countries established universal male suffrage in the 19th century, while full universal suffrage, including women, had to wait until the first half of the 20th century.

Suffrage led to the emergence of political parties as power groups. Political parties control the representatives in parliament, and the head of a winning party could accede to the control of state power as president or prime minister. The workers' movement and the increased political participation through the extension of the right to vote at the turn of the 20th century forced political parties to mobilize new strategies to attract the mass society. In turn, mass society began to dispute the power of the bourgeoisie and introduced new social issues, such as the women's question, for which women began to claim their rights and recognition in the public space. This was known as the transition from what was called liberalism to democracy.

Nationalism represented another challenge to liberalism. Germany and Italy joined the traditional major nation-states resulting from unification processes characterized by the confluence of political, social and economic interests. Alongside, small nation-states appeared, dismembered through wars, alliances and other power movements. At the turn of the 20th century, the national problem spread and became radicalized, provoking broad movements for autonomy and independence all over Old Europe. This nationalism generated much tension and eventually led to the onset of the First World War. Small states were not called upon to decide on war and peace, but they would have an increasing instrumental value as buffers and balancers in these processes.

The "Great War" of 1914 caused the disintegration of old empires, profound changes in the belligerent countries' systems of government and a crisis in democratic regimes. The political, social and ideological crisis of the interwar period paved the way for the triumph of totalitarianism in which a single party imposed itself on all citizens, the exaltation of leaders who took possession of all the mechanisms of the State and control over all facets of public and private life by force. In Russia, the first communist dictatorship was installed as an alternative to monarchies and parliamentary democracies. While in other countries such as Italy, Germany and Spain, mass populist movements mobilized to overthrow parliamentary governments and install authoritarian, fascist and national socialist regimes (Altrichter & Bernecker, 2014).

Once again, tensions transcended the national level, polarizing international relations and generating a new war. The Second World War far eclipsed the first one, extending the battlefield to the entire globe; the use of genocide or of weapons of mass destruction (the atomic bomb) were some of its most characteristic features. Europe went from being the center of world politics to a double periphery within a bipolar world order dominated by the Soviet Union and the United States. The image of this division would remain present in a divided Germany, converted into the border between two worlds. NATO and the Warsaw Pact, as supranational bodies, positioned countries around these two power blocs during the Cold War, reproducing two antagonistic systems characterized by party pluralism on one side and communist power monopoly on the other and market economy versus socialist planned economy (Altrichter & Bernecker, 2014). This situation continued until the fall of the Berlin Wall in 1989.

The collapse of the USSR provided an opportunity for former communist countries to transform themselves into liberal democracies, thanks to the pressure exerted by civil society pressure on political elites to act in accordance with democratic norms and the processes of integration into NATO and the European Union (Carpenter, 2020). The European Union began in the 1950s to promote economic cooperation and, as an evolving institution, grew into a union that now encompasses many policy areas. In the EU, member countries utilize solidarity to condition their state powers to achieve supranational efficiency.

The European Union has achieved more than half a century of peace, stability and prosperity. However, peace has not been complete on the continent. The conflicts in Yugoslavia, Kosovo, Georgia and the more recent one in Ukraine mean that war remains part of Europe's current reality. Likewise, processes such as *Brexit* sow the idea of geopolitical unity with uncertainty and others question one of its fundamental principles, democracy. Immersed in liquid modernity (Bauman, 2000) conditioned by new global powers, nomadic elites and in which every value becomes unstable and not eternal, we are witnessing the clash between liberal democracy, populism and oligarchies that can be authoritarian and/or illiberal. The discourse regarding the degradation of European democracy has degenerated into a structural crisis that forces us to reconsider the very existence of the European project (Innerarity et al., 2018). All this notwithstanding, and in an era of post-truth where the media have become political actors and social networks mean that the masses can influence democracy, what future awaits democracy in Europe?

Didactic objectives

- To understand the varying possibilities of people to participate in societal decision-making process.
- To reflect on the implications of the power systems in the freedoms and rights of people.
- To deliberate on the reasons for excluding segments of society from participation.
- To be able to identify and describe the possibilities and challenges of democratic structures.
- To be able to examine the changes and continuities in societal structures in Europe.
- To be able to recognize the different representations of power.
- To understand the mechanisms and the historical context that explain the emergence of power systems.
- To be able to analyze the causes and consequences of power systems and revolutionary movements.

Historical concepts

TABLE 10.1 Historical concepts associated with the topic of power and powers in Europe

Power				
Autocracy	Authoritarianism	Democracy	Republic	Feudalism
Centralism	Constitutionalism	Nationalism	Totalitarianism	Dictatorship
Communism	Liberalism	Populism	Absolutism	Supranationalism
Fascism	National socialism			
Representation of power				
Aristocracy	Nobility	Oligarchy	Monarchy	Church
Castes	Corporations	Elites	Nation-state	Parliament
Political party	European Union	State	Assembly	Bourgeoisie
Participation				
Suffrage	Revolution	Elections	Manifestation	Citizenship
Protest	Sovereignty	Mass movement		

Note

1 This research is a result of Grant PID2020–113453RB-I00 funded by MCIN/AEI/10.13039/501100011033.

References

Akrigg, B. (2019). *Population and economy in classical athens*. Cambridge: Cambridge University Press. https://doi.org/10.1017/9781139225250

Altrichter, H., & Bernecker, W. (2014). *Historia de Europa en el siglo XX*. Madrid: Marcial Pons.

Andersen, M. S., & Wohlforth, W. C. (2021). *Balance of power: A key concept in historical perspective*. London: Routledge. doi:10.4324/9781351168960-27

Bachrach. P., & Baratz, M. S. (1970). *Power and poverty: Theory and practice*. New York: Oxford University Press.

Bailey, M. L., & Barclay, K. (2017). *Emotion, ritual and power in Europe, 1200–1920: Family, state and church*. London: Palgrave Macmillan.

Bauman, Z. (2000). *Liquid modernity*. Cambridge: Polity Press.

Beard, M. (2021). *Twelve caesars: Images of power from the ancient world to the modern*. Princeton, NJ: Princeton University Press.

Bentzen, J., & Gokmen, G. (2020). *The power of religion*. CEPR Discussion Paper No. DP14706. Available at SSRN: https://ssrn.com/abstract=3594341

Berkhofer III, R. F., Cooper, A., & Kosto, A. J. (2005). *The experience of power in medieval Europe, 950–1350*. London: Routledge.

Blanning, T. C. W. (2002). *The culture of power and the power of culture: Old regime Europe 1660–1789*. Oxford: Oxford University Press.

Blockmans, W. P. (1997). *A history of power in Europe: Peoples, markets, states*. New York: Abrams Books.

Bolton, B. M., & Meek, C. E. (2007). *Aspects of power and authority in the middle ages*. Turnhout: Brepols.

Boone, M., & Howell, M. (Eds.). (2013). *The power of space in late medieval and early modern Europe. The cities of Italy, Northern France and the Low Countries*. Turnhout: Brepols.

Bovey, A. (2015). The medieval Church: from dedication to dissent. *The Middle Age*. www.bl.uk/the-middle-ages/articles/church-in-the-middle-ages-from-dedication-to-dissent

Cámara, A., García, J. E., Urquízar, A., Carrió-Invernizzi, D., & Alzaga, A. (2015). *Imágenes del poder en la Edad Moderna*. Madrid: Editorial Universitaria Ramón Areces.

Carpenter, M. (2020). *The Europe whole and free: Europe's struggle against illiberal oligarchy*. https://pism.pl/publications/The_Europe_Whole_And_ Free_Europes_Struggle_Against_Illiberal_Oligarchy

Cartwright, D. (Ed.). (1959). *Studies in social power*. Ann Arbor, MI: University of Michigan.

Dardanelli, P. (2017). *Restructuring the European State – European integration and state reform*. Montreal: McGill-Queen's University Press.

Dinneen, N. (2018). The corinthian thesis: The oratorical origins of the idea of the balance of power in herodotus, thucydides and xenophon. *International Studies Quarterly, 62*(4), 857–866. https://doi.org/10.1093/isq/sqy037

Duby, G. (1973). *Hommes et structures du Moyen Âge*. Paris et La Haye: Mouton.

Dumitroaia, G. (2012). Valoración expositiva del patrimonio de la Cultura de Cucuteni en el territorio de Rumania. *RdM. Revista de Museología, 54*, 15–22.

Dunstan, W. E. (2011). *Ancient Rome*. Lanham, MD: Rowman & Littlefield.

Dwyer, P. (2008). *Napoleon: The path to power*. New Haven, CT: Yale University Press.

Elliott, J. H. (1992). A Europe of composite monarchies. *Past and Present, 137*, 48–71.
Erler, M., & Kowaleski, M. (Eds.). (2004). *Women and power in the middle ages*. Athens, Georgia: University of Georgia Press.
Evans, R. (2017). *The pursuit of power: Europe, 1815–1914*. London: Penguin.
Fokkens, H., & Harding, A. (2013). *The Oxford handbook of the European bronze age*. Oxford: Oxford Press.
Foran, J. (1997). *Theorizing revolutions*. London: Routledge.
Fox, J. (2011). Separation of religion and state and secularism in theory and in practice. *Religion, State and Society, 39*(4), 384–401. https://doi.org/10.1080/09637494.2011.621675
Gulick, E. (1967). *Europe's classical balance of power: A case history of the theory and practice of one of the great concepts of European statecraft*. New York: W. W. Norton & Company.
Gusejnova, D. (2016). *European elites and ideas of empire, 1917–1957*. Cambridge: Cambridge University Press.
Hamerow, T. D. (1989). *The birth of a New Europe. State and society in the nineteenth century*. Chapel Hill (North Carolina) and London: The University of North Carolina Press.
Hayden, B. (2018). *The power of ritual in prehistory. Secret societies and origins of social complexity*. Cambridge: Cambridge University Press.
Hazen, C. (2017). *The French revolution and Napoleon*. Charleston, SC: Arcadia Press.
Hobsbawm, E. (1978). *The age of revolution: Europe 1789–1848*. London: Abacus.
Huskinson, J. (Ed.). (2000). *Experiencing Rome. Culture, identity and power in the roman empire*. London: Routledge.
Imízcoz, J. M. (Coord.) (1996). *Elites, poder y red social: las élites del País Vasco y Navarra en la Edad Moderna*. Bilbao: Universidad del País Vasco.
Innerarity, D., White, J., Astier, C., & Errasti, A. (Eds.). (2018). *A new narrative for a new Europe*. Lanham, MD: Rowman & Littlefield.
James, L. (2010). *Aristocrats: Power, grace, and decadence: Britain's great ruling classes from 1066 to the Present*. New York: St. Martin's Press.
Johns, S. M. (2003). *Noblewomen, aristocracy and power in the twelfth-century Anglo-Norman Realm*. Manchester: Manchester University Press.
Kelly, L. (2015). *Knowledge and power in prehistoric societies*. Cambridge: Cambridge University Press.
Lamal, N. Cumby, J., & Helmers, H. J. (Eds.). (2021). *Print and power in early modern Europe (1500–1800)*. Leiden; Boston: Brill.
Larres, K. (2021). *Dictators and autocrats. Securing power across global politics*. London: Routledge.
Lefebvre, H. (1974). *La production de l'espace*. Paris: Éditions Anthropos.
Little, R. (2007). *The balance of power in international relations: Metaphors, myths, and models*. Cambridge: Cambridge University Press.
Maicas, R. (2019). The bone industry of Los Millares. From Luis Siret to present. *Cuadernos de prehistoria y arqueología de la Universidad de Granada, 29*, 203–218. https://doi.org/10.30827/cpag.v29i0.9773
Martínez, J. (2006). La Corte de la Monarquía Hispánica. *Studia Historica: Historia Moderna, 28*, 17–61. doi:10.14201
Meiksins, E. (2012). *Liberty and property: A social history of western political thought from the renaissance to enlightenment*. Cambridge: Cambridge University Press.
Mennen, I. (2011). *Power and status in the roman empire*. Leiden; Boston: Brill.
Miller, D., & Tilley, C. (2008). *Ideology, power and prehistory*. Cambridge: Cambridge University Press.
Mills, C. W. (1957). *The power elite*. Oxford: Oxford University Press.
Monod, P. K. (1999). *The power of kings: Monarchy and religion in Europe, 1589–1715*. New Haven, CT: Yale University Press.

Nexon, D. H. (2009). *The struggle for power in early modern Europe: Religious conflict, dynastic empires, and international change*. Princeton, NJ: Princeton University Press.

Pérez-García, M. (2021). *Blood, land and power. The rise and fall of the Spanish nobility and lineages in the early modern period*. Cardiff, Wales: University of Wales Press.

Pomeroy, S. B. (2012). *La antigua Grecia: historia política, social y cultural*. Barcelona: Crítica.

Ringrose, D. (2018). *Europeans abroad, 1450–1750*. Lanham, MD: Rowman & Littlefield.

Russell, B. (1938). *Power: A new social analysis*. 1st impression. London: Allen & Unwin.

Sánchez-Pardo, J., & Shapland, M. (Eds.). (2015). *Churches and social power in early medieval Europe. Integrating archaeological and historical approaches*. Turnhout: Brepols.

Scales, L., & Zimmer, O. (Eds.). (2009). *Power and the nation in European history*. Cambridge: Cambridge University Press.

Sheehan, M. (2005). *The balance of power. History and theory*. London: Routledge.

Starkey, D., Morgan D. A. L., Murphy, J., Weight, O., Cuddy, N., & Sharpe, K. (1987). *The English court from the wars of the roses to the civil war*. London: Addison-Wesley Longman.

Tripp, Ch. (2013). *The power and the people. Paths of resistance in the middle east*. Cambridge: Cambridge University Press.

Vincent, M. (2007). *Spain, 1833–2002: People and state*. Oxford: Oxford Press.

Digital Resources

Europeana. Consulted in: www.europeana.eu/

Historic Figures. Consulted in: www.bbc.co.uk/history/historic_figures/

House of European History. Consulted in https://historia-europa.ep.eu/

Modernalia. Recursos para la enseñanza de la Historia Moderna. Consulted in: www.modernalia.es/

Power, Justice, and Tyranny in the Middle Ages. Consulted in: https://artsandculture.google.com/story/power-justice-and-tyranny-in-the-middle-ages/nQXxtYLVVjYGxQ

The Exploration and Conquest of the New World. Consulted in: https://courses.lumenlearning.com/boundless-ushistory/chapter/the-exploration-and-conquest-of-the-new-world/

The Medieval Church. Consulted in: www.worldhistory.org/Medieval_Church/

The Power in Louvre Museum. Consulted in: https://collections.louvre.fr/en/

The Rise of the Nobility. Consulted in: https://courses.lumenlearning.com/suny-hccc-worldhistory2/chapter/the-rise-of-the-nobility/

The Struggle for democracy. Consulted in: www.nationalarchives.gov.uk/pathways/citizenship/struggle_democracy/making_history_democracy.htm

Woman Suffrage and the 19th Amendment. Consulted in: www.archives.gov/education/lessons/woman-suffrage

Women's suffrage timeline. Consulted in: www.bl.uk/votes-for-women/articles/womens-suffrage-timeline

11
UNDER A CLOAK OF TERROR

Violence and armed conflict in Europe

*Cláudia Pinto Ribeiro Luís Alberto Marques Alves
Helena Vieira Ana Isabel Moreira Diana Martins
Daniela Magalhães Lara Lopes*

First words . . .

In *The Art of War* (2009), written by Sun Tzu more than 2000 years ago, the warrior-philosopher prophesied one of the most widely generalized maxims, accepted by those who see in the military exercise an authentic form of "artistic expression". In fact, the great strategist states "the ability to obtain victory by changing and adapting according to the opponent" in a Darwinian logic applied to conflict. As Tim Newark writes, "adaptation to changing circumstances is indeed the key to military success. In war, victory depends more on ingenuity, creativity and innovation than on brute-force" (Newark, 2011: 6). In other words, the outcome of a war depends on how many weapons and soldiers are placed on the battlefield.

Carl von Clausewitz (1780–1831) can also be mentioned, when he stated that "war is a mere continuation of policy by other means", anticipating "two centuries of increasingly pointless, financially disastrous, and above all, lethal conflicts . . . culminating in the discovery and proliferation of nuclear weapons, have rendered this venerable institution virtually incapable of performing any of the roles classically assigned to it" (Clausewitz, 1984: 6).

The paradigm of war shifts as it becomes more surgical, deadly, and "clean". The professionalism of those who handle this machine take on grotesque contours in a time when, in the words of Zbigniew Brzezinski: "war today is a luxury that only the weak and the poor can afford" (O'Connell, 1989: 4).

In fact, over the last 70 years, is safe to say that the war between powers holding a nuclear arsenal would only happen by "accident or madness", mainly because, in such scenario, murders and suicides would happen. Therefore, the possession of nuclear and chemical weapons has turned out to be convincing enough to dissuade the most powerful countries from embarking on a path of no return.

However, deterrence is neither infallible nor capable of preventing conventional warfare between countries that do not possess nuclear arsenals. And there are numerous examples that show "the ingenuity, creativity and innovation" of those who create weapons with what they have "more at hand". Rape or the sterilization of human beings may not be new, but the width and science invested in the profitability of this "weapon of war" has certainly gained expressive contours. In fact, this would only be surprising if we were unaware that "weapons are among man's oldest and most significant artefacts; it makes sense that their development would be affected by their users' attitudes toward them" (O'Connell, 1989: 4–5).

The war . . . always war . . .

War was already an ancient practice when the first civilizations appeared, around 3000 BCE. However, with the advent of Civilization, war became essential to its development. The history of "civilised" warfare, perhaps not the most accurate term, began with the development of complex societies, made possible by the production of agricultural surpluses, in large part due to the irrigation of agriculture. From Ancient Egypt in its imperial phases and the warlike city-states of Mesopotamia, through the Greek-speaking world around the Aegean Sea and its "civic militarism", and the grandeur of the mighty kingdom of Macedonia, with an unparalleled army, created by Philip II, bequeathed to his son Alexander the Great, power and military organization made a difference in the advances and retreats, rise and fall of kingdoms and empires. It was war, always war.

The Greek contribution to the art of war was more innovative, but it was with the Romans that the exercise of force came to be seen as a normal feature of society. The Greeks had a preference for offensive tactics over strategies. The Romans used both. Taking advantage of the Greek contribution, the Romans added a capacity for aggression that has never been seen before. "The Roman Republic's ability to wage war was unparalleled before, and was not equaled until the emergence of the modern nation state" (Newark, 2011: 41).

Between the 5th and 1st centuries BCE, the Roman Republic conquered an empire around the Mediterranean, dominated exclusively by the use of military force. Constantly at war, the Romans gradually subdued the other peoples on the Italian Peninsula, fought mercilessly against Carthage, their great rival, finally imposing their rule over the Greek states of the eastern Mediterranean.

The legions' thirst for conquest led the Romans to a conflict with Carthage, in the 3rd century BCE, for the conquest of the sea. The Punic Wars unfolded major naval and land battles, ending with the destruction of Carthage, at the end of the trilogy. After these epic battles, the Gaul and Dacia campaigns, the Roman civil wars, and the threats of revolt or invasion by the Roman Empire wrote some pages in the history of one of the most powerful and enduring empires that saw war as a way of life.

During the 3rd century, a series of invasions by Germanic peoples took place and nearly destroyed the empire. The instability in the governance of Rome, with the succession of numerous emperors, greatly contributed to the poor resistance offered to the invading peoples. The Germans, who settled within the borders of the empire, were recruited by the Roman army, keeping in its ranks about half of Germanic soldiers, some of them reaching the highest leadership of the military command. At the end of the 5th century, the Germanic tribes that had settled in the territory of the empire no longer saw the need to recognize the authority of an emperor and, thus, the Western Empire fell.

With the taking over of Rome by Odoacer, in 476, instead of an empire in the West, there was a series of kingdoms founded by the different Germanic tribes. Unable to manage their fair share of land, the ancient Roman administration quickly became homesick.

The Middle Ages were marked by the difficulty of states and empires to integrate, or to dominate in a decisive way, the peoples that pressed their borders. This incapacity left them exposed to disastrous invasions and made them passively watch absolute conquests. Most western European states were unable to maintain active professional armies and were far from having a monopoly on armed force. This fragility made it difficult to distinguish between war and conflict, as local lords or mercenary chiefs fought to satisfy their own interests.

The rapid Muslim advance, which took place in the 7th and 8th centuries, is proof of this difficulty. Two decades after the formation of the first Muslim state, in 622, the Arabs had conquered the Sasanian Persian Empire, the eastern Mediterranean, and Egypt. Even though the Byzantine Empire resisted (in 717–718, the siege of Constantinople was lifted after the demoralized troops of Maslama ibn Abd al-Malik endured terrible ordeals and realized how impermeable the city walls were), North Africa and most of the Iberian Peninsula were swept away by the mantle of Islam. Asturias resisted, at the expense of Pelagius, in 718, in the Battle of Covadonga, and the rest of western Europe, with Charles Martel stopping the Muslim advance, at Poitiers, in 732. Both armies still hesitated to enter the field, but the Muslims eventually attacked. The Muslim army was repelled by Frankish soldiers who fought on foot, forming a compact frame, which they defended with their swords, their spears and their shields against the enemy cavalry.

The Vikings, who go down in history between the 8th and 9th centuries, terrorized Europe from Dublin to Constantinople. Skilled men in the art of the sea, they were merchants, robbers, explorers and settlers: the period of quick and surgical looting was followed by the settlement of these peoples from the North, culminating in the foundation of Normandy in 911, a concession by the Frankish king Charles III in exchange of good behaviour. Despite the appeal, the Normans continued their conquests from England (Battle of Hastings, in 1066) to Sicily (Battle of Civitate, in 1053).

In 1095, Pope Urban II's appeal to Christian knights to liberate the holy city of Jerusalem, after 400 years in Muslim hands, begins the first Crusade. More than 100,000 volunteers, who responded to Urban II's appeal, were moved by the expectation of material gains and the promise of a place in heaven for those killed in combat, fought in hostile territory and made possible the establishment of Christian states in Palestine and in Syria. However, the precarious situation and the constant harassment of Muslim troops forced other Crusades to defend the gains already achieved. As a process rather than an episode, the Crusade was part of mediaeval Christian life.

In the western Mediterranean and, by this time, in the Iberian Peninsula, the Christian kingdoms of Castile, Leon, Aragon, and Portugal were carrying out their own Crusade against the Infidel. The Christian reconquest movement in the Iberian Peninsula unfolded over more than four centuries, with the conquest of Granada in 1492, with Isabella of Castile and Ferdinand of Aragon ruling Christian Spain.

War did not stop from being felt in Europe between 1100 and 1500. For men of the nobility, making war was a natural activity, a result of the European political division of the time. The latent antagonisms of kingdoms, duchies, cities, popes, and emperors animated a continent in constant turmoil.

The beginning of modern warfare was determined by the growing importance of gunpowder weapons. If the war on land gained new contours, at sea, boats equipped with cannons revolutionized naval battles. The development of the fleets of Spain, France, England, and the Netherlands turned the naval battles into authentic cannon-fire duels. The defeat of the Invincible Armada by the powerful naval fleet of Elizabeth I of England (1588) or the Battle of Lepanto that resulted in the victory of the Holy League over the Ottomans (1571) challenged the cunning "naval engineering" and the military leaders.

On land, a series of conflicts swept across Europe such as the religious wars between Catholics and Protestants in the late 16th and early 17th centuries; the Thirty Years' War (1618–1648), which discussed the struggle for European supremacy between France, Sweden, and the Habsburgs of Spain and Austria; the English civil war; the dynastic wars that dotted the European continent (France, Ireland, Spain, Austria); and the Great Northern War (with the military campaigns carried out by Charles XII of Sweden against Denmark, Prussia, Saxony, Hannover, Poland, and Russia for dominating trade in the Baltic).

During the 18th and 19th centuries, different continents were the scene of numerous wars that contributed to the birth of modern nations. The military power of Europe and the countries resulting from European colonization (such as the United States) acquired an indisputable preponderance in terms of military technology and organization. This period was launched by the Seven Years' War (1756–1763), considered the first "truly world war". In fact, the war was fought in Europe, in the Indian Ocean, and in North America. The birth of the United States of America owes much to war: the war for independence against the British crown (1775–1783), the war against Mexico and against indigenous populations, and the Civil War (1861–1865). French Revolution and Napoleonic Wars (1792–1815) contributed to the spread of a new concept of the state – liberalism – and gave an autonomous meaning to the word "freedom". In colonial empires, western powers imposed their power mainly by force of arms: over the populations of the Indian Ocean and West Africa, by the British, or by the French in Southeast Asia and West Africa.

Between 1815 and 1914, Europe experienced a period of peace between the great powers, a calm feeling that contrasted with the course of previous centuries. If we ignore insurrection phases related to the unification of Germany and Italy, between 1845 and 1871, we can consider that the armed conflicts had little expression because they remained in marginal lands of the interior or surroundings of the Ottoman Empire. However, this climate of rotten peace does not disarm countries during times of peace, which allow themselves to be invaded by a wave of nationalism aggravated by the growth of tensions.

Europe considered itself to be on a stage of war, either hot or cold, several times throughout the 20th century. The Great War, with its muddy trenches; the Spanish Civil War, with Guernica serving as a training center for German aviation; World War II, sweeping almost the entire old continent as if a cloak of terror had fallen over the whole land; and the relocation of conflicts to other stages after 1945 (there was not a single day without a conflict in any part of the world – Korea, Vietnam, colonial, and post-colonial wars, etc.) as a result of a new world order, are the great moments that mark the history of war and peace during the last two centuries.

Borders as "scars of history": changes and permanence in Europe

Space: stability and tension on Europe's borders

The European Union has around 14,000 km of borders. The continent, from the Atlantic to the Urals, has more than 37,000 km and about 90 km of borders between states. The multiplicity of political borders, which often have the same amount of languages, has always been the hallmark of Europe.

Some are among the oldest in the world (Portugal-Spain; Spain-France; Andorra; Switzerland; Norway-Sweden), but half of them are very recent, dating from 1989 onwards. Representing a quarter of world borders and recognized states by the UN, it has only about 8% of the world's population, which does not prevent it from playing a very particular and important role in the world context.

Structural fragmentation is still seen in our contemporary world, such as in the war in Ukraine, the return of the post-Brexit secession of Scotland or other regions in the United Kingdom, whether abroad or within the European Union, as proved by the case of Spain or Belgium.

The impact of the collapse of the Iron Curtain, even before the disintegration of the Soviet Union, the bloody dismemberment of the Yugoslav Federation, the autonomy of spaces in Czechoslovakia, and the constant tension between territories led the historian Krzysztof Pomian to state in 1990 that "l'Histoire de l'Europe est celle de ses frontières".

This uncertainty and tension is reflected in the memories of its inhabitants. The feelings that this situation provokes are profoundly disturbing and traumatizing: exalted passions, memories recovered in the present, individual experiences that become collectivized, institutional records that claim ownership of certain territories, pedagogical and didactic concerns so that future generations can live together democratically, and cultural memories that convey representations and imply individual and collective behaviour due to the borders.

The long-time signs: the cultural frontier, the religious frontier, the political frontier, and the ambiguities of the present times

In ancient times, borders were not clear lines, yet they were simple fluid markings that delimited boundary spaces. The development of modern borders emerges in the modern era. It during the Peace of Westphalia, 1648, that the first borders were negotiated between empires. The Treaty of the Pyrenees, 1659, will be the first example of this modern delimitation, occurring simultaneously with the great evolution of cartography. At that time, borders served not only to control the entrances, often for health reasons, but also to guarantee a district where tax collection became fundamental to feed the new needs of the modern State, amongst which the professionalization and equipping of armies stood out, that, in return, would guarantee the maintenance of borders.

The undefined cultural boundary that had marked the difference between the Western and the Slavic Kingdoms in the year 700 (roughly corresponding to the division between the Western and Eastern Roman Empire) gave way to a religious boundary that will distinguish the western territory of Christianity from the Eastern Orthodoxy at the beginning of the 16th century. When looking at spatial demarcations in 1990, we find a political border where Western countries and the communist bloc almost coexisted in the territories previously "occupied" by the last two designations. The fall of the Berlin Wall and the current invasion of Ukraine (2022) are temporal limits of a time where ambiguities call Europe into question, not only what concerns spatial concept, but above all on a political, ideological, and institutional meaning. It seems that we have returned to a new fluidity, yet dangerous, because it is supported by imperialist, ideological, and military views that cast doubt on not only Europe as a signifier, but perhaps its own meaning.

On the other side of the war: economic and social consequences for civilians in armed conflicts

According to Arendt (2006: 124), "we know these processes of devastation throughout history", as it is mainly in this curricular component that armed conflicts of greater or lesser scale and their consequences are studied.

In fact, wars, such as other subjects that oscillate between history and memory, more than being analysed in a logic of regret or guilt in the face of a painful or uncomfortable past/present (Traverso, 2012), need to be thought of historically, "sin simplificación ni falsificación de ningún tipo" (Morin, 2009: 92), stimulating skills such as empathy, argumentation, or multiperspective.

In this sense, with regard to history teaching and learning at the secondary level, the study of 'the other side of the war' can focus on, without "denying the shocking facts of the facts, [or] eliminating the unprecedented from them" (Arendt, 1989: 12), the geopolitical, social, and economic changes resulting from the armed conflicts that took place. The development of their historical awareness, preferably approaching the ontogenetic level (Rüsen, 2010), will involve a thoughtful analysis of aspects such as different ideological models, different economic conceptions and contrasted, even antagonistic, visions of social organization.

Going back in time, before the barbarians, the Western Roman Empire experienced the disastrous consequences of looting and war, in a struggle for survival. Already after the effective collapse, in the 5th century, the western economy and society, deeply marked by that vast political and territorial domain, suffered the inevitable impacts. The economic disruption resulted from abandoned fields, paralysed industries, and an unstable and fragile market. At a social level, the population suffered from famines and epidemics, and the climate of instability and fear pressured them to return to the countryside, a space of refuge and survival, to the detriment of former cities, or else seeking shelter from militarized classes and lords. The cultural setback took place through the reduction of the relevance of literature, the arts, and simple achievements in the daily life of individuals. Perhaps the only resistance came from the Catholic Church, especially in monastic spaces of religious orders, capable of reinforcing its role and position amongst individuals.

The European expansion brought another type of conflict, unequal in terms of armament and devastating in terms of economic and social consequences for the colonized peoples. If some European economic sectors and social groups benefited from this "attack on the American and African continents", in demographic terms there is a ravage in African and American communities as a result of new diseases without adequate defences, while in Europe there is a return to the growth of cities, due to commercial, industrial, and financial development.

Afterwards, in the 18th and 19th centuries, the French Revolution and, later, Napoleon's imperialism caused conflicts that, in some way, allowed the rise of liberalism and its founding principles. Consequently, the shock of those with the most conservative and anti-nationalist ideas, which had an echo in Europe, favoured the emergence of new revolutionary waves.

At the end of the 19th century, territorial disputes by European countries, especially in relation to Africa, but also to Asia, represented a climate of "armed peace". Later came the military alliances that, to a certain extent, anticipated a full-scale armed conflict. In fact, at the time, nationalisms also contributed to the aggravation of this scenario of crisis and put world security in jeopardy.

Those 4 years of WWI shook the foundations of Europe, now marked by an unprecedented world conflict, contributing to the end of old empires and the emergence of new states. If in various parts of Europe parliamentary democracy gained ground, in the Soviet Union a dictatorship of communist nature emerged. Even so, the economic (inflation, public debt, constraints on investments and exports, etc.) and social difficulties resulting from that conflict, as well as the problems associated with the expansion of socialism around the world, favoured the emergence, in power, of authoritarian or totalitarian regimes, controllers of public life and repressors of individual liberties.

With regard to the Second World War, the "total war" not only involved the military, but also led millions of civilians to situations of mass execution, forced labour, or deportations in absentia. Therefore, it proved to be a fertile ground for massive violations of human rights, as stated by Amnesty International (https://www.amnesty.org/en/). In turn, the weakening of fundamental political institutions or the alteration of the current social fabric has become a fundamental element for the reformulation of norms, values, or ideologies previously defended (Colletta & Cullen, 2000).

From then on and until 1989, with the fall of the Berlin Wall, the world became bipolar at political, economic, and social levels. If, on the one hand, with the West being influenced by the United States, liberalism was affirmed based on the principle of individual freedom, on the other hand, the East dominated by the Soviet Union, prevailed the Marxist conception that emphasized collectivity to the detriment of the individual.

It is important to stress, after World War II, the creation of the European Economic Community (EEC, or European Union nowadays), especially as a symbol of the union that aimed at economic prosperity and, again, greater political influence disappeared in the meantime as a result of world armed conflicts.

Even considering that "pensar la barbarie es contribuir a recrear al humanismo" (Morin, 2009: 94), the investigation of topics such as the outbreak of the first independence movements for the emancipation of colonized people from the first to the second half of the 20th century will be inevitable, as well as the persistence of religious, ethnic, or nationalist tensions at the end of the Cold War. Those movements, with an unequivocal impact on Sub-Saharan Africa, looked to the recovery of the national and cultural identity of the countries occupied by European colonists in a logic of self-determination and action against economic backwardness. In the Balkans, after the end of the division of the world into two distinct blocks, various crimes including genocide and war took place in the form of bombings against local populations, concentration camps, and violent massacres of civilians. Religious rivalries or ethnic cleansing actions have spread to countries such as Slovenia, Croatia, and Bosnia, as well as to the Kosovo region.

Despite efforts in this direction, the United Nations, created in 1945 with the aim of maintaining international peace and security and repressing acts of aggression, has not been able to counteract such harmful effects on the lives of many civilians. Regardless of the work being done in the opposite direction to the armed conflicts, "la barbarie de la guerra resulta por lo demás inseparable de los tiempos históricos" (Morin, 2009: 17).

In turn, the transformations related to the mentality of individuals, whether their visible reflections in behaviour, in the arts, in literature or in science, deserve didactic exploration, so that history is not interpreted as the subject that only studies wars and battles, alienating from other parallel and distinct memories (Traverso, 2005).

Still, in the first half of the 20th century, following the world conflict, Europeans also began to interpret the world from other lenses: female emancipation took place, namely through the conquests of the right to political participation; positivism was questioned, with science being 'fallible' and knowledge subjective; visual arts and literary manifestations acquired subversive contours, sometimes showing more refined techniques and breaking the old canons. Since the mid-century, it is possible to recognize the emergence of a global society, marked by the role of information and communication technologies or by the generalized civic commitment against environmental degradation and social exclusion, as well as by recurrent scientific innovations or by the urban culture with reflections in several artistic domains.

Then there are the daily changes, banal and linked to each one's life, such as illnesses associated with the Hiroshima and Nagasaki radiation or the psychological effects resulting from daily experiences of war, such as anxiety, depression, or obsessive-compulsive disorders. In addition to all the points mentioned, wars, whether from another century or the current conflicts that, for example, put Russia and Ukraine in confrontation, are responsible for situations of greater insecurity for civilians, poor mobility, or reduced job opportunities. Furthermore, the refugee status repeatedly becomes a reality, due to the destruction of housing, the absence of sanitary and food conditions, or the high levels of pollution.

To observe, discuss, and understand such scenarios, perhaps in the context of the classroom, is, in some way, to agree with Morin (2009: 94), "pensar la barbarie es contribuir a recrear el humanismo".

How can we approach this topic in the classroom?

The approach of this topic in History classes, in secondary education, requires, in the first place, the definition of clear objectives that allow serious, consistent work aligned with a logical thread for teachers and students. The historical understanding of this problem goes beyond the location in time and space in order to perceive the complexity of the process marked by continuities and ruptures, advances and setbacks, and, mainly, by the implicit power games that make each conflict a particular context.

In this sense, it is essential that students understand weapons, soldiers, and war fields as key elements in understanding a war, know the different moments of the colonization process, describe the evolution of the European political map across the borders of its countries, assess economic and social consequences of armed conflicts, show the importance of propaganda in the development of an armed conflict, and be able to identify examples of moments of terror and disrespect for human rights in the 20th century European history.

The contents, when approached according to this objective logic, develop in students' skills that contribute to the construction of historical knowledge, insofar as they are based on the use and interpretation of historical and historiographical sources and on the expectation that students will identify the historical evidence that supports the validation of knowledge. In other words, the learning experiences conceived by the teacher must privilege the diversity of rich and challenging didactic resources for the construction of historical knowledge, in the sense of promoting the performance of complex mental operations that allow the student to think historically.

There are numerous skills that students can develop when approaching this topic and that are not limited to the specific skills of History, but which seek to go further:

- To analyse sources of different nature, distinguishing information, implicit and explicit, as well as the respective limits for knowledge of the past.
- To analyse historiographical texts, identifying the author's opinion and taking it as an interpretation susceptible of revision in the light of historiographical advances.
- To use operational and methodological concepts of the discipline of History.
- To situate relevant events and processes chronologically and spatially, relating them to the contexts in which they occurred.
- Identify the multiplicity of factors and the relevance of the action of individuals or groups, in relation to historical phenomena circumscribed in time and space.
- Relate the history of Portugal to European and world history, distinguishing dynamic articulations and analogies/specificities, whether of a thematic nature or of a chronological, regional, or local scope.
- To problematize the relations between the past and the present and the critical and grounded interpretation of the current world.
- To express openness to the intercultural dimension of contemporary societies.
- To develop the capacity for reflection, sensitivity, and critical judgement.
- To develop awareness of citizenship and the need for critical intervention in different contexts and spaces.
- To promote respect for difference, recognizing and valuing diversity: ethnic, ideological, cultural, and sexual.
- To value human dignity and human rights, promoting diversity, interactions between different cultures, justice, equality, and equity in the enforcement of laws.

Addressing a topic that is both complex and sensitive like this one with secondary school students requires rigour and clarity in the conceptual domain. In this specific domain, concepts such as imperialism, colonialism, propaganda, total war, genocide, socially acute questions (SAQ), and resentment are unavoidable.

Throughout history, from ancient to contemporary times, imperialism and colonialism practices have given rise to serious war conflicts that have marked the memory of humanity. The practice of imperialism has a wide meaning. It was practised by Greeks and Romans, having been perpetuated with the absolutist monarchies of the modern period and maintained by the main European powers of the 19th and 20th centuries. Imperialism can be understood as a policy of territorial expansion of a State with a view to enlarging its borders, in which that same State exercises military, political, economic, and cultural dominion over another(s), frequently resorting to propaganda to justify its dominance and discredit the dominated state. On the other hand, colonialism is a political and economic system whereby a state or a nation conquers and colonizes specific territorial areas across borders – the colonies – in order to exploit its economic resources and expand its markets. In this process, there is an extension of the way of life from the metropolis to the colony.

Total war means a war without restrictions regarding the type of weapons used, the territories invaded, or the soldiers and civilians involved; it accepts the disregard of the conventionally established rules of war, considering that the means justify the ends, with a view to a complete victory. In this conception of war, genocide is frequent.

The concept "genocide" was coined by Polish lawyer Raphäel Lemkin (1944) following the Nazi "final solution to the Jewish question" during the Holocaust (or Shoah), but not forgetting the systematic murder of certain groups of people that took place before World War II, such as the massacre of the Armenian people by the Turks or the "Great Famine" (Holodomor) in 1931–32 to which Ukraine was destined by Stalin's will.

In 1946, the General Assembly of the United Nations recognized "genocide" as a crime under international law, and on the 9 December 1948, it achieved its own status as an independent crime in the Convention on the Prevention and Punishment of the Crime of Genocide, ratified by 152 States (data from July 2019).

As is easily understood, topics that address genocide and war crimes are sensitive and arouse pain and resentment.

"Resentment" is a painful memory related to an event or an experience that deeply marks the state of mind of an individual or a group that feels victimized or the target of injustice, giving rise to feelings such as pain, resentment, and rage. These feelings can generate hostile attitudes on the part of victims towards their aggressors or their supporters. On the other hand, we cannot forget that the traumas of war are often perpetuated by the following generations who feel the need not to forget the violence and injustices experienced by their ancestors. War memories are precisely an example of this desire to perpetuate the memory of victims, with the aim of not forgetting the traumatic experiences faced by a group in times of war, while waiting for their status as victims of war to be recognized and due reparations are made, not so much economic, but above all social and moral (Frotscher et al., 2014).

Thus it is indisputable that when working on a topic as painful and delicate as war, we are entering the specific field of socially acute questions.

Simonneaux (2019) proposed this term to describe the complex issues open to controversy and integrated in real context. These issues place social and scientific controversy, complexity, consistency of knowledge, evaluation of evidence, uncertainty, and risk at the center of the teaching-learning process.

These aspects are considered "alive" when they are controversial in the following three areas:

- In society, as they generate debate. There is media coverage of these issues and therefore students may have superficial knowledge.
- In research and in the professional world.
- In the classroom, they are often perceived as "alive". In this context, teachers often find it difficult to approach them in the classroom because they cannot rely solely on the use of consistent scientific facts and fear that they will not be able to manage students' reactions.

In the end . . .

Talking about narratives and uncomfortable heritage leads us to remember that "history is a narrative, a writing of the past according to the modalities and rules of a craft . . . that tries to answer questions raised by memory. History is born, therefore, from memory, freeing itself from it by putting the past at a distance" (Traverso, 2012).

Often, the narratives of the most uncomfortable legacies are crystallized because of the subjectivity of memory, seizing the strength of the lived experience, anchored in what we witness, either as protagonists or as extras.

> Memory is qualitative, singular, little concerned with comparisons, with contextualization, or with generalizations. Whoever carries it does not need to provide evidence. Reports of the past given by witnesses – as long as they are not conscious liars – will always be their truth, which is the image of the past deposed in them.
>
> *Traverso, 2012*

Therefore, the different narratives and representations of a phenomenon, a process, or an event often bring to a boil the feeling of reckoning with the past, as if there were debts to settle whenever discordant voices are heard.

Alongside individual narratives – and not forgetting collective memories – there are official memories, supported by States, which perpetuate or withhold the "ghosts of the past", making them underground, hidden, and forbidden.

Recently, Johann Michel, in the article "Le devoir de mémoire" ("Sciences Humaines", no. 315, June of 2019, pp. 20–25) took stock of the conceptual framework that the Social Sciences and Humanities and, in particular, History were incorporated in the approach of these themes. This article is particularly interesting because it brings us face to face with some dangers that are sometimes forgotten or underestimated, such as the fact that "le devoir de mémoire peut conduire à un culte du passé plus ressassé que réfléchi qui risque d'inhiber le présent" or that "a saturée mémoire par la douleur empêche la construction de nouveaux horizons d'attente et charrie avec elle le repli des individus et des groups sur eux-mêmes" (p. 25).

Even so, observing the pain of "others" – assuming that we are oblivious to our own pain – does not leave us indifferent. At least it should not.

Ignorance and contempt for the "ghosts of the past" can lead to ignorance, fanaticism, and the instrumentalization of History. But also to "resentment in History", in line with what Marc Ferro (2007) wrote at the beginning of the new millennium, trying to find in the remote past the roots of actions observed in the present.

References

Arendt, H. (1989). *Origens do Totalitarismo*. São Paulo: Companhia das Letras.
Arendt, H. (2006). *O que é política?* (6.ª ed.). Bertrand Brasil. http://arquivos.eadadm.ufsc.br/somente-leitura/EaDADM/UAB_2017_1/Modulo_1/Ciencia%20Politica/Material%20Complementar/O%20que%20%C3%A9%20pol%C3%ADtica%20Hannah%20Arendt.pdf
Clausewitz, C. (1984). *Da guerra*. Tradução para o inglês de Michael Howard e Peter Paret. Tradução do inglês para o português de Luiz Carlos Nascimento e Silva do Valle. [S.I.; s.n.].
Ferro, M. (2007). *O Ressentimento na História. Compreender o nosso tempo*. Teorema.
Frotscher, M., Stein, M., & Olinto, B. (2014). *Memory, resentment and the politization of trauma: narratives of World War II*. Revista Tempo, v. 20. www.scielo.br/j/tem/a/jwtF54gbSRzr7BbJDtvKxBs/?format=pdf&lang=pt
Lemkin, R. (1944). *Axis rule in occupied Europe: Laws of occupation - Analysis of Government - Proposals for redress*. Carnegie Endowment for International Peace.
Michel, J. (2019). "Le devoir de mémoire ». *In Sciences Humaines*, *315*(June), 20–25.
Morin, E. (2009). *Breve historia de la barbarie en el occidente*. Paidós.
Newark, T. (2011). *História Ilustrada da Guerra*. Sao Paulo, Brazil: PubliFolha.
O'Connell, R. L. (1989). *Of arms and men a history of war weapons and aggression*. Oxford University Press.
Pomian, K. (1990). *L'Europe et ses nations*. Paris: Gallimard.
Rüsen, J. (2010). *Jörn Rüsen e o Ensino da História*. Editora UFPR.
Simonneaux, J. (2019). *La Démarche d'Enquête. Une contribution à la Didactique des Questions Socialement Vives*. Dijon: Educagri Editions.
Sun Tzu (2009). *A Arte da Guerra*. Lisboa: Bertrand Editora (tradução portuguesa)
Traverso, E. (2012). *O passado, modos de usar*. Lisboa: Unipop.

12

PERSECUTED BY JUSTICE AND POWERS

Outcasts, rebels and criminals in the history of Europe

Carla van Boxtel

Introduction

The painting *The Outcast* (1851) by Richard Redgrave portrays a sad and anxious looking young girl carrying a baby who is cast out into the cold by her furious father. In the front you can see another female family member, probably the girl's sister (dressed in yellow), who tries to prevent this, begging the father to change his mind. Redgrave's painting might have functioned as a warning to other women to avoid a similar fate. However, because the painter puts hope for a change in the foreground of the painting, it might also have been meant to evoke sympathy for the young mother abandoned by her family.

In the sixteenth and seventeenth century, both in Catholic and Protestant regions, the state took increasing control over religious matters, including the discipline of marriage and sexuality (Headley et al., 2016). Extramarital sex was punishable by law. Moral courts imposed sanctions such as monetary fines, shaming punishment or dismissal of the city (Muurling et al., 2020). In the time of Redgrave, the new English poor law forced unwed mothers and their illegitimate children to live and work in workhouses (Williams, 2018; The National Archives, n.d.). Unwed mothers are often portrayed as vulnerable and isolated women. The last decades, however, historians have revised this negative image and stress the agency of unwed mothers, the choices they made and how they tried to improve their lives (Van der Heijden et al., 2021). Furthermore, research in Finland, Sweden and the Southern Netherlands, has shown that unwed mothers were a heterogeneous group and were not always isolated (De Langhe & Mechant, 2009).

This example raises questions about what was seen as crime and what punishments were thought appropriate and how that changed over time. Throughout history, different groups in Europe have been considered undesirable and part of them were persecuted by justice. This chapter is about crime, rebellion and punishment in the history of Europe and particularly about those who were cast out and persecuted and those who used violence against the powers. The chapter will first give a brief overview of the topic and the issues that are addressed by historians. The second part discusses approaches to teach about these topics.

Major changes in crime and punishment

It should be noted that providing a brief overview does of course not sufficiently reflect the complexity of developments in crime and punishment and the differences that existed between different areas within Europe. Following current approaches in writing the history of crime and punishment, the focus in this chapter is on the interaction between law, ideas, the political and social structures of the society and cultural representations of crime.

What was considered a crime?

When a penal code prescribes punishment for an act it can be considered crime. Therefore, we start with looking at the first penal codes. The first states, enabled by grain-based agriculture, had different officials who specialized in, for example, the collection of taxes but also in the administration of justice (Scott, 2017). People started making laws and much of early law was penal. For example, in the Code of Hammurabi (ca. 1755–1750 BCE), which included long lists of crimes and penalties, it was stated that "if a man steals an ox or a sheep, a donkey, pig or goat, he shall repay it thirtyfold if it belongs to a temple or a palace, and tenfold if it belongs to a free man. If the thief couldn't pay with anything, then he would be put to death" (The Code of Hammurabi, n.d.). The first laws in agricultural societies were meant to protect the well-being of individuals and their property and reflect the notion that humans should not lie, steal, break contracts or use violence against other human beings. At this point, there is a lot of continuity throughout history. Later, the Romans had punishments for the same types of crime. Since family and preserving the honour of the family were considered highly important in Roman culture, the Romans had special, cruel punishments for killing a father, mother or grandparent.

Due to the rise of the Catholic Church and the dominant role of Christianity in the Middle Ages, crime was increasingly identified with sin. Life was perceived a continuous struggle between good and evil forces, and people could be 'drawn into' evil. The practice of trial by ordeal illustrates that God was considered the ultimate judge. New types of 'criminal' figures, such as heretics, vagabonds and witches, became targets of arrest and punishment. In early modern time, religious tensions and conflicts intensified the persecution of heretics. After the scientific revolution, crime became less associated with religion or demonic manipulation. Humans were considered rational beings whose behaviour, including criminal behavior, is the result of free will and rational choice (Arrigo & Williams, 2006).

In the twentieth century, as more people work in the service sector, new types of crime develop. In the 1930s, criminologist Edwin Sutherland (1940) coined the term "white-collar crime", referring to crime commonly committed by people, for example, professionals in business or government who possess a high social status. One form of white-collar crime is fraud. Since the invention of the Internet, contemporary societies are increasingly faced with cybercrime, for example, hacking of websites or computers, identity theft, data breaches, credit card fraud and sending false invoices. After the Second World War, there is also an expansion of internationally organized crime. An example is human trafficking. Most human trafficking in Europe is related to forced labour and sexual exploitation (Wylie & McRedmond, 2010).

For a long time, the motives for committing a crime received little attention. In modern time, social scientists developed several theories to explain crime (Melosi, 2008). They emphasized, for example, the role of upbringing, peer group and role models (socialization), unfair economic structures and capitalism (social conflict), predispositions that stimulate engagement in crime (biological trait) and neurophysiologic dysfunctions.

From corporal punishments to imprisonment

A key change in European countries is the shift from corporal punishment and the death penalty to imprisonment (Rousseaux, 2013; Shapiro, 2020). Scholars have, however, criticized a 'narrative of progress' (e.g. Bretschneider, 2019; Meranze, 2003). A one-sided focus on major crimes and horrific punishments can give a distorted impression of past society as violent. And while harsh punishments, such as the whip and public executions, were forbidden in European countries, European authorities continued to use them in the colonies. And despite the changing ideas on severe penalties, in modern times punishments did not necessarily become humane, as evidenced by, for example, the use of penal colonies, and asylums for 'fallen women'.

In ancient times, punishment included fines, forced labor, exile and corporal punishments, including the death penalty (e.g. crucifixion, fighting with animals) which was often a public execution (Carucci, 2017). Imprisonment was only used for persons condemned to death or arrested awaiting trial or when the condemned couldn't pay the imposed fine. Although there is a perception that punishment was extremely cruel in the Middle Ages, such as burning alive, trial by water or fire, breaking a person on the wheel or cutting off a hand, historians point out that extremely harsh methods were rather exceptional (Broers, 2022). For a long time, medieval laws were based largely on the principle of compensation: the perpetrator was asked to compensate (called a "weregeld" or later "man's compensation") the victim for wrong done.

In early modern time the notion that wrongdoers should be excluded from society, whereas it should simultaneously benefit society, gained ground (Broers, 2022). The Dutch Dirck Volkertszn Coornhert (1522–1590) argued that harsh punishments did not prevent or decrease criminal behaviour and that an important reason why people committed criminal offences was their reluctance to work.

FIGURE 12.1 T'Rasphuys in 1662, a workhouse where delinquents had to shave wood from the brazilwood tree, rasping it into powder which was delivered to the paint industry From Melchior Fokkens, Beschrijvinge der wijdt-vermaarde Koop-stadt Amstelredam.

Workhouses became popular in urban areas throughout Europe. In the Amsterdam houses of correction, the so-called "rasp house" (see Figure 12.1) and "spinning house", young delinquents who were punished for begging, vagrancy or engagement in prostitution or petty theft were made to rasp wood or spinning. Although later they were often portrayed as places of hunger, humiliation, sexual and physical assault, the houses also provided relief for poor, old and sick persons and security and education.

Despite the workhouses, before the eighteenth century, punishments were mainly corporal. Influenced by the Enlightenment philosophers, such as John Locke's idea that life and liberty must be considered unalienable 'natural rights' of every human, French reformists called for less violent punishments. The Italian aristocrat Cesare Beccaria, writer of *Dei delitti e delle pene* [On crimes and punishment], published in 1764, criticized torture, the death penalty and inequality in criminal law (Harcourt, 2013). Beccaria's principles of equality in law and punishment, legality (only the law should prescribe punishment) and proportionality (punishment of a certain crime should be in proportion to the severity of the crime itself) became important pillars of modern criminal law, together with the introduction of independent judiciary (Gerber, 2011). At the beginning of the nineteenth century, in the Netherlands, seven Colonies of Benevolence were established. Large numbers of people, vagrants, beggars and orphans were sent there to work in agriculture and learn discipline (Colonies of Benevolence, n.d.).

Banishment was seen as a humane alternative to the death sentence and was widespread among imperialist European countries in the nineteenth and twentieth century. The most known examples are probably the British penal colonies Australia and New Zealand. The French had several prisons in Devil's Island, French Guiana, where more than three-quarters of the exiles eventually died. Banishment helped to manage domestic populations and eliminate the unwanted from European societies. Furthermore, it turned out to be an important tool in the colonization process. It provided cheap labor and was essential to overseas infrastructural development.

Most European countries abolished the death penalty in the second half of the twentieth century. Portugal abolished capital punishment for ordinary crimes much earlier, in 1867, and the Netherlands in 1870. In 2012 Latvia was the last European Union member that abolished the death penalty. The abolishment of the death penalty is in line with the European Convention of Human Rights. Several factors played a role in the abolition. First, democracies with a parliamentary system with proportional representation were among the early abolishers (Sandholttz & McGann, 2012). The abolition was also pushed by the activism of non-governmental and transnational organizations such as Amnesty International (founded in 1961) and Human Rights Watch. Finally, incentives provided by European political institutions, such as the Council of Europe and the European Union, played a role.

Since the 1990s, in Europe crime rates dropped nearly by two thirds. There is no agreed upon explanation, but Farrell et al. (2014) conclude that improved security and crime prevention is the best explanation. Policy is increasingly informed by results from scientific research in the discipline of criminology.

Outcasts: prejudice and persecution

Throughout history, people were not only punished for theft, murder or committing violence against other people but also because they deviated from the norm and were seen as a threat. There is a rich historiography on the history of outcasts and marginalized groups in Europe. In the 1960s historians called for writing 'history from below'. They aimed at history from a non-elite perspective, with a particular focus on groups who have suffered oppression and were persecuted by the authorities and wanted to write the stories of those who did not get the chance to author their own story (e.g. Hitchcock, 2004). This turned out to be a challenging task because access to sources is crucial and documents and images are mostly providing the perspective of the elites and those who have power. Historians have become increasingly aware that writing the stories of marginalized groups of people is also about examination of power relations. The cultural turn of the 1980s and 1990s brought a stronger focus on meaning and forms of perception (Eley, 2008). In *Vice, Crime, and Poverty: How the Western Imagination Invented the Underworld*, the French historian Dominique Kalifa (2019) shows, for example, how the "underworld" of beggars, thieves, convicts, prostitutes and pimps was partly real and partly fantasized and how social imaginary, the way in which societies perceive groups and classes, instantiates structures of power. Kalifa describes the "underworld" as a literary creation and explains why it was precisely in the nineteenth century that so many stories about the miserable, corrupt and dangerous were produced. The political and industrial revolutions resulted in deep social change and uncertainty among the elites, and the rise of newspapers and popular fiction contributed to the spread of the "underclass" mythology.

An example of a group that was considered undesirable by the authorities and has been studied extensively by historians are the vagabonds (Beier & Ocobock, 2008; Hitchcock, 2012; Woodbridge, 2001). People moved around in search of work and often lived by beggary or thievery, but some did have a profession, for example, as actor, healer or musician, and some suffered from mental illness. In the late Middle Ages vagrancy began to be considered a crime. Later, the elites increasingly saw vagrancy as "asocial behavior" and a result of poor behavior or eugenics and less as a result of poor economic and social conditions. In the English act of 1572 it was mentioned that vagabonds were to be whipped and burned through the gristle of the right ear with a hot iron. In early modern time, authorities send vagabonds to workhouses. In Finland and Sweden, however, vagabondage was often punished with forced labour or military service. When imprisonment became a more common punishment, vagabonds were imprisoned. In nineteenth century France, for example, the penal code considered vagabondage punishable by 3 to 6 months imprisonment. In our own time, there is still criminalization of what are now called "homeless people", reflected in removing them from particular areas, restricting the areas in which sleeping is allowed or the prohibiting of begging.

Another group that was outcast are the "fallen women". The term implied work in prostitution, young women who became pregnant outside of marriage, were victims of rape or young girls and teenagers who had no family support. Disciplining organizations were also established for this group (Bigman, 2016). In the Magdalene asylums or Magdalene laundries in Ireland, for example, tens of thousands of women were forced, sometimes by the Irish government, to be institutionalized (Magdalene Asylum in Northern Ireland, n.d.). Though the institutions were run by Catholic orders, they were supported by the Irish government, which funneled money toward the system in exchange for laundry services. In 1996 the last 'laundry' closed. Only recently these practices were seriously being questioned in Ireland. In 2014, the remains of at least 796 babies were found in a septic tank of the Bon Secours Mother and Baby Home in Tuam.

Often the Nazi concentration camps are seen as a separate and unique phenomenon in European history. The scale on which the Nazis used camps to exile and exterminate minority groups and political prisoners was and is unprecedented; however, concentration camps were not a new phenomenon. Camps were used on a large scale in the nineteenth and twentieth centuries by European colonial empires. The French colonial regime forced Arabs, Berbers and Jews to leave their villages and held them in camps in order to replace them with French settlers (Gallois, 2013). In the nineteenth century, about a quarter of the native Algerians died in these camps. This didn't stop after World War II. During the Algerian War of Independence (1954–1962), "centres de regroupements" were created, to relocate more than one million Algerians including children in order to create free fire zones for the French forces (Henni, 2016). Other examples are the infamous British camps for the Boer population in South Africa, camps in the Dutch East Indies for both Dutch and indigenous Indonesians and the large-scale system of Spanish camps in Cuba.

Violence against the powers: rebels and terrorists

Historiography 'from below' was also fundamental to the increased study of uprisings and revolt in since the 1970s and 1980s. As was discussed earlier, the terminology used is important because it reflects ideological perspectives and affects the analysis and representation of historical phenomena. Access to the actions of rebels and terrorists is mediated by the texts that report them (Firnhaber-Baker & Schoenaers, 2017). Many terms are being used to describe politically motivated violence against the state or state institutions, for example, riot, uprising, insurrection, revolution, protest, rebellion and terrorism. It is not easy to draw clear lines between these concepts. The choice of which word to use depends often on which subjects perceive the phenomenon.

Peasant and urban uprisings

What riots, rebellions and uprisings have in common is that they are collective actions of groups of people who – in pursuit of common interest – try to gain power by violence to realize concrete improvements in their lives or to prevent something to happen. We will use here the term uprisings, following Balibar (2007) who defined it as short-lived instances of highly visible, militant, and autonomous collective action. Mostly, popular uprisings – unlike revolutions – did not result in structural changes in the institutions of government or in society as a whole. The participants of popular uprisings often had a local frame of reference and were aimed at rectification of local injustices.

Peasant uprisings were mostly a reaction to the intensification of landlordship, increased taxes, religious conflicts and serfdom. In the fourteenth and early fifteenth centuries there were popular uprisings throughout Europe, which were almost always defeated. Examples are the peasant revolt in Flanders (1323–1328), the Jacquerie in France (1356–1358) and the English Peasants' Revolt or Great Rising (1381) (Scott, 1985). Peasants used various means to protest, such as refusal to pay taxes or render services, but also armed revolt. Their uprisings had to be planned in advance because they lived in dispersed villages. Sometimes a general assembly, often with the aid of someone who could write, drew up a set of demands. In the seventeenth century, the scale of warfare greatly increased, and war increasingly stretched over decades. Although the armies were much bigger, logistical support was often inadequate. Soldiers devastated civilian areas. In some cases this resulted in protests of the local population. Catalan peasants, for example, were suffering from the presence of the royal army during the war between the Kingdom of France and the Monarchy of Spain. Personal property was destroyed, and women raped by soldiers. In 1640, Catalan peasants revolted against the quartering of soldiers on their land. In the eighteenth century, several peasant uprisings were part of the French Revolutionary Wars, such as the Peasants' War of 1798 in the Southern Netherlands (Flanders and Brabant).

Urban uprisings or riots were often the result of poor working or living conditions or oppression by the city's administration. In the Middle Ages, due to urbanization, the number of urban uprisings increased. Dissatisfaction with the administration was expressed through petitions or, in some cases, violence. In early modern time, urban uprisings often took the form of food riots. There was a peak in food riots in the eighteenth century, particularly in France. These riots must be understood in a wider political and economic context of changing governmental policy and a movement towards a formation of a national market. This national market resulted in distribution problems. Furthermore, there were larger demands for food for the (growing) armies and administrative centers. The citizens who participated in the food riots were mainly artisans and proto-industrial workers. Both men and women played a role in the food riots. One of the significant events of the French Revolution, the march on Versailles on October 5, 1789, started as a march of women working at the street markets of Paris protesting against the high price and scarcity of bread. In many cases, the riots were successful in the short-term and resulted in lower prices and more food in markets and bakeries.

The question of differences in uprisings between rural and urban settings, once a major historiographical focus, has been less urgent in recent years as historians have emphasized relationships between town and country and even partnerships between urban and rural rebels (Firnhaber-Baker & Schoenaers, 2017).

Uprisings of enslaved people in the European colonies

Outside Europe, in European colonies, uprisings of enslaved people took place. An early example is the major revolt in 1522 during the Christmas season on a sugar plantation owned by one of Christopher Columbus' sons in the Spanish colony of Santa Domingo (now the Dominican Republic and Haiti). People who were forced to work on the plantation were from the West-African Wolof ethnic group. The uprising was a well-planned, collective and multilocal effort (Stevens-Acevedo, 2019).

The uprising was violently crushed and ended in harsh punishments and execution of the alleged leaders, and the governor immediately issued a set of ordinances. These are the oldest known recorded laws on black slavery in the Americas and aimed at preventing any further occurrence of uprisings. The laws restricted physical mobility, minimized access to weapons, prescribed harsh punishment in the form of physical torture and executions and regulated an increase in Black women with whom the enslaved males could engage in the formation of family.

The Enlightenment and French Revolution gave a new impulse to uprisings of enslaved people with ideas about the natural, inalienable and sacred rights of man. In 1791, for example, enslaved people of the colony Domingue (belonging to France) started a major revolt led by François-Dominique Toussaint Louverture. In Curaçao, a Dutch colony, Tula gave lead to a strike on the Knip plantation (Fatah-Black, 2013).

Terrorism

Across the world, and also in European countries, terrorism developed as a new form of political violence against the authorities (European Council, n.d.). The hijacking of several passenger jets and their subsequent use as missiles against the towers of the World Trade Center and the Pentagon on September 11, 2001, has been widely understood as terrorist acts (9/11 Memorial & Museum, n.d.). It is, however, difficult to provide a clear definition of terrorism (e.g. Millington, 2018). The term terrorism comes from the Latin *terrere*, "to shake", which corresponds with the arousal of extreme fear. It is sometimes difficult to distinguish terrorism from other forms of political violence, guerilla warfare or freedom fighting. Labeling an act of violence as "terrorism" is also a political act since it influences the audience. What instances of terrorism have in common is the threat or use of unlawful force and violence by non-state or state actors and the intention to achieve political, economic, religious or social objectives through fear, coercion or intimidation.

Political scientist David Rapoport (2001) identified four waves of modern terrorism (see also Book talks: Waves of global terrorism with David C. Rapoport, 2022). The anarchistic wave started in Russia at the end of the nineteenth century. Mikhail Bakunin, a revolutionary socialist and anarchist, advocated the abolition of the state and private ownership of means of production, which should be owned collectively. The anarchists traveled extensively, and the telegraph, newspapers and railroads helped spread their ideas. The People's Will was probably the first terrorist organization. They tried to assassinate the csar and, after a number of failed events, eventually succeeded in 1881 by throwing a homemade bomb of dynamite (a recent invention) into his carriage. More assassinations followed. In 1898, empress Elisabeth of Austria was murdered with a sharpened needle file by an Italian anarchist. The First World War ended this first wave of terrorism.

The anticolonial wave had its peak after the Second World War. The idea of self-determination, promoted by the American president Woodrow Wilson, motivated people all over the world to work on driving out the occupier and establishing self-government. Several groups adopted violence as a means to implement their ambitions. This was the case in European colonies (e.g. in Algeria) but also in Europe itself. In Spain, the ETA waged a bloody campaign aimed at Basque independence. In Northern Ireland, the Irish Republican Army (IRA) fought against the dominance of the United Kingdom. In Cyprus, the nationalist organization EOKA used violence to end the British rule and unite Cyprus with Greece.

In the 1970s and 1980s, there was a new left wave of terrorism. Criticizing the 'Establishment' and the 'System', the hard left stream committed to political and social activism, sometimes inspired by ideas of Mao Zedong and Che Guevara. New left protests mainly consisted of strikes, demonstrations and occupations of universities. Some groups, however, adopted the idea that revolutionary violence would have a positive transformative effect. In Germany, for example, the left-wing terrorist group Rote Armee Fraktion used hijacking, kidnapping and bombing in its fight against capitalism, imperialism, fascism and NATO. In Italy, a bomb explosion in the center of Milan in 1969 initiated two decades – also known as 'The Years of Lead' – of political terrorism of both far-left and far-right groups. In the 1980s this wave of terrorism gradually ebbed away.

The last wave that Rapoport describes is the religious wave that started in 1979. In Europe the number of attacks and deaths were relatively low, although several attacks caused enormous human suffering and impacted daily life. Scholars have pointed out that it is problematic to use the term Islamic terrorism because it can demonize all Muslims and reinforce the stereotype that Islam encourages terrorism. They suggest terms such as Islamism or fundamentalist terrorism, although these terms are also criticized. Islamists view Islam as a political system in addition to a religion. They demand the strict application of the prescription of Sharia law, advocate for a jihad against 'bad' Muslims and rulers in order to establish an Islamic state or Caliphate, oppose to the secular values that dominate the non-Muslim world and belief in a transnational Muslim community. Most Islamism terrorist attacks were related to Al-Qaeda, the Taliban and the Islamic State (IS), but there were also attacks of so-called lone wolves who used guns or vehicles (Hoffman, 2017). Characteristic of this wave is the use of self-bombing.

Discussing these waves of terrorism, makes it clear that terrorism is not something very recent and that terrorists had different kinds of motives and used different techniques. A disadvantage of this discussion in waves is that it draws less attention to other forms of terrorism, such as terrorism from far-right groups, cyber terrorism and eco-terrorism.

Teaching about crime and punishment

How can we teach about particular groups of outcasts, rebels and terrorists and more broadly about (ideas about) crime and punishment? We discuss four approaches emphasizing different types of objectives.

Deepen understanding of significant developments and key concepts

Novices in the domain of history have difficulties understanding abstract colligatory historical concepts such as the Enlightenment that actually encompass a large range of events or ideas (Lévèsque, 2008). Teachers can enhance students' understanding by providing concrete examples, asking students to use the concepts to analyze concrete cases and by connecting these concepts to other concepts (van Boxtel & van Drie, 2018, 2012).

Exploring questions related to crime and punishment and concrete examples of violence against the authorities can deepen students' understanding of particular eras and key developments in European history, such as centralization, humanism, the Reformation, urbanization, the scientific revolution, the Enlightenment and the development of an information society because these developments affected what people considered crime and suitable punishment (see Table 12.1). Students can also develop their understanding of general concepts used in the broader domain of social studies, such as law, justice, social exclusion, uprising and revolt. In upper secondary education, teacher can aim at developing the understanding that concepts used in history and social studies do not have a fixed meaning and that the meaning may vary with time and place and frames how we understand a particular phenomenon (Limón, 2002). This is certainly true of concepts such as crime, social exclusion, riot or terrorism.

Enrich and challenge mainstream narratives about the past with perspectives and experiences from ordinary people and marginalized groups

Historians want to acknowledge the multiplicity of perspectives and voices and address issues of power in the past (Bergmann, 2000). In history education, studying historical phenomena from different perspectives is important because it contributes to a richer understanding but also to avoid processes of exclusion. When the experiences and voices of, for example, females, ethnic and social minorities are neglected, students may feel that their actions matter less, which is detrimental to their development of agency (Den Heyer, 2018; Wilke et al., 2019).

Research has, however, shown that history textbooks present a rather closed and 'one-sided' narrative, often dominated by states, "great men" and the perspectives of the elites instead of those of ordinary people (e.g. Carretero, 2017; Foster, 2012; Kropman, 2020). Mainstream narratives can be enriched and challenged by focusing on different historical agents. Paying attention to groups that were marginalized in the past and nonconformists such as vagabonds; persons accused of heresy or witchcraft; people who were send to workhouses, penalty colonies or asylums or rebelling peasants and craftsmen can enrich the often one-sided narratives and do more justice to different experiences and perspectives. One should be careful, however, not to isolate the experiences and perspectives of a particular marginalized

TABLE 12.1 General and historical concepts related to the history of crime and punishment and violence against the powers, organized in periods and themes

	Criminal justice, repression and punishment of crime	Persecuted by justice	Violence against the powers
General concepts	state, law, power, justice, crime, police, punishment, imprisonment	(in)justice, (in)equality, social imaginary, social exclusion	uprising, riot, rebellion, revolt, terrorism, violence
Prehistory	agricultural revolution, (penal) law, officials in administration of justice, fines, corporal punishment	e.g. theft, damaging of another one's property, harming someone physically, murder	
Classic Antiquity	Roman law, trial by jury, capital punishment, public executions, fines, exile	e.g. early Christians, enslaved people who had run away, prisoners of war	e.g. Spartacus slave rebellion, Jewish revolt, Bagaudae uprisings
Middle Ages	Christianity/Catholic Church, centralization, urbanisation, common law, trial by ordeal, principle of compensation	e.g. vagabonds, Jews, persons accused of heresy or witchcraft	e.g. Peasants revolt in Flanders, the Jacquerie, Great Rising*
Early Modern Time	humanism, reformation, scientific revolution, Enlightenment, increased scale of warfare, formation of a national market, workhouses	e.g. vagabonds, Jews, persons accused of heresy or witchcraft, unwed mothers	urban uprisings, food riots, uprisings of enslaved people (e.g. Santa Domingo, Dominque, Curaçao)
Modern Time	industrialization, urbanisation, population growth, information society, imprisonment, penal colonies, concentration camps, task penalty, police system, white-collar crime, cybercrime, human rights organizations	e.g. victims of human trafficking, homeless people, prostitutes	wave of terrorism: anarchist (e.g. People's Will), anticolonial (e.g. ETA, IRA, EOKA), new left (e.g. RAF, Years of Lead), religious (e.g. Al-Quada, Taliban, IS)

Source: *see for a list of peasant uprisings https://en.wikipedia.org/wiki/List_of_peasant_revolts

group or person. Students may develop the idea that social changes result from heroic acts of iconic individuals (Den Heyer, 2018).

Develop historical thinking and reasoning skills through inquiry learning

Topics related to the history of crime and punishment provide a powerful context for the development of historical thinking and reasoning skills. In history, there are different types of reasoning, such a reasoning about continuity and change, causes and consequences and differences and similarities (van Boxtel & van Drie, 2018). When teaching about crime and punishment or rebellion or terrorism, students can learn to engage in these different types of reasoning. They can, for example, compare what we consider crime in our contemporary times and what was considered crime in the past or explore how attitudes about punishment have changed. They can identify causes and consequences of different waves of terrorism. When focusing on those in power and who rebelled or were persecuted, students explore multiple perspectives and can learn about positionality.

In inquiry-based learning students consider, evaluate and weigh information from multiple sources and develop or evaluate interpretations of the past (van Boxtel et al., 2021). Inquiry tasks can focus on a particular uprising, type of crime (e.g. vagabondage, witchcraft or human trafficking) or terrorist group. There is a large variety of historical sources that can be used in inquiry tasks, such as diaries, pamphlets, images (e.g. of vagrants), newspapers, cartoons, legal documents and documentaries. Teachers have to be aware that many sources come from urban, royal or national powers and do not include the voices of those who were prosecuted or who rebelled against the powers.

Promote reflection on enduring issues and moral reasoning

Gert Biesta (2015) emphasizes that education should support students in becoming more independent in their thinking and acting in the world to allow them to make sense and develop agency. Exploring how the powers in the past defined and fought crime, and how people expressed their displeasure, sometimes choosing to use violence, can enhance reflection on what students consider important themselves, how they can contribute to change or continuity or how that may be difficult or which means are permitted. Students can look at a historical urban uprising and the discourses surrounding them to better understand examples of recent uprisings. In England, Benwell et al (2020) discussed, for example, the uprisings in Liverpool in 1981 in order to reflect on recent uprisings in 2011.

An important means to connect past, present and future and to help students orientate in current society is to define and focus on enduring issues. Enduring issues are persistent societal problems related to, for example, (in)equality, (in)justice, sustainability or war and peace (van Straaten, 2016). When teaching about crime and punishment and rebellion, teachers can ask students to reflect on enduring issues related to (in)justice, (in)equality and social exclusion. For example, they can reflect on and discuss different views on crime and punishment in past and contemporary society, including personal views and underlying values such as equality, fairness, freedom, humanity, justice and respect. Inquiry into groups that were considered outcasts can spark a dialogue about social exclusion and inclusivity.

When highlighting particular historical agents, for example, rebels, it is important to realize that one should not set them apart or isolate them as if they acted alone. There is the risk of transforming them into heroes or heroines. It is better to acknowledge the significance of all and to locate the individuals in networks of allies, family or friends.

Crime and punishment are also about human suffering and teaching about these topics can stir emotions. Accounts of violence, rape and executions can trouble students even when they occurred in the past. Students can identify with either the victim or the perpetrator. The topic may evoke anger, for example, because it involves victims who are defenseless or because people are unjustly punished, in their opinion. There may also be fear, for example of becoming a victim of terrorism themselves or students may look up to the perpetrator. When a topic evokes strong emotions, teachers need to construct and maintain a safe classroom climate, cultivate and develop positive civic dispositions, develop critical consciousness by analyzing social inequality, develop the ability to explore multiple perspectives and provide information to support contextualization (Wansink et al., 2021; Stylianou & Zembylas, 2021).

In conclusion, we can say that the study of crime, rebellion and punishment provides an interesting window into the history of Europe. The topics can be powerful contexts for teaching historical thinking and reasoning skills and enrich the mainstream one-perspective narratives that are often taught in the history classroom with experiences and perspectives of ordinary people and marginalized groups. Furthermore, crime, uprisings and political violence are amongst the complicated challenges and concerns of both past and contemporary societies and can support meaningful connections between the past, present and future and promote reflection on moral issues.

References

Arrigo, B. A., & Williams, C. R. (2006). *Philosophy, crime and criminology*. University of North Carolina.
Balibar, E. (2007). Uprisings in the Banlieues. *Constellations, 14*(1), 47–71.
Beier, A. L., & Ocobock, P. (Eds.). (2008). *Cast out: Vagrancy and homelessness in global and historical perspective*. 1st ed. Ohio University Press. https://doi.org/10.2307/j.ctt1rfsq2g
Benwell, M. C., Davies, A., Evans, B., & Wilkinson, C. (2020). Engaging political histories of urban uprisings with young people: The Liverpool riots, 1981 and 2011. *Politics and Space, 38*(4), 599–618. https://doi.org/10.1177/2399654419897916
Bergmann, K. (2000). *Multiperspektivität. Geschichte selber denken*. 2008 ed. Wochenschau Verlag.

Biesta, G. (2015). What is education for? On good education, teacher judgement, and educational professionalism. *European Journal of Education Research, Development, and Policy, 50*(1), 75–87. https://doi.org/10.1111/ejed.12109

Bretschneider, F. (2019). Pieter Spierenburg's contribution to the history of confinement in early modern Europe. *Crime, History & Societies, 23*(2), 123–130. www.jstor.org/stable/45283230

Broers, E. (2022). The Evolution of criminal law in continental western Europe. *International Journal of Law and Society, 5*(1), 35–44. doi: 10.11648/j.ijls.20220501.15

Carretero, M. (2017). Teaching history master narratives: Fostering imagi-nations. In M. Carretero, S. Berger & M. Grever (Eds.), *Palgrave handbook of research in historical culture and education* (pp. 511–528). Springer nature.

Carucci, M. (2017). The spectacle of justice in the Roman Empire. In O. Hekster & K. Verboven (Eds.), *The impact of justice on the Roman Empire: Proceedings of the thirteenth workshop of the International Network Impact of Empire (Gent, June 21-24, 2017)* (pp. 212–233). Leiden/Boston: Brill. https://doi.org/10.1163/9789004400474_013

Den Heyer, K. (2018). Historical agency: Stories of choice, action, and social change. In S. A. Metzger & L. McArthur Harris (Eds.), *The Wiley international handbook of history teaching and learning*. John Wiley & Sons, Inc.

De Langhe, S., & Mechant, M. (2009). Vulnerable women? Unmarried mothers in the Southern Netherlands during the eighteenth and first half of the nineteenth century. *Economy and society in the low countries before 1850* (4th Flemish-Dutch Conference, Leiden) (pp. 20–30). Januari.

Eley, G. (2008). Dilemmas and challenges of social history since the 1960s: What comes after the cultural turn? *South African Historical Journal, 60*(3), 310–322. https://doi.org/10.1080/02582470802417391

Farrell, G., Tilley, N., & Tseloni, A. (2014). Why the crime drop? *Crime and Justice, 43*(1), 421–490. doi:10.1086/678081.

Fatah-Black, K. (2013). Orangism, patriotism, and slavery in Curaçao, 1795–1796. *International Review of Social History, 58*, 35–60.

Firnhaber-Baker, J., & Schoenaers, D. (Eds.). (2017). *The Routledge history handbook of medieval revolt* (1st ed.). Routledge. https://doi-org.proxy.uba.uva.nl/10.4324/9781315542423

Gallois, W. (2013). Genocide in nineteenth-century Algeria. *Journal of Genocide Research, 15*(1), 69–88. https://doi.org/10.1080/14623528.2012.759395

Gerber, S. D. (2011). *A distinct judicial power: The origins of an independent judiciary, 1606–1787*. Scott Douglas Series.

Foster, S. (2012). Re-thinking history textbooks in a globalized world. In M. Carretero, M. Asensio & M. Rodriquez-Moneo (Eds.), *History education and the construction of national identities* (pp. 49–62). Information Age Publishing.

Harcourt, B. E. (2013). Beccaria's 'on crimes and punishments': A mirror on the history of the foundations of modern criminal law. *Coase-Sandor Institute for Law & Economics* (Working Paper No. 648). https://chicagounbound.uchicago.edu/cgi/viewcontent.cgi?article=1633&context=law_and_economics

Headley, J. M., Hillerbrand, H. J., & Papalas, A. J. (2016). *Confessionalization in Europe, 1555–1700*. Routledge.

Henni, S. (2016). On the spaces of Guerre Moderne: The French army in Northern Algeria (1945–1962). *Spaces of Conflict*, 37–56.

Hitchcock, D. (2012). A typology of travellers: Migration, justice, and vagrancy in Warwickshire, 1670–1730. *Rural History, 23*(1), 21–39.

Hitchcock, T. (2004). A new history from below. *History Workshop Journal, 57*, 294–298.

Hoffman, B. (2017). *Inside terrorism*. New York: Columbia University Press.
Kalifa, D. (2019). *Vice, crime, and poverty: How the western imagination invented the underworld*. New York: Columbia University Press.
Kropman, M., van Boxtel, C., & Van Drie, J. (2020). Narratives and multiperspectivity in Dutch secondary school history textbooks. *Journal of Educational Media, Memory, and Society*, *12*(1), 1–23, 10.3167/jemms.2020.120101
Lévesque, S. (2008). *Thinking historically. Educating students for the twenty-first century*. University of Toronto Press.
Limón, M. (2002). Conceptual change in history. In M. Limón & L. Mason (Eds.), *Reconsidering conceptual change: Issues in theory and practice* (pp. 259–289). Kluwer.
Melosi, D. (2008). *Crime, punishment and migration*. London: Sage.
Meranze, M. (2003). *Michel Foucault, the death penalty and the crisis of historical understanding*. Alfred University.
Millington, C. (2018). Were we terrorists? History, terrorism, and the French Resistance. *History Compass*, *16*(2). http://dx.doi.org/10.1111/hic3.12440
Muurling, S., Kamp, J., & Schmidt, A. (2021). Unwed mothers, urban institutions and female agency in early modern Dutch, German and Italian towns. *The History of the Family*, *26*(1), 11–28. https://doi.org/10.1080/1081602X.2020.1767677
Rapoport, D. C. (2001). The fourth wave: September 11 and the history of terrorism. *Current History*, *100*(650), 419–424.
Rousseaux, X. (2013). A history of crime and criminal justice in Europe. In S. Body-Gendrot, M. Hough, K. Kerezsi, R. Levy, & S. Snackes (Eds.), *The Routledge handbook of European criminology* (pp. 38–54). Routledge. www.routledgehandbooks.com/doi/10.4324/9780203083505.ch3
Sandholttz, W., & McGann, A. J. (2012). Patterns of death penalty abolition, 1960–2005: Domestic and international factors. *International Studies Quarterly*, *56*(2). https://doi.org/10.2307/23256781
Scott, J. C. (2017). *Against the grain: A deep history of the earliest states*. Yale University Press.
Scott, T. (1985). Peasant revolts in Early modern Germany. *The History Journal*, *28*(2), 455–468. doi:10.1017/S0018246X0000323X
Shapiro, I., & Foucault, M. (2020). *Discipline and punishment. The birth of the prison*. Modern Classics.
Stevens-Acevedo, A. (2019). *The Santo Domingo slave revolt of 1521 and the slave laws of 1522. Black slavery and black resistance in the early colonial Americans*. Dominican Studies Institute. www.dominicanlandmarks.com/Slave-Revolt-1521-Slave-Laws-1522-Monograph.pdf
Stylianou, P., & Zembylas, M. (2021). Engaging with issues of death, loss, and grief in elementary school: Teachers' perceptions and affective experiences of an in-service training program on death education in Cyprus. *Theory & Research in Social Education*, *49*(1), 54–77. https://doi.org/10.1080/00933104.2020.1841700
Sutherland, E. H. (1940). White-collar criminality. *American Sociological Review*, *5*(1), 1–12.
Van Boxtel, C., & Van Drie, J. (2012). "That's in the time of the Romans!" knowledge and strategies students use to contextualize historical images and documents. *Cognition and Instruction*, *30*(2), 113–145. 10.1080/07370008.2012.661813
Van Boxtel, C., & Van Drie, J. (2018). Historical reasoning: Conceptualizations and educational applications. In S. Metzger, & L. McArthur Harris (Eds.), *International handbook of history teaching and learning* (pp. 149–176). Wiley-Blackwell.
Van Boxtel, C. A. M., Voet, M., & Stoel, G. L. (2021). Inquiry learning in history. In C. A. Chinn, & R. Golan Duncan (Eds.), *International handbook of inquiry and learning* (pp. 296–310). Routledge.

Van der Heijden, M., Schmidt, A., & Vermeesch, G. (2021). Illegitimate parenthood in early modern Europe. *The History of the Family, 26*(1), 1–10. https://doi.org/10.1080/1081602X.2020.1853586

Van Straaten, D., Wilschut, A., & Oostdam, R. (2016). Making history relevant to students by connecting past, present and future: A framework for research. *Journal of Curriculum Studies, 48*(4), 479–502. https://doi.org/10.1080/00220272.2015.1089938

Wansink, B., De Graaf, B., & Berghuis, E. (2021). Teaching under attack: The dilemmas, goals, and practices of upper-elementary school teachers when dealing with terrorism in class. *Theory & Research in Social Education, 49*(4), 489–509. https://doi.org/10.1080/00933104.2021.1920523

Wilke, M., Depaepe, F., Van Nieuwenhuyse, K. (2019). Teaching about historical agency. An intervention study examining changes in students' understanding and perception of agency in past and present. *International Journal of Research on History Didactics, History Education, and Historical Culture, 5*(1), 53–80.

Williams, S. (2018). *Unmarried motherhood in the metropolis, 1700–1850*. Palgrave Macmillan. https://doi.org/10.1007/978-3-319-73320-3_4

Woodbridge, L. (2001). *Vagrancy, homelessness, and English Renaissance literature*. University of Illinois Press.

Wylie, G., & McRedmond, P. (2010). *Human trafficking in Europe. Character, causes and consequences*. Palgrave Macmillan.

Digital resources

Bigman, F. (2016). 'Fallen Women' at the Foundling Museum www.historyworkshop.org.uk/fallen-women-at-the-foundling-museum/ and www.youtube.com/watch?v=04T3nG55ysA

Book talks: Waves of global terrorism with David C. Rapoport (2022). https://podcast.app/book-talks-waves-of-global-terrorism-with-david-c-rapoport-e312274153/

Colonies of Benevolence, video 'The 7 colonies of Benevolence'. https://www.kolonienvanweldadigheid.eu/en/movie-7-colonies-benevolence

European Council, The EU's response to terrorism. https://www.consilium.europa.eu/en/policies/fight-against-terrorism/

Magdalen Asylum in Northern Ireland. www.history.com/news/magdalene-laundry-ireland-asylum-abuse and www.history.com/news/magdalene-laundry-ireland-asylum-abuse

The Code of Hammurabi. https://avalon.law.yale.edu/ancient/hamframe.asp; https://manyheadedmonster.com/2013/07/22/david-hitchcock-why-history-from-below-matters-more-than-ever/

The National Archives, 1834 Poor Law. www.nationalarchives.gov.uk/education/resources/1834-poor-law/

9/11 Memorial & Museum, www.911memorial.org/

13
WOMEN, GENDER, AND THE FIGHT FOR GENDER EQUALITY IN EUROPE

Ingmarie Danielsson Malmros Marianne Sjöland

Theoretical perspectives

Concepts like gender, sexuality, and family relations are closely connected to constructions of identities and meaning. This approach was not common either in traditional women's history or in history education before the last three decades. The introduction of the concept historical consciousness in history didactic theory has created new prerequisites for relating gender history to history education. Historical consciousness is an ability that each human being is gifted with, and it is fundamental for interpreting historical experiences for the purpose of orientating in time and life (Jeisman, 1980; Rüsen, 2005). An aspect of this is that history is formed both by scientific history and individuals' sense-making questions to the past.

Historical consciousness is not easy to operationalize in an actual teaching situation. Nonetheless, the concept is highly present when teachers select historical content and methods. From an existential perspective, which history content is the most urgent one for the students? Which history knowledge is essential for students as citizens? What interests them? Those questions generate different answers in different social, economic, and not least historical-cultural contexts. Regardless which choice is made as a teacher or a student, it always means a kind of deselection. In a historical perspective, this has usually meant excluding women, children, indigenes, and poor people, in other words, people with a lack of power. This chapter focuses on gender history in the aforementioned aspects and with an intersectional approach.

This text offers starting points that could be useful for teachers working with gender history. The first is to avoid using the term 'women's history.' It can result in women and their roles as historical agents being seen as an addendum rather than an integral and natural part of all the studied change processes. It can, of course, be appropriate to look in detail at women as agents (Wiesner & Willoughby, 2018).

DOI: 10.4324/9781003289470-16

Naturally, women have a place in history education. However, new perspectives are needed in order to understand the driving forces of history. Therefore, the approach in this chapter is aligned with the historiography of today (Meade & Wiesner, 2021). For example, when we discuss power, sexuality, and the capacity of various individuals to act from a gender perspective, it is important to point out to students that these are always relational constructions; changes in women's power and influence should be understood in relation to men's power. Therefore, the concepts *power* and *power structures* are crucial for analyzing and understanding gender history.

It is also important for students to comprehend that history cannot be interpreted in terms of simple relationships between men and women. The struggle for justice and equality has created various power correlations throughout history, including many cases where poor people have come together to challenge wealthy men and women. Understanding such movements involves always putting agents and groups in context in the power hierarchy that is present in each situation. Understanding history from an *intersectional* perspective makes it easier for students to consider that these movements involve various interests and different forms of injustice, vulnerability, and fighting spirit (Crenshaw, 1989). An intersectional approach also helps to problematize a simplified version of history and, thus, understand how someone can maintain power in one situation but lack it in another.

An agent's position within the power hierarchy is determined by the underlying economic, legal, and ideological structures. The latter can include both political and religious ideas as well as inherent doctrines that steer how individuals understand their reality and how they ought to live and act. Individual agents existing within these structures are influenced by them, but individuals also challenge structures. A reciprocal view of the concepts *agency* and *structure* is important for understanding the view of history presented in this chapter. Students need to understand the limitations that these structures have placed on the agents' possibilities to affect a situation at a given time in a specific society.

Furthermore, it is important to discuss how language influences our understanding of people's thoughts throughout history. Students need to comprehend how different concepts have been used with different meanings in different historical contexts, as well as how the meaning of a concept can change and lead to new visions and utopias (Koselleck, 2002). The concept *historical empathy* can be a helpful tool to understand agents' actions in relation to the society they lived in, which is probably significantly different from the students' own (Wiesner & Willoughby, 2018). Historical empathy can be both the most complicated and important concept to apply – complicated because becoming familiar with the diverseness within history is a demanding work and important because it can ultimately lead to a deeper historical understanding that we all interact in and are influenced by a context formed by history (Van Sledright, 2001). With such insight, it can be easier to teach students that many historical perspectives are characterized by either continuity or very gradual changes. Historians usually analyze changes in terms of cause and consequence. Phenomena that remain largely unchanged are given less attention. A blinkered focus on changes hampers historical understanding in two ways. First, gender history becomes a success story, starting gloomy and, thanks to present-day changes, resulting in an almost total gender equality. Second, students will then struggle to understand why we are still experiencing gender inequality. The mechanisms and structures holding society back from becoming more equal become invisible when we only focus on the changes. There is a risk that students' understanding of history gets caught up in one-dimensional accounts in which differences, nuances, and discontinuities disappear. Focusing on changes also creates a clear-cut interpretation in which women's victories and influences in previous eras are hidden. One of the ambitions of this chapter is to problematize such one-dimensional accounts.

The concepts *continuity*, *change*, *agent*, and *structure* are closely connected to the purpose of understanding and discussing what has happened in the past, that is, gaining knowledge. In historical didactic theory, this approach to teaching history is called a genetic perspective – you understand present processes and events by turning to the past with questions for scientific or educational reasons. The concept *historical empathy* concerns another aspect of history, namely the existential one. When students are confronted with gender history, it can awaken thoughts and questions about identification and emancipation rather than inquiries about what really happened in the past. This *genealogic perspective* highlights the subjective elements in people's needs and constructions of the past (Karlsson, 2020).

Finally, this chapter contains several dives into history meant to enable students to recognize continuities and change processes over time. However, we have absolutely no intention to cover large parts of gender history, and the global perspective is not represented either. Instead, our ambition is to point out important changes and slow continuous processes that are sometimes relevant in large parts of Europe and sometimes relevant only in a limited area. As described above, concepts provide a starting point for the students' understanding of history and can be the glue keeping the different themes, epochs, and geographical areas together.

Field of research

A text on gender history must start with a reference to Joan Wallach Scott's important article "Gender: A Useful Category of Historical Analysis" (Scott, 1986). This paper came to be a pioneering work since Scott applied a gender perspective on history which offered a changed view and understanding of the past.

Most of the recent academic literature on gender history has a global synthetical perspective focusing on worldwide inequalities. An important work in the field is *A Companion to Global Gender History* (Meade & Wiesner, 2021). It contains both thematic and conceptual overviews in addition to more traditional chronological chapters. The work offers two key points: to avoid generalization about gender and to put an intersectional perspective on gender issues. The authors provide evidence for both fluidity and rigidity in gender structures, which we also discuss in the present text.

Another work with a global perspective is *Gender: A World History* (Kent, 2021). The significant contribution of this text is that gender is interpreted in a context of history of ideas and strictly connected to existential questions and construction of meaning. Like us, the author emphasizes that ideas about gender are always constructed in a context and rooted in power relationships.

Wiesner-Hanks, together with Urmi Engineer Willoughby, has also written *A Primer for Teaching Women, Gender & Sexuality in World History* (Wiesner & Willoughby, 2018). This is a guide for teaching gender history in college and senior high school, focusing on how to design and develop courses. In the last chapters, the authors discuss challenges and opportunities, including historical empathy, which they present as means to help students handle different ethical and historical contexts.

In contrast to the works above, *Gender: Antiquity and its Legacy*, by Brooke Holmes (2012), discusses a single epoch, namely classical antiquity. One important approach in this work is the conceptual history. Holmes points out that research on the antiquity has contributed to the development of gender as a category of analysis. Another important perspective is that the present-day gender debate must be understood in light of the past, what in this text is defined as a genealogical perspective on history.

Prehistory

In the past few decades, researchers have published theories about the emergence of patriarchal structures, which throughout history have shaped and still shape our society today. Previous research has claimed that these structures were a result of social changes that occurred in the transition from hunter-gatherer societies to agricultural societies about 12,000 years ago. When the surplus that people could gather started increasing, so too did the need to control how this surplus was distributed across generations (Stearns, 2015). As men demanded more control over the passing on of possessions and power, this also led to them taking control over the lives of women in general and their sexuality in particular. On the other hand, more recent research has emphasized that these processes have varied greatly in different areas and that the structure of gender relations has been much more multifaceted than was previously thought. Nonetheless, there is still relative agreement that the Neolithic period brought a change in how work was divided between the sexes and that this led to shifts in status, the emergence of new rituals, and an increased struggle for power and prestige. In the long term, this resulted in an institutionalization of asymmetrical power relationships in general (Knutsson, 2017). Therefore, the concept of intersectionality is significant for analyzing prehistoric cultures as well. How gender relations were influenced is unclear and much debated, but the fact remains that *patriarchal* systems emerged around the world during this time. However, due to the unavailability of sources, the cause and effect in these change processes is harder to prove.

Ancient societies

The view of gender roles and gender relations changed during the end of the 5th century BC. During this period, it became more important to differentiate between male and female behaviour, which resulted in limiting women's freedom of movement (Dirke, 2018). The image of the ideal man also changed from the Dionysian emotional expressiveness to the more Apollonian restraint. It may also be worth introducing the poet Sappho and her importance as a symbol of lesbian love. However, there is a lack of sources about Sappho's life and love life (Wiesner, 2011). To what extent are the accounts about her an embodiment of subsequent exotification and sexual fantasies or, in more recent times, an understandable need from the LGBTI community to embrace historical figures who seem relevant from an identity perspective? There is a fine line between avoiding anachronisms and depriving people of important opportunities for historical identification. We believe that the solution is to initiate this type of discussion with the students. What do we gain and lose by highlighting different historical content? How can we understand the different values and norms that were prevalent during different periods? Again, this is related to the central discussion about the main purpose of the subject of history.

However, it is important to avoid getting caught up in anachronistic narratives based on the contemporary view that sexuality is part of a person's identity (Olaison, 2018). Instead, it is vital to highlight for students that sexual expression was regarded as unique or repeated actions that may or may not have been categorized as sin in relation to a religious, social, or cultural system of rules. This view could lend itself to a discussion about historical empathy and how this concept differs from the everyday definitions of 'empathy' and 'sympathy'. How can we comprehend how people from earlier times have looked at existential questions? How can we make sure that the teaching of history has relevance when our starting point is present-day issues, without assigning our contemporary mindset to people from the past?

Another perspective that is important to raise is the continuous impact of the Abrahamic religions on gender relations in Europe. Judaism, Christianity, and Islam are based on the views of the world, human beings, and ethical rules depicted in the narratives of the Old Testament, and these views have great influence on gender constructions and social relations on many levels. European societies have developed under a strong influence from Christianity in particular, but Judaism and Islam have also influenced European societies and ways of thinking at different times. Teachers usually focus on the characteristics of the religions and the differences between them, but it is also important to show the major similarities between the religions in terms of views about gender relations, sexuality, and allocation of power between the sexes.

Middle Ages to 1700s

Christianity and the church as an institution remained the most important elements in the history of Europe during this period. The church shaped the view of the family and what was considered male and female. These views did not change significantly during the Middle Ages and the Early Modern Age, but there were changes in the views on marriage and family which affected gender roles. Until the 1500s, the church had decreed that marriage was only binding if there was an agreement between the spouses, although many parents did influence their child's choice of husband or wife. At the same time, an opinion started to form amongst priests that marriage was a holy covenant with God, which made matrimonies hard to dissolve and premarital relations illegal (Wiesner, 2011). How strictly these rules were observed depended on where in Europe a person lived.

Most women in the Middle Ages and Early Modern Age had limited influence over their own lives, but some women could at certain times gain greater power and authority and thereby greater freedom. This generally happened during times of war when men were gone for long periods of time or once the women became widows. The historian Dick Harrison states that queens and noblewomen in the Nordic countries during the late Middle Ages had greater influence than women in similar roles in the 1700s and 1800s. In particular, he points out Queen Margaret of Denmark, Norway, and Sweden and the Norwegian-Swedish duchess Ingeborg, who was active in politics at the national and county level (Harrison, 2010). Margaret was never given the title of queen in her lifetime because it was synonymous with being the wife of the king, not a female regent. Instead, she was proclaimed Margaret 'Sovereign Lady and Rightful Ruler' as the widow of the Norwegian king. This example may be interesting to study from a conceptual perspective, possibly by examining the titles men and women got, how titles could reinforce or challenge the gender order, and how they changed over time. Queens who reigned 200 to 300 hundred years after Margaret bore the title of queen.

A new economic system was introduced around the 11th century, namely merchant capitalism. In contrast to the feudal economy, this system was based on money. This change led to the rise of the bourgeoisie, with a new range of professions for men, such as doctors and lawyers. Women were not allowed into any of these professions, which meant that the power and public offices that women in the upper classes of society could hold during the Middle Ages disappeared along with feudalism. During the Renaissance, kings and court administrators appointed male public officials from the bourgeoisie based on their qualifications rather than through inherited rights as was done in the Middles Ages. Therefore, the ability of women in the aristocracy to exercise power also disappeared, and their primary role during the Renaissance was that of wife or mistress. Of course, some women could gain political power indirectly through their husbands, but in public life, this possibility was greatly restricted.

However, the majority of women lived under completely different conditions in which family care and gathering food were the most important duties. The latter could provide a certain margin for manoeuvres and influence for women in the lower classes. Women's responsibility for food supplies meant that they had to leave their homes regularly to go to markets where they could bargain and protest collectively about high bread prices. Rioting was not unusual but rarely led to punishment because the actions of the women were seen as a way to take responsibility for the family's survival (Blom et al., 2006). Highlighting the common forces that drove women to action during different periods and adding a class perspective can help students to understand what struggles could lead to.

What was considered as male and female was also affected by other materiality, such as long-distance trade, which involved transportation of valuable and heavy goods over long distances from Europe to Asia and vice versa. Because women did not generally produce goods for trade or work far from home, it was unthinkable that they would engage in long-distance trading. Again, we see a gender divide in society into a public sphere for men and a private sphere for women. As we have seen, the divide can be traced back to Prehistoric and Ancient societies.

In the 16th and 17th centuries, manufacture took place in the form of cottage industries, but during the 18th century paid labour in newly built factories became more common. As capitalism gained ground, corporations and guilds were developed in order to increase the skills of craftspeople and to reduce competition. The members of the corporations were almost exclusively men even though many women worked in the textiles industry. A woman's wage was roughly half of a man's wage (Wiesner, 2011). Industrialization did not lead to any fundamental changes in gender roles even though the process in itself is considered one of the most crucial in the history of humankind. Thus, there is a clear link between gender and division of work, which even today sustains the differences in status between what is seen as typical professions for men and women.

The arena where women were most active was the home, but there were boundaries there as well for what they could do. The husband was the guardian of his wife's and children's lives, but neighbours and relatives could also exert some control. Women who were considered to have broken norms and rules were frequently the subject of rumours, prosecution, and punishment, which was documented by the church or the legal system (Blom et al., 2006). Extensive witch hunts are an example of how such rumours could have terrible consequences for individual women and, in parts of Europe, for individual men, too. The witch hunts began in several places in Europe during the 1450s, but they reached their height at the end of the 1500s and early 1600s. Both the Roman and Protestant churches spread ideas about women's complicity with the devil, but the persecution was especially prominent in the Protestant northern and central Europe (Wiesner, 2011).

The 1700s and the Enlightenment

In the Western accounts of history, the Age of Enlightenment, the French Revolution, and the American Revolution all stand for reason, liberty, and the fight for human rights. These movements shook the political order as well as the balance between the sexes. Within the general hope for achieving justice and putting an end to the old aristocratic structures, there was also a hope and demand for justice for women. It was a time of change in which traditional and modern thought competed and hopes for peace coincided with hate and warmongering. There was a bitter struggle about the term citizen: about who would be accepted and what would be included in the rights of citizens.

During the Age of Enlightenment, the old autocracy and religious society were criticized. There was a growing belief that human reason, rather than the divine will, should guide society and development. The Enlightenment promoted thoughts about individuality and accompanying rights for life, freedom, and property. Notably, in the beginning, these ideas circulated within a very limited group of people in western Europe. As we have already seen, the effect of the changes should be considered from the perspective of class and estate.

Many of the political and philosophical texts that were written during this time addressed the hierarchy and relationship between the sexes as well as what characterized being male and female. Despite the reason-based approach, there were varying thoughts about what women could do and what role they should adopt. Progressive thoughts about complete equality shared space with opinions that a woman was a different type of human with other duties in society. Thus, the male and female roles cemented in ancient and early modern societies persisted but were being challenged. By applying historical empathy and an intersectional perspective, students can try to understand how opinions about gender roles that we would identify as old-fashioned and irrational could share space with the ideas that we now embrace.

The divisions between individual and political rights as well as between male and female had influence on the interpretation and implementation of the Declaration of the Rights of Man and of the Citizen from 1789 and the new constitution from 1791. The active citizen, understood to be a tax-paying man, held both political and individual rights, whereas the passive citizen, who is any woman, child, or man who did not pay tax, only held the rights for individuals. Thus, the idea of gender became entwined with citizenship (Blom et al., 2006).

The British writer and philosopher Mary Wollstonecraft had an impact on contemporary discourse with her progressive texts, for example, *A Vindication of the Rights of Women* (Wollstonecraft, 2008 [1792])where Wollstonecraft demanded the same rights for women and men. In contrast to Rousseau, she believed that boys and girls should be raised the same way. Alongside these progressive ideas, Wollstonecraft defined a woman's place as in the home (Tomaselli, 2007). She thus combined clear ideals of gender equality with ideas that seem outmoded nowadays. Interestingly, Wollstonecraft connected women's situation to that of the working classes and believed that both faced the same powerlessness.

Between 1790 and 1793, there were several reforms that reinforced a woman's legal position within the family and marriage, making it possible to get divorced and have a civil wedding ceremony. Accordingly, this period could be seen as a success for equality for certain groups of women. However, in 1793, there were tensions between various groups of women with different interests. Issues such as hunger and food were more pressing than the fight for rights for certain women (Desan, 2007).

The Napoleonic Code (or Civil Code), which was established in 1804 after Napoleon came to power, eliminated feudal privileges. Women also lost their remaining rights, which were initially brought about by the revolution. The Code reverted to Roman law in which women were seen as minors and without rights outside of the family. The main principle was that it was the man's duty to protect the woman and the woman's duty to obey the man (Blom et al., 2006).

Despite how it ended, the French Revolution had created the possibility to understand and grasp the relationship between men and women in a different way than the patriarchal way. Women had taken part in the revolution as citizens. They did not hold the right to take part in the public sphere, so they demanded it. History students can see this if they use the concepts *continuity* and *change*.

1800s and 1900s

The 19th century in Europe was a time when living conditions changed radically for many groups of the population. Thoughts that had emerged in the intellectual circles of the Enlightenment during the 1700s now spread to a wider segment of the population. A large population increase in northern Europe, along with the redistribution of lands through land reforms, forced people into seeking a living in industries within cities, mills, or on the other side of the Atlantic. This migration affected previous gender contracts concerning work duties, family dynamics, and the balance of power. The relocation of people on what was previously an unthinkable scale was now possible thanks to new modes of transportation. For many people, the rural social unit of production, consumption, and socialization was replaced by a life in which work and education took place outside of the home. All of this led to exchanges of culture and views, which shattered the old ways of thinking in various ways.

The 1800s were the golden age of the bourgeoisie, which also affected gender relations. The view of the public man and the private woman was spread to larger groups within the growing middle class. Based on this view, the husband should provide for and represent the family in society while the virtuous wife should take care of the family and home, away from the public gaze. Although this is a description of the gender roles in a new class in society, we still recognize the divide into a public male sphere and a private female sphere. A patriarchal, bourgeois intellectual construct emerged where the family was organized as a microcosm mirroring the macrocosm of society. The healthy, fertile body of a woman also came to represent the middle-class woman and contrasted with the licentious, immoral upper-class and lower-class woman. Both the nobility and the working class become emblems of a threatening immorality that could jeopardize the order of society (Larsson, 2018; Rydström & Tjeder, 2013).

Another archetypal 19th century woman was the worn-out factory worker providing cheap labour in the expanding industrial society. Working-class women had, of course, always worked and supported themselves and their families in various ways, but during the industrialization and urbanization of the 1800s, they became a more visible category in society. The rules governing marriage and childbirth, which were rigid for middle-class women, were reinterpreted by working-class women. For example, many working-class women in Sweden rejected marriage because, until 1874, a husband had the wife's income at his disposal and was, until 1921, also her guardian. Instead, some men and women lived (and had children) as cohabitants, and the women could thus maintain a certain amount of freedom. This was referred to as 'Stockholm marriage' (*Stockholmsäktenskap*) because more than 40% of the children born in Stockholm during the 1840s were 'illegitimate' (Ohlander & Strömberg, 2002).

Despite their presence in the labour force, women were excluded from the growing labour movement at the time. The first Social Democrats and labour unions prioritized better conditions for men and viewed women workers almost as a threat that caused wage cutting. Low wages for women were a reality not only in the 1700s, during the first stage of industrialization, but also during the 1800s. The working-class man's goal was to copy the middle-class family model and strive for a wage that was enough to support the whole family. This was often impossible, until the middle of the 1900s, and the wife's sub-contracting, childminding, and taking in lodgers was necessary to make the family's finances work. It was not until the early part of the 1900s that women's demands were heard within the labour movement. As recently as the economic crisis of the 1930s, women were being fired with the approval of the labour movement to improve the job market for men (Charpentier Ljungqvist, 2012; Blom et al., 2006).

The women's movement was much more of an international effort than what is often portrayed in literature. Looking at democratization from an overtly Eurocentric perspective can obscure the fact that the first countries in the world to give women the vote were New Zealand in 1893 and Australia in 1902 (Wiesner, 2011). Notably, from an intersectional perspective, the indigenous people in Australia, both men and women, did not get the right to vote until 1962. An important milestone for the women's movement was the Seneca Falls Convention in America in 1848, which can be seen as the beginning of modern feminism. Those who were involved in this movement, like the Quakers Elisabeth Cady Stanton and Lucretia Mott, were often also abolitionists (Svanström, 2017; Blom et al., 2006). This shows how various movements supporting equality for all were intertwined and, in most cases, boosted each other. Women's struggle for equal voting rights eventually achieved results after World War I in northern Europe and the United Kingdom and after World War II in southern Europe. The efforts of the British suffragettes paved the way for these changes in many respects. The most well-known figure was probably Emmeline Pankhurst. However, it took until 1928 for women in Britain to be granted equal voting rights. Traditionally, much of the focus on the women's rights movement has been on northern and western Europe. It is also important to point to the struggle conducted within the context of the Catholic Church, for example. In the Mediterranean countries, a difference feminism emerged in which supporters wanted better rights for women without challenging the influence of the church over family structures (Karlsson, 2017).

When teaching about 20th century Europe from a gender perspective, teachers cannot ignore the large influence that both world wars and non-democratic ideologies have exerted on the construction of gender for both men and women. For instance, appalling crimes against humanity, especially against women, took place during the Armenian genocide (1915–1917) in the Ottoman Empire during the Young Turks regime; thousands of Armenian women were raped, forced into marriages, murdered, and had their children taken away (Lundgren, 2009).

Conventional history teaching describes how women entered the job market because men were in the trenches during World War I. The war broke out at a time when the male role was under renegotiation. Many saw the war as a purification and a way to restore a forgotten masculinity. Of course, experiencing the horrors of war caused these ideas to nosedive, and instead, a whole generation of European men were traumatized by their experiences during the war (Englund, 1996). This was also a time when the modern, independent woman started to enter public life.

Nonetheless, women's progress on the labour market did not become permanent because the Great Depression in the 1930s generated massive unemployment, even though female coded professions did not suffered from the same high rate of unemployment as male coded professions (Berggren & Greiff, 2009). Nazism and fascism also emerged in this context, and they greatly affected conditions for men and women. These ideologies had a similar agenda in that they were about controlling all aspects of a person's behaviour, including in the bedroom. Women were encouraged to stay at home and have many children for the nation's sake. Even legislation was influenced in various ways to ensure that these gender roles were performed.

World War II affected civilians in a way that few wars had until then. Recent research has shown how badly mass rape affected women in Germany. According to the German historian Miriam Gebhardt (2017), estimates show that the number of German rape victims was approximately 860,000 women and that the crimes were committed by armies from both east and west. Similar crimes occurred across the whole war-torn world.

The Holocaust has an important place in European cultural history as well as in history teaching in schools. We believe that the Holocaust must also be examined from a gender perspective because its horrific short-term and long-term consequences have gender dimensions as well. Discussions about how the roles of perpetrator and victim can relate to gender constructions are important to bring up with the students. In addition, it is important for history teachers to actualize an intersectional perspective and show students how the Holocaust also affected those who did not fit the heteronormative mould or were considered as 'the other' in Nazi ideology (Kent, 2021).

On the other hand, World War II had positive effects for women in the long term because it, once again, allowed for women to have a working life. Of course, there was a crucial difference between the countries that were drawn into the war and those that were lucky enough to keep out of it, although men were on standby in the latter countries as well. There continued to be major differences, even after the war because countries that did not fight in the war had the economic resources to invest in various welfare reforms, which improved the position of women.

It was also at this time that the second wave of granting women the right to vote occurred in Europe. For instance, Italian women got the right to vote in 1946 and Greek women in 1952. Most countries overtaken by communism gave women the vote around this time, for example, Bulgaria in 1944 and Rumania in 1946. We believe it is important to draw students' attention to the late introduction of equal voting rights in Switzerland (in 1971) and Portugal (in 1976), as well as to discuss the reasons for the delay in the progress towards democracy and equality. In connection with this, it is important to point out to students that these victories should not be taken for granted and that even today there are various threats to democracy.

A hot topic regarding the post-war era has been the attitude towards family planning and abortion. After World War II, many European states changed their political agendas on these issues. Long continuities surrounding motherhood, family, and the role of women were challenged, which influenced legislation. For instance, abortion was first legalized in communist countries, but legalization gradually spread west of the Iron Curtain. These changes came to be associated with various discourses: in some countries, the discussions were about women's right to choose over their bodies, and in others, it was more about responsible motherhood and the unborn baby's social conditions (de Zordo et al., 2017).

In summary, gender issues are relevant to the subject of history as they affect the social conditions of all individuals, and the work to promote gender equality is a constant, ongoing process. In these respects, this chapter has shown crucial historical changes and continuities that have been influenced by the actions of particular individuals and groups as well as by the surrounding structures of society. Like the historical agents, the students are both a part of history and makers of it. They are agents who can have an impact on history through their opinions, values, and actions, which are in turn influenced by the students' present as well as the past.

References

Berggren, L., & Greiff, M. (2009). *En svensk historia från vikingatid till nutid*. 2nd ed. Lund: Studentlitteratur.

Blom, I., Sogner, S., & Rosenbeck, B. (2006). *Kvinnor i västvärlden från renässans till nutid: renässans, reformation och revolution* (1 uppl.) Stockholm: Liber.

Charpentier Ljungqvist, F. (2012). Klimat, missväxt och extremt väder 1830–1920. In B. Stråth (Ed.), *Nordstedts Sveriges historia 1830–1920*. Stockholm: Nordstedts.

Crenshaw, K. (1989). *Demarginalizating the intersection of race and sex. A black feminist critique of antidiscrimination doctrine, feminist theory and antiracist politics* (Vol. 1989, pp. 139–167). University of Chicago Legal Forum.

Desan, S. (2007). The politics of Intimacy: Marriage and citizenship in the French revolution. In S. Knott & B. Taylor (Eds.), *Women, gender and enlightenment* (pp. 630–648) Houndmills: Palgrave Macmillan.

De Zordo, S., Mishtal, J., & Anton, L. (Eds.). (2017). *A fragmented landscape: Abortion governance and protest logics in Europe*. New York, NY: Berghahn.

Dirke, K. (2018). Kön och känslor. Antika idéer om kvinnor och män. In L. Lennerhed (Ed.), *Från Sapfo till cyborg: idéer om kön och sexualitet i historien* (2nd ed., pp. 11–28). Hedemora: Gidlund.
Englund, P. (1996). *Brev från nollpunkten: historiska essäer.* Stockholm: Atlantis.
Gebhardt, M. (2017). *När soldaterna kom: våldtäkterna mot tyska kvinnor vid andra världskrigets slut.* Stockholm: Karneval förlag.
Harrison, D., & Eriksson, B. (2010). *Sveriges historia. Digerdöden, Kalmarunionen, heliga Birgitta och Vadstena kloster, bondeuppror, Stockholms blodbad, Gustav Vasa, Vasakungar, reformationen, Dackefejden, krig, skatter, riksdag] 1350–1600.* Stockholm: Norstedt.
Holmes, B. (2012). *Gender: Antiquity and its legacy.* London: I.B. Tauris.
Jeisman, K-E. (1980). Geschichtbewuβtsein. In K. Bergmann et al. (Eds.), *Handbuch der Geschichtsdidaktik* (pp. 42–44). Düsseldorf: Schwann.
Karlsson, B. (2017). Tre regioner ett hav. In Maria Sjöberg (Ed.), *En samtidig världshistoria* (2nd ed., pp. 766–791). Lund: Studentlitteratur.
Karlsson, K.-G. (2020). Lessons of history. An impossible equation? Towards new perspectives on historical learning. *The Historical Review, XVII,* 351–382.
Kent, S. K. (2021). *Gender: A world history.* New York, NY: Oxford University Press.
Knutsson, K. (2017). Jordbrukets framväxt. In M. Sjöberg (Ed.), *En samtidig världshistoria* (2nd ed., pp. 94–113). Lund: Studentlitteratur.
Koselleck, R. (2002). *The practice of conceptual history. Timing history, spacing concepts.* Stanford, CA: Stanford University Press.
Larsson, M. (2018). Om en kvinna som befunnits tillhöra genus masculinum: synen på kön, klass och sexualitet i 1800-talets medicin och kultur. In Lena Lennerhed (Ed.), *Från Sapfo till cyborg: idéer om kön och sexualitet i historien* (2 nd ed., pp. 109–134). Hedemora: Gidlund.
Lundgren, S. (2009). *I svärdets tid: det osmanska folkmordet på kristna minoriteter* (2nd ed.) Otalampi: Sahlgren.
Meade, T. A., & Wiesner, M. E. (red.) (2021). *A companion to gender history.* Malden, MA: Blackwell Publishing.
Ohlander, A., & Strömberg, U. (2002). *Tusen svenska kvinnoår: svensk kvinnohistoria från vikingatid till nutid.* 2nd ed. Stockholm: Prisma.
Olaison. N. (2018). Otukt är världens lön: kön och sexualitet i den kristna traditionen. In Lena Lennerhed (Ed.), *Från Sapfo till cyborg: idéer om kön och sexualitet i historien* (2nd ed., pp. 29–57). Hedemora: Gidlund.
Rüsen, J. (2005). *History: Narration, interpretation, orientation.* New York, NY: Berghahn Books.
Rydström, J., & Tjeder, D. (2013). *Kvinnor, män och alla andra: en svensk genushistoria.* 1st ed. Lund: Studentlitteratur.
Scott, J. W. (1986). Gender: A useful category of historical analysis. *The American Historical Review, 91*(5), 1053–1075. www.jstor.org/stable/1864376
Stearns, P. N. (2015). *Gender in world history.* 3rd ed. New York, NY: Routledge.
Svanström, Y. (2017). En ny världsordning. In M. Sjöberg (Ed.), *En samtidig världshistoria* (2nd ed., pp. 734–764). Lund: Studentlitteratur.
Tomaselli, S. (2007). Civilization, patriotism and enlightened histories of woman. In S. Knott & B. Taylor (Eds.), *Women, gender and enlightenment* (pp. 117–135). Houndmills: Palgrave Macmillan.
Van Sledright, B. (2001). From empathetic regards to self-understanding; Im positionality, empathy, and historical contextualizations. In O. L. Davis Jr., E. A. Yeager & S. J. Foster (Eds.), *Historical empathy and perspective taking in the social studies* (pp. 51–68). Lanham: Rowman & Littlefield

Wiesner, M. E. (2011). *Gender in history: Global perspectives*. 2nd ed. Oxford: Wiley-Blackwell.
Wiesner, M. E., & Willoughby, U. E. (2018). *A primer for teaching women, gender, and sexuality in world history: Ten design principles*. Durham, NC: Duke University Press.
Wollstonecraft, M. (2008 [1792]). *A vindication of the rights of women*. New York: Cosimo Classics.

Digital resources

https://archive.org/details/narrativesofsorc00wrig/page/108/mode/2up, (01–06–22)
https://blog.britishmuseum.org/suffragettes-and-the-british-museum/, (01–06–22)
https://chnm.gmu.edu/wwh/, (01–06–22)
https://eh.net/encyclopedia/women-workers-in-the-british-industrial-revolution/, (01–06–22)
https://historiana.eu/case-study/womens-voting-rights/search-equality#, (01–06–22)
https://history.hanover.edu/texts/wurz.html, (01–06–22)
https://worldhistorycommons.org/long-teaching-module-women-early-modern-world-1500–1800, (01–06–22)
www.bbc.com/news/magazine-16945901, (01–06–22)
www.bbc.com/news/world-42879161, (01–06–22)
www.nationalgeographic.com/science/article/prehistoric-female-hunter-discovery-upends-gender-role-assumptions, (01–06–22)
www.uft.org/teaching/classroom-resources/womens-history-curriculum-resources, (01–06–22)
www.worldhistory.org/article/927/women-in-ancient-greece/, (01–06–22)

14
TRAVEL STORIES AND TRAVELERS

Transdisciplinary approaches and proposals for a history of Europe

Beatrice Borghi and Rosa Smurra

Histories of transcontinental movements in the history of Europe

It was in the second half of the last century that a new historiographical paradigm was inaugurated that radically altered the traditional approach to political, cultural, and social history. Indeed, it was in 1949 when Fernand Braudel published the volume *La Méditerranée et le monde méditerranéen à l'époque de Philippe II*. The protagonist of the French historian's investigation is the Mediterranean, the subject and no longer solely the object of analysis, which passes under Braudel's lens over a long period of time, where the marriage of history and geography is fundamental for understanding the same social and cultural dynamics. It is a methodological approach that Lucio Gambi (1972) called "the historical values of environmental frameworks," i.e., the interaction between humans and nature, interpreted and revived by the Anglophone school by focusing on the dimension of individual histories of which David Abulafia (2013), Monique O'Connell and Eric Dursteler (2016) are spokespersons.

Mobility is the key to understanding human history, and many scholars have focused on migration flows in recent years. As mentioned by Ian Coller (2020), the French Revolution produced multiple outcomes in many ways and far beyond the territories occupied by Napoleonic troops; as well as other significant revolutionary frictions. The transnational approach and the use of biographical sources are the methodological choices of 19th-century historians such as Maurizio Isabella (2011), Konstantina Zanou (2018), Julia Clancy Smith (2013), and Michael Broers (2014) and are capable of constructing a "new thalassology" of the Mediterranean, which chronicles the impact of Mediterranean migrations on the construction of European identity (Guarracino, 2007).

It is now well established that voyages, conquests, and economic expansions are not a phenomenon of the Modern Age but have occurred over millennia.

DOI: 10.4324/9781003289470-17

Piracy and related forms of maritime violence, for example, are almost 3,000 years old: from the late Mediterranean Bronze Age to the eve of the 21st century. The phenomenon should therefore be studied from a long-term global and historical perspective, although the importance of specific historical factors should not be overlooked, as M. Bloch (1953) has pointed out. Piracy can also be studied from an economic perspective in the context of which market access is of paramount importance (Leeson, 2009).

Human history is a history of mobility, and the cipher of modernity and actuality is mobility itself (Clancy-Smith): studying it allows us to continue the reflections of one of the promoters of world history. Christopher Bayly (2019) recalls "the idea that there is some contradiction between the study of the social fragment or the powerless and the study of the great processes that have constructed modernity." In this sense, the teaching and learning of history today can only start from the recovery of the value of contamination between cultures, which means first and foremost rediscovering the roots of European identity for an education for peace and for active and democratic citizenship that is able to stimulate the younger generations to investigate and reflect on the present and guide them on how to work together as citizens for effective integration policies.

The routes of history: itineraries, routes, and cultures

From the very origin of travel in human history, roads – at first roadways – and routes represented, as they do today, the expression of man's great mobility and were the means that made possible the encounter of different cultures. Explorers, conquerors, merchants, refugees, bandits, corsairs, wayfarers, pilgrims, students, and the curious, with their movements and exchanges over millennia, have composed the varied and rich cultural mosaic of our continents; from that distant journey of humans from Africa, we will take a great journey through time in the footsteps of men and women who were able, with their testimonies, to forge the European identity, starting from the relationship between nomads and the sedentary and between the moment of invention and the moment of construction and preservation.

Among the routes of history, the focus is on the routes of faith, which were constituted on the ancient Roman roads and represented an articulated system that contemplated multiple possibilities of connection between the different routes, allowing the ideal link that enabled the "holy places" to be united to each other also on a more concretely itinerary level.

As is well known, the agricultural revolution coincided with the first and greatest global demographic transformation that established a close and indissoluble link between the increase of foodstuffs and population growth that implied new agricultural frontiers, new territories, and thus considerable transformations of the environment. Relations among humans fostered, mainly through trade, the spread of ideas, techniques, and goods. Indeed, thanks to trade, groups of humans colonized territories permanently and transmitted their knowledge to other human groups (e.g., the effects of trade in the Danube valley). The theme therefore would extend to the sea and trade routes, which in the second half of the 15th century expanded considerably. The most intense and important traffic of wide-ranging trade involved and connected the ports of Flanders and England to those of the Near East in a network involving major ports with ample receptive capacity and a considerable number of smaller ports of call, where, unlike the major ports of call, reception facilities were limited and services were mainly oriented to inland and local transport.

For many centuries it was the sea routes that conveyed the long-distance links, and there was no long-distance link that was not made through a sea route; and only exceptionally did the land ones have a dimension that holds up to comparison. It was on the trade routes, often coinciding with devotional routes and thus the ancient Roman road axes, that the encounter of humanity on the move began. These included the amber, silk, gold, and salt routes.

Sea travel and trade: production, transportation, markets, and stakeholders

The earth's surface is composed of about 30 percent land and 70 percent water, of which about 97 percent is ocean. The connection with this element of nature has been – and continues to be – fundamental to the survival of the human species. The sea has also been the main carrier of commerce for centuries: propelling a boat over water requires infinitely less energy than land transport. There is a wide assortment of vessels, and numerous trade routes have begun to emerge since prehistoric times. It is believed that the Egyptians were among the first Mediterranean civilizations to engage in river and sea transportation. The earliest boats were probably rafts made from papyrus reeds, while wooden boats are speculated to have been adopted during the Neolithic period (6,000 BCE), around the same time as the introduction of agriculture and animal husbandry.

The gradual development of increasingly large port infrastructures in various parts of Europe, Africa, and Asia meant that as early as the Hellenistic period (323–31 BCE), there was an entire network consisting of main ports (Ancient Coastal Settlements) intended for international trade (emporiums) and "secondary" facilities. Huge transformations in the scale and complexity of Roman maritime trade, and the associated infrastructure, occurred between the 3rd and 2nd centuries BCE. The economic, social, and cultural pattern that then developed in the Roman world created an unprecedented demand for consumption (Young Gary, 2001). The new needs triggered the development of new infrastructure and profound innovations in construction techniques, making it possible to create artificial harbors. Indeed, in the 2nd century BCE a major technological revolution took place: the introduction of hydraulic concrete enabled the construction of completely artificial harbors with imposing concrete piers; they could be located on open coasts that were not naturally protected.

Archaeological research on the coasts of northern Germany and southern Scandinavia has uncovered several dozen sites from the Viking Age (750–1050 CE) embedded in a supra-regional network of trade and communication in the North

Sea and Baltic Sea area. Numerous boat landing places have been identified. In written sources they are usually described as trading posts or market places. Significant finds of Arab silver coins, dated from the late 8th century onward, reflect the gradual growth of trade with the Arab world.

Beginning in the 11th century CE, strong urban growth and significant trade development is attested in Europe where Mediterranean ports become crucial to the economy. There is a major restructuring of equipped landings and ports of call that gradually enter a complex system linking production and market areas, providing a strong stimulus to the economy and investment. In this scenario an important role is played by the already mentioned Vikings, whom we can point to as the first European merchants and navigators who connected seas and oceans around the year 1000. However, it should be remembered that before that period, sources record Viking attacks (793) on monasteries such as Lindisfarne, on the coast of Northumberland in the British Isles, and St. Philibert, at the mouth of the Loire (799). History is also inextricably linked to maritime violence (Williams, 2000).

As already mentioned, from the 11th century there was a considerable growth in productive activity that was evident in the expansion of maritime trade (Simbula, 2009). The commercial success of Italian port cities, which were among the major beneficiaries of this expansion, produced not only prosperity but also more aggressive maritime strategies.

Improvements in technology in the 12th century enabled ships to make longer and more frequent voyages with longer sailing seasons, relying on the compass, nautical instruction books, and maps. In ancient times sailors used the position of the stars to know the location of places; instruments such as periples are also known, such as that of the Red Sea (1st century CE) describing navigation routes across that sea and, to some extent, across the Indian Ocean and the Persian Gulf. In the Middle Ages pilot books and nautical charts became more widespread.

This combination of factors and technological advances made both warships and cargo ships more effective. Competition for trade guided the naval policy of the so-called maritime republics and other geopolitical entities as well. The maritime economy and naval strength allowed Venice a thalassocracy that lasted several centuries during which the city was able to rely on a widespread distribution of trading bases and colonies; in addition, the Venetians knew how to adapt ships to specific missions.

The port system and trade network showed full structuring in the 14th century when the Mediterranean became a set of interconnected sea and land routes and, at the same time, was the shared setting of three distinct economic and cultural areas (West, East, Islam). The trading companies of the maritime republics of Genoa and Venice not only integrated the various networks of the Mediterranean but expanded them to the Atlantic and the North Sea.

The business records produced over a 50-year period (1380–1410) of activity by the companies of Prato merchant Francesco di Marco Datini highlight how Western and Southern Europe and the Near East were at that time already connected by established networks.

Fernand Braudel (1949) speaks of a "northern invasion" in the Mediterranean in referring to the Dutch and English who, beginning in the late 16th century, maintained control of the Mediterranean throughout the seventeenth century.

Although a base of livelihood and source of wealth, the sea is also perceived as a threat, so much so that numerous myths of sea monsters and sea gods have arisen. Every culture that has had contact with the sea has at least one sea monster in its mythological history. Shipwrecks testify to how real these fears were, and, on the other hand, underwater archaeology, crucial to the study of seafaring, shows how wrecked ships can enrich our knowledge of international contacts and networks developed among the various players in maritime trade in centuries past (Jowitt et al., 2020).

Among the threats, besides shipwrecks, piracy has never been absent. The presence in all the world's languages of the word 'pirate,' which derives from the Greek verb *peiràn* and means 'to assault,' testifies that piracy is a phenomenon as old as shipping itself and is recurrent in universal history (Braccesi, 2004). There are different types of piratical activities: an initial, though rather fluid, distinction can be made between privateers and pirates. A privateer can be defined as one who, provided with authorization from an official government, acts against enemy ships of the state he serves; a pirate, on the other hand, is one who assaults ships solely for his own interest and without legitimacy from monarchs, local governors, or other minor officials. But the blurry line between pirates and privateers could easily be crossed, and many acts of piracy were committed under false pretenses against non-enemies and in peacetime.

Maritime predation became very intense between 1620 and 1720, a period known as the Golden Age of Piracy. It took place mainly in the Caribbean and in the waters off the American colonies. The exploits of pirates inspired creation of many legendary figures and a genre of literature, including Robert Louis Stevenson's *Treasure Island* (1883) or Emilio Salgàri's *Pirates of Malaya* (1896).

Other terms have been used to refer to types of marauders of the sea: buccaneers and filibusters. In the Caribbean islands, buccaneers got this name from the boucan, a tool used to smoke meat. Although piracy declined dramatically in the 19th century, serious incidents occurred off the coast of Africa, particularly in Somalia, where in 2008 acts of piracy included the hijacking of ships belonging to different countries, which caused warships from different navies to intervene. In late 2008, the European Union organized Operation Atalanta for the freedom of navigation of merchant traffic and in particular for the transport of World Food Program humanitarian aid in Somalia and the Horn of Africa. The naval military operation, which has included among its objectives the fight against arms and drug trafficking, will end on December 31, 2022.

Travel and mirages: slavery of yesterday and today

Human history has long been, and unfortunately still is, a history of various forms of slavery. Although condemned by the Geneva Convention of 1926, it continues to exist in some countries. In particular, Article 1 (FedLex – Confederazione

Svizzera: https://www.fedlex.admin.ch/eli/cc/46/696_714_724/it) of the aforementioned Convention defines slavery as "the state or condition of an individual over whom the prerogatives of the right of ownership are exercised," while the slave trade includes:

> Any act of capturing, purchasing an individual for the purpose of reducing him or her to slavery; any act of purchasing a slave for the purpose of exchanging or selling him or her; any act of transferring for sale or by exchange a slave purchased for the purpose of being sold or exchanged, as well as, in general, any act of trading in or transporting slaves.

Wars, invasions, and colonization were among the main causes that fueled, in every different time and place on the planet, a profitable trade with slaves being the cheapest labor force. A journey that differs greatly from those analyzed so far in that it actually concerns a forced migration, that is, when people are compelled by force to leave their land of origin (Ceccatelli & Tirini, 2020).

Probably initiated with the sedentarization of man, and thus with the emergence of agriculture, slavery was present in the ancient Mesopotamian civilizations of the Assyrians, Sumerians, and Babylonians; in the Near Eastern civilizations of the Hittites and Hebrews; and in Egypt, India, and China. Indeed, slavery requires large lands to be exploited, economic surpluses, and high population density. It is because of these factors that it started from the Neolithic period and specifically about 11,000 years ago.

Slavery was not identical in every civilization; in some cases the slave had no rights and in others he or she was partially protected by law.

The phenomenon of slavery from the agricultural revolution to the present day is a practiced and accepted reality. Between the 16th and 20th centuries 12 million Africans, herded onto slave ships, many of whom died during the crossing, were deported to America as forced labor. In the 16th century, for the first time, Western civilization surpassed the Arab slave trade in export volume through the Atlantic slave trade of African slaves.

The spread of capitalism also moved through slave ships, which, with its many uses, played the role of transporting goods, men, and weapons; the vessels were, as they were called in the Igbo language, true "owba cococoo" (monstrous ships): places, therefore, of labor, confinement, trade, and plunder, of men who changed from slaves to submissive laborers and, through violence, forced subjects. Numerous were the revolts and mutinies.

As noted, slavery has existed as long as human history has existed. However, various forms of abolitionism were adopted over the centuries, i.e., movements aimed at abolishing slavery. In 1863, A. Lincoln issued the Emancipation Proclamation, which freed slaves held in the Confederate States.

Human history is a history of movement, and climate has been responsible for many of the profound transformations of the planet and human movements. During planetary migration, humans have extended and expanded natural frontiers;

they have, thanks to technological advances, explored the planet by plying seas and tracing pathways.

The peopling of the earth has involved continuous migrations. From the need for food, control of territory and conquest of other spaces, the desire to explore and the natural desire for adventure, and climate change humanity's journey began as early as 70,000 years ago when Homo sapiens successfully carried out a great planetary migration that reached and populated Eurasia from East Africa in a short time. All humans share a very high percentage of DNA that attests to the fact that we are all descendants of this group of African humans.

While humans traveled long distances, accomplishing the global migration that populated planet Earth, others continued to move daily within relatively small areas; many of these movements were linked to the changing seasons, the life cycle of plants, and to the very migrations of the animals on which humans fed.

Globalization is a very long process that has taken place over the last tens of thousands of years, from the earliest movements of the earliest human communities, constantly searching for resources to sustain themselves (Ambrosini, 2005). Although far less numerous and dense than today, they had to move to ever new areas in which to gather, hunt, and fish since they were still unable to produce their own food. Thus it was that from their areas of origin in East Africa they reached by groups the various continents, distributing themselves and placing themselves in all the habitable areas of the planet. They assumed from the climatic and environmental contexts those somatic differences that characterize the races, but which in reality have not changed the almost absolute identity of the human species, today confirmed by genetic investigations. It was in the horizons circumscribed by their rays of displacement the different linguistic strains arose and radiated.

Those millennia could be considered the times of separation since almost all the peoples who inhabited the different parts of the Earth were ignorant of the existence of the distant ones or at most had some legendary notion of it through those who initiated long-distance exchanges, assuming the function of mediators. One can thus designate those peoples who inhabited the hinge areas between continental contexts and who derived their livelihood precisely from the transportation and trade of products and raw materials of remote origin. Examples among the most recent include those peoples who between Asia and Europe activated the mythical routes of silk, spices, incense, and amber, which by overland tracks, river routes, and sea routes brought goods of distant origin to the extreme ends of Eurasia.

The climatic changes of the first centuries of the Vulgar Era, particularly the lowering of temperatures between the 5th and 6th centuries CE, certainly influenced the movements of peoples in northern and eastern Europe who precisely then broke through the Rhine/Danube front that bounded the Roman Empire to the northeast. In the five centuries between 800 and 1300 global temperatures averaged at least one degree higher than today. Just within this period – and especially from the 11th century onward – Europe's population increased to levels later reached only with the Industrial Revolution. The "warm Middle Ages" ended in the early 14th century with a sharp drop in temperatures (mini-glaciation) that was accompanied by famines and followed by extensive plague epidemics and consequent sharp population decline. The mini-glaciation had its coldest period in the 1600s and continued until 1850 with average temperatures of 2.5 to 3 degrees lower than today (Ashtor, 1982).

The sea is also the scene of several illicit trades. Since ancient times among the "merchandise" transported have appeared slaves. Homer refers to Phoenicians moving through Greek waters, between Libya, Ithaca, and Lemno, landing at ports to sell slaves and products of their metallurgy. For the Middle Ages we can mention, to limit ourselves to a very few examples, the flourishing slave market operated by Vikings, or that of 12th and 13th-century Spain, which traded Muslim slaves.

Of gigantic magnitude was the transatlantic slave trade that ran for more than 400 years (16th–19th centuries), involving millions of people mostly originating from the African coast, enslaved and deported to the Americas and the Caribbean islands (Curtin, 1969).

Speaking of the present-day Mediterranean, it must be remembered that it is a crossroads of the illicit drug trade. There are multiple trafficking streams: the two-way use of the Balkan route has recently been noted, which has seen an increased flow of drugs from Western Europe to Central and Southern Europe and Turkey.

Another truly global concern is migrant smuggling in which profit-seeking criminals take advantage of migrants willing to take risks in search of a better life when they cannot access legal channels of migration. It has been estimated that in 2020 alone, nearly 3,200 people lost their lives along global migration routes despite movement restrictions caused by the Covid-19 pandemic. Unfortunately, this is not an accurate figure since it is not possible to count the victims of the ghost shipwrecks, barges that sank of which it is not possible to document the number of victims.

A history of Europe: teaching objectives and skills for participatory citizenship education

In the field of historiography, in order to make full use of the acquisitions of analytical research and local insights, it is necessary to broaden the horizons and reflection to the main outcomes of human history by seeking to detect and compare the climatic and environmental characters that have influenced the population and migratory movements, the economic and social dynamics that have resulted, and the political relations that have developed from them, observing in different contexts the influences of natural disasters, health events, and technological evolutions as well, of course, as the manifestation of cultural aspects and artistic expressions. These are key themes of World History, a discipline recognized as such in the 1980s and geared toward learning about historical unfolding and the connections underlying the constitution of the international order and the interdependencies between economic, political, social, and diplomatic factors in different areas of the world.

An attitude that fully emphasizes the study of world history, based on two main approaches, is considered fundamental: on the one hand, integration (syncretism) through which historical processes are emphasized that enable the comparison and identification of relationships between different cultures, between communities around the world that reveal similarities and kinship; and on the other hand, difference (discrepancy), by which the variety and thus the peculiarities of different human experiences and social patterns are emphasized. In short, it involves recognizing, distinguishing, and comparing the constants and variants, the general and the particular aspects that connote the evolutions of human affairs in all areas of the world.

History is understood as a continuous succession of changes over time, proceeded by evolutionary or transformational processes through incessant transitions in which developments, phenomena, events, motivations and accidentalities, environmental and human factors, and contrasts and coincidences intertwine, collide, rebound, deform, disappear, and reappear. It is influenced by causal relations but also by randomness. They are enacted according to an unfolding that is sometimes foreseen and sometimes unpredictable. All this converges to form "conjunctures," in other words, those heterogeneous combinations of situations and facts which, precisely because of their internal complexity, are unrepeatable. Each period of history can be seen as the combination of a wide range of concomitant conditions, circumstances, factors, trends, and variations of remote, recent, or contemporary origin.

Recognizing that the reality in which we live is only one of a number of possible worlds, both with respect to the past and with respect to other contemporary and future societies, implies an awareness of the relative and provisional nature of civilizations. Social systems are complex and in motion; it is up to us to identify the conditions that favor or limit change or permanence (Borghi, 2016).

History becomes primarily the discovery of a pure otherness: at a given time, in a certain place, there were men and women who spoke a particular language, ate certain foods, inhabited and lived in certain dwellings, and were organized in given social forms, professing specific cults and religions; people and groups who have left us a heterogeneous heritage of experience and knowledge, as they contributed, as our ancestors, to shaping what we are today, influencing all aspects that affect us on a daily basis, from the tools and services we have to the communications and connections we use, from the words we use to the foods we eat.

Some transdisciplinary content: travel between devotion, curiosity, and necessity

In proposing the theme of "travel and travelers" over time and in order to better master the infinite variety of facts that concurred to such outcomes, we have identified some general aspects that in different historical periods have undergone remarkable transformations, such as the arrangements of peoples, their relationships with resources, and their cultural and religious references. These are useful overviews to introduce and then follow in continuity their more minute transformations through the chronological succession of the essential events that affected them. An initial summary review of such strands can indeed usefully outline the frames of subsequent diachronic profiles to be conducted at different scales of magnitude: planetary, continental, national, and territorial.

The main objectives of the approach by outcomes of history are to offer a critical approach to the phenomenon of travel considered decisive for the elaboration of European societies and to gain insight into the complex relationships existing between different cultures through an approach by outcomes of history.

Identifying the fundamental phenomena of travel in the history of humankind and its intertwining of economic, social, and cultural aspects thus defines the indicators that make it possible to define the characteristics of societies and compare them with others. Knowing the fundamental moments and processes of the European history of travel with glimpses into world history, also starting from personal and local history, offers the opportunity to expound historical knowledge by making connections and arguing one's own reflections and to develop education for democratic citizenship through critical and responsible behavior inspired by the values of freedom and solidarity at all levels of organized life (local, national, European, and world).

Among the skills we can mention those of attributing meaning to the main forms of the journey through history and comparing them with current aspects as the result of an ultra-millennial process; of understanding the relationships between historical events and processes by distinguishing between historical unfolding, micro-histories and sectorial or thematic histories, to grasp the relationships between local history and national, European, or world history; of using in a relevant way and essential key steps in periodization and temporal organizers.

Also of particular relevance is the understanding and use of the methodology of historical research and to know how to use historical sources of different types (e.g., visual, multimedia, and dedicated websites) to construct historical knowledge, making use of disciplinary sectoral vocabulary. Experiential activities that enable students to recognize the historical component in current migrations and other forms of travel by implementing comparisons, comparisons and grasping persistence, continuity and discontinuity, and the variety and historical development of the phenomenon of travel and travelers to identify relationships with European and world contexts and intertwining with environmental, demographic, and social variables.

Skills and competencies should be aimed, therefore, at recognizing the contexts that induced humanity to move by identifying the evolutions of travel and in the traces of the present (material and immaterial heritage), the phenomena, and evolutions of the hybridization of past histories and cultures (Baumann, 2003).

Among the themes that can be proposed in a secondary school context, that of pilgrimage is of great and significant relevance (Cardini, 1996); representation of a typical religious, cultural, social, and economic expression that did not concern only the Middle Ages nor only Christians, but that in that era and among those faithful involved women and men of all ages and social conditions on their way to the kingdom of heaven (Richard, 2002). The motives that drove them to face the countless hardships of pilgrimage can be summed up in that commitment of faith, that voluntary act toward a shrine, which is a deepening of one's existence; the religious dimension of a path of prayer and meditation; the personal desire to be *advevae et peregrini* in "adventure" toward God, toward that otherworldly goal that is the true homeland.

The earliest pilgrims are men who fade into myths and legends from the Bible to the *Odyssey* to the *Epic of Gilgamesh*, from the Dolmen to Stonehenge. These are journeys linked to places that are objects of devotion in order to make contact with natural centers and with illustrious personages; to celebrate precise events; to draw from them information about destiny; to hope for a recovery from an illness; to venerate sacred images, objects, parts of a body, or relics. The exodus from Egypt is the model for excellence of pilgrimage in both Jewish and Christian traditions in which Egypt was a symbol of sin and of slavery from which the pilgrim frees himself by turning toward the authentic homeland: the Promised Land that becomes a great occasion for equality and brotherhood among all the children of Israel and a recognition of Jewish identity.

Traveling in today's times with male and female students is not unlike what wayfarers once did along ancient roads or plying the seas. Reflecting on the reasons why one chooses to embark on a journey, reach a place, be received in a facility, what to bring on a journey, and what one actually needs means constantly recalling the similarities and differences between the past and the present. It means, first and foremost, having a cultural experience and, as recalled by UNESCO (Unesco – World Heritage Convention: https://whc.unesco.org/en/convention-text), understanding the nature of tangible and intangible heritage by assuming the responsibility of caring for it, protecting it, and enhancing it; that is, sharing the knowledge of our common history in order to build mutual respect and common dialogue among communities.

Another topical issue that brings us back to sea travel again is maritime violence that has been accepted and/or tolerated for much of history. The raiding mentality, present in many societies around the world, even served to justify maritime violence, for example by conferring religious sanction on it and elevating the social status of the perpetrators, at least when the victims of such violence were foreigners or outsiders. Only with the formation and development of states in classical antiquity did piracy become more clearly defined and fully condemned. During the late Roman Republic, particularly beginning with the Greek historian Polybius (c. 200–118 BCE), piracy came to be defined as a particularly despicable activity, distinct from both other forms of violent crime and acts of war. According to Cicero (106–43 BCE), who is associated with the expression "pirates are common enemies of mankind," they were a threat to the social and political order of civilization, and consequently did not deserve to be treated with respect or decency but to be exterminated. Piracy was defined as a crime against the laws of all men (natural law) and their suppression was, according to Cicero, an obligation for all states.

The idea of pirates as enemies of mankind weakened with the fall of the Roman Empire, and it had to wait until the 15th century with the rediscovery of Cicero's writings. During this period, which coincided with the beginning of European expansion, the condemnation of piracy as contrary to natural law re-emerged; this condemnation also served to justify imperial expansion. It was not until the mid-19th century, however, that the major European powers renounced piracy as a means of exercising power over the sea.

References

Abulafia D. (2013). *Il grande mare. Storia del Mediterraneo*. Mondadori.
Ambrosini M. (2005). *Sociologia delle migrazioni*. Il Mulino.
Ashtor E. (1982). *Storia economica e sociale del Vicino Oriente nel medioevo* (trad. it. Einaudi).
Baumann G. (2003). *L'enigma multiculturale. Stati, etnie, religioni*. Il Mulino.
Bloch M. (1953). Towards a comparative history of european societies. In F. C. Lane, & J. C. Riemersma (Eds.), *Enterprise and secular change: Readings in economic history* (pp. 494–521). Allen and Unwin.
Bono S. (2021). *Schiavi. Una storia mediterranea (XVI-XIX secolo)*. Il Mulino.
Borghi B. (2016). *La Storia. Indagare, apprendere, comunicare*. Pàtron.
Braccesi L. (Ed.). (2004). *La Pirateria nell'Adriatico antico*. L'Erma di Bretschneider.
Braudel F. (1949). *La Méditerranée et le monde mediterranée à l'époque de Philippe II*. Lib. A. Colin.
Broers M. (2014). *Europe under Napoleon*. Bloomsbury Publishing PLC.
Cardini F. (1996). *Il pellegrinaggio. Una dimensione della vita medievale*. Vecchiarelli.
Ceccatelli G., & Tirini S. (2020). *Atlante delle migrazioni. Dalle origini dell'uomo alle nuove pandemie*. Edizioni Clichy.
Ciardi, M. (Ed.). (2008). *Esplorazioni e viaggi scientifici nel Settecento*. Rizzoli.
Clancy-Smith J. A. (2011). *Mediterraneans: North Africa and Europe in an age of migration, C. 1800–1900*. University of California Press.
Clancy-Smith J. (2013). *The modern Middle East and North Africa: A history in document*. Oxford University Press.
Coller I. (2020). *Muslims and citizens: Islam, politics and the French revolution*. Yale University Press.
Curtin P. (1969). *The Atlantic slave trade: A census*. University of Wisconsin Press.
Gambi L. (1972). *I valori storici dei quadri ambientali* (pp. 3–57). Einaudi.
Griffo M., & Tagliaferri T. (Eds.). (2019). *From the history of the empire to world history the historiographical itinerary of Christopher A. Bayly*. FedOA-Press.
Guarracino S. (2007). *Mediterraneo. Immagini, storie e teorie da Omero a Braudel*. Mondadori.
Isabella M. (2011). *Risorgimento in esilio. L'internazionale liberale e l'età delle rivoluzioni*. Laterza.
Jowitt C., Lambert C., & Mentz S. (Eds.). (2020). *The Routledge companion to marine and maritime worlds 1400–1800*. 1st ed. Routledge.
Leeson P. T. (2009). *The invisible hook: The hidden economics of pirates*. Princeton University Press.
O' Connel M., R. Dursteler (2016). *The Mediterranean world: From the fall of rome to the rise of Napoleon*. Johns Hopkins University Press.
Richard J. (2002). *Il santo viaggio. Pellegrini e viaggiatori nel Medioevo*. Jouvence.
Simbula P. (2009). *I porti del Mediterraneo in età medievale*. Bruno Mondadori.
Williams G. (2000). *The Viking ship*. British Museum Press.

Young Gary K. (2001). *Rome's Eastern trade international commerce and imperial policy 31 BC – AD 305*. Routledge.
Zanou K. (2018). *Transnational patriotism in the mediterranean, 1800–1850*. Oxford University Press.

Digital resources

Ancient Coastal Settlements, Ports and Harbours: A catalogue of Ancient Ports. Link: www.ancientportsantiques.com/

Operation ATALANTA: Contributes significantly to the suppression of piracy, as well as the protection of the vessels of the World Food Programme (WFP), African Union Mission in Somalia (AMISOM) and other vulnerable shipping. Link: https://eunavfor.eu/

15
CHURCHES AND RELIGION IN EUROPE

Interdisciplinary methods and approaches for a European history

Filippo Galletti and Manuela Ghizzoni

Introduction

At the end of the year 2018 the Eurobarometer 90.4, aimed at analyzing the attitudes of Europeans toward biodiversity, awareness, and perceptions of customs and perceptions of antisemitism (European Commission, 2018), photographed the presence of religions in the European Union in this way: the majority religion was Christianity, practiced by 72.8 percent of the population (in turn divided into Catholic Christianity, 44.5 percent; Orthodox, 10.2 percent; Protestant, 9.9 percent; and other Christianity, 5 percent). The percentage of citizens who declared themselves non-religious or agnostic reached 17 percent of the consensus, while atheists were 9.3 percent. The population of Muslim faith stood at 2.1 percent; Hindu at 1 percent; Buddhist at 0.6 percent; and Jewish at 0.2 percent. Compared to these data, the Pew Research Center (2017), a think tank that conducts surveys and demographic research in the social sciences, estimated instead that Muslim adherents reached 4.9 percent of the population (about 26 million): a number destined to increase in the next three decades also as a result of the migration phenomenon, despite the Union's own initiatives to limit it by funding, for example, "inclusive education strategies" in Turkey (530 million euros) and "measures to support migration and border management" (30 million euros), again in Turkey, where an estimated 4 million refugees, mainly Syrians, are hosted (European Commission, 2021a). The aforementioned surveys were conducted in the countries of the European Union, thus excluding several territories whose population is for the most part Muslim or is otherwise characterized by a significant portion of the population following the precepts of Islam (e.g., Turkey, Kosovo, Bosnia and Herzegovina, Albania, Russia, Serbia, and Montenegro). It follows that the European continent possesses a truly remarkable and, above all, changing multiculturalism and spiritual/religious richness, since migrations of peoples – and this can

DOI: 10.4324/9781003289470-18

be observed even now with the terrible crisis in Ukraine from where more than 6 million people have fled and were promptly taken in by neighboring countries, especially in Poland (United Nations High Commissioner for Refugees, 2022) – are a constant in European history.

The different ratios of practiced or declared faiths, therefore, stem from the historical, social, economic, and demographic evolutions that have strongly contributed to shaping the material and immaterial identities and heritages of European countries and their common horizon. Understanding, studying, and analyzing these developments allow us to grasp in a diachronic and synchronic key trends, perspectives, and common elements, which lay the groundwork for enhancing an intercultural dialogue and strengthening appropriate paths for the formation of an active, responsible, and participated citizenship.

For this reason, in order to orient oneself among the challenges of the contemporary world and consciously design the key tools of global citizenship, the history of religions constitutes a relevant thematic area combining social, economic, institutional, and cultural history and can become an integrating background for genuine mutual collaboration among European and world citizens.

It is, however, a history that is not always peaceful. In the name of religion, as will be seen later, people have been killed and conflicts, even bloody ones, have been triggered, but this violent characteristic can be reshaped in the educational context of the 21st century. Studying religious conflicts, within the same community or the one toward "others," can be useful, as well as reflecting about the many similarities between faiths, to re-imagine the teaching of European history, to promote civic education and historical consciousness projected toward building an attainable future, to avoid the rise of new clashes, and to resolve conflicts through dialogue and participation.

But let us take one thing at a time

The history of religions has a very ancient origin. Although its understanding has sometimes been hindered by an inaccurate methodological approach and it was only in the Modern Age that it achieved the status of an autonomous academic discipline, as Filoramo, Giorda and Spineto (2020) recall, it is believed that the first historians of religions, albeit budding, were the ancient Greek historiographers such as Herodotus and Hecataeus of Miletus (Harrison, 2010). To them we owe the elaboration of the relativistic conception of religion, that is, they were the first to hold and put in writing that all religiosity is to be considered relative to the population under consideration and that therefore there is no universal and absolute religion. A more organic study of the system of religions was later addressed by Aristotle and his school.

The ancient Romans, on the other hand, wondered about the etymological signification of the term "religion," which, coming from the Latin *religio*, indicated a type of conduct in the face of certain realities (Fugier, 1963: 172–179; Lieberg, 1974). According to Cicero (De natura deorum, II, 28, 72), the word derived from the verb *relegere*, i.e., "to go over again" or "to reread," meaning a new and careful reflection on what concerns the worship of the gods. On the other hand, Lucretius (De rerum natura, I, 930) made *religio* originate from the root of *re-ligare*, to indicate "the ties that unite men to certain practices"– an explanation that was later also accepted by Lactantius (Divinae institutiones IV, 28), however with the meaning of "to bind oneself in regard to the gods." Considering the interpretations, it thus seems possible to link the origin of the lemma to the pair of terms *religere/relegere* understood as "to collect again," "to reread," "to scrupulously and conscientiously observe the performance of an act," and thus diligently perform the "religious act" (Filoramo, 2004).

As a result of these orientations, philosophical-religious analysis became more careful; religions began to be compared and anthropomorphic connotations removed from deity, resulting in traditional gods often being judged as lesser divine entities (Jordan, 1905; Schmidt, 1938; Bros, 1953; James, 2007).

Christianity willingly accepted the latter belief, which was capable of explaining and later offering the theological basis for combating pagan religions (Filoramo & Menozzi, 2002). The interpretations gradually perfected by Christian theologians of the late Antique Age and reaching into the Middle Ages were essentially traced back to two theories. The first, called "of plagiarism," predicted that the ancient pagans had intuited the religion revealed to Moses but, at the same time, had imitated it erroneously; the second, called "of divine condescension," considered that God had deliberately granted some pagan forms, since the ancients were not yet able to understand the authentic faith, but on the condition that paganism was then supplanted by Christianity.

Only in the 18th century, thanks mainly to missionary activity, was the horizon of observation broadened, allowing for more refined studies and insights. Giambattista Vico, for example, assumed the idea that the origin of mythology resided in human beings, who, in order to explain life, the universe, and natural phenomena, had recourse to imagination and tradition (Schaeffer, 2019). For thinkers of the Enlightenment, on the other hand, there was the belief that revealed religion (like Christianity, Islam, Judaism, and all religions) as originating from a common natural religion, that is, founded on human reason, later modified due to human weakness and the various interests of organized clergy. Still in the 18th century, again, David Hume (1757) held that monotheism was a later development than polytheism, which was considered a more backward form of religiosity.

In the first half of the 19th century, aided by the blossoming of numerous studies in philology, archaeology, and historiography in a modern key, the history of religions was able to count on valuable theoretical-scientific contributions and finally obtained the status of an autonomous discipline.

From this time, several currents ran through and continue to influence the history of religions, always connected to large-scale historiographical movements. The development of the "proto-Indo-European" theory was the basis for the reflections of Max Müller (1892) and Edward Burnett Tylor (1994), who identified a common primitive religion among Indo-Europeans along the lines of linguistic commonality among the various families of the population. The evolutionary strand continued to have its own following, which saw the history of religions as a path toward progress and marked by the stages of animism, polytheism, and, finally, monotheism. It was followed, then, by an ethnological approach, based not on a single evolutionary line but on "qualitatively different cultural-historical cycles" (Frobenius, 1898; Gräbner, 1905), which mostly indicated characteristics inherent in mentalities (Lévy-Bruhl, 1922). The sociological approach dominated the research of many Francophone scholars, such as Hubert and Mauss (1899) and Durkheim (1912). At the same time, the psychological studies of Rank (1909), Freud (1927), and Jung (1970) gave an important impetus to the interpretation of individual religions (Kerényi, 1951).

In sum, all these influential schools of thought have made it possible to delineate a reasonable concept of religion, and historiographic analysis shows that religions are ultimately inseparably intertwined with all aspects of human cultures, from political and social institutions to economic structures, from arts and techniques to customs; even individual peoples' views on nature, the environment, and history are closely related to religious conceptions.

For this reason, nowadays, on the one hand, the concept of religion is believed to be definable only within a historically determined cultural position and with reference to specified historical formations; on the other hand, methodological problems derived from the postmodern turn, combined with the ever-increasing sectoriality and specialization of scientific research, continue to pose some interesting problems of an interpretative nature (Alles, 2007; Antes et al., 2004; Whaling, 1985).

Specific narrative strands in the history of religions

In a recent survey conducted by the European Commission (2021b), published in Special Eurobarometer Number 508, just over half of European citizens (53 percent) identify with their religion or religious belief; 21 percent maintain a neutral stance; and 24 percent say they do not identify with their faith. Although there are numerous differences between countries – more than seven out of ten respondents in Cyprus (79 percent), Italy and Slovakia (both 74 percent), Bulgaria and Poland (both 72 percent), and Romania (71 percent) identify with their religion, while respondents in Sweden (19 percent), Luxembourg (26 percent), Denmark (27 percent), Germany (35 percent), Finland and Belgium (both 36 percent), and Ireland (37 percent) are less likely to do so – religion represents a significant cultural and identity value, which can be a fertile common ground for dialogue with a view to active and responsible citizenship.

Indeed, historical culture, as mentioned above, is basic to the achievement and continuous regeneration of the concepts of freedom, democracy, equality, and human dignity on which the value pact of European citizenship is based. Critical knowledge of events and the practice of the basic methodologies of historical research constitute a fundamental cultural and cognitive background for orienting oneself in the present with awareness and responsibility, for being free and autonomous in current and future choices, for fostering the broadest coexistence in respect for diversity, and for developing the critical capacities necessary to assume dialogue and confrontation as instruments of democratic exercise. In this context, knowledge of religious phenomena in a long-term historical perspective, in connection with the current religious and spiritual characteristics of Europe, can become a common ground for educating in intercultural dialogue and inclusiveness. The critical exercise of defining similarities and differences between cults and the different social and political contexts in which they are embedded – carried out over a very long time span and in a space of continental dimension – represents an opportunity to promote paths of education in active, responsible, and democratic citizenship.

Therefore, in the light of the most recent contributions of historiography and with the aim of designing the teaching of a collective European history, it is proposed to unravel religious phenomena through the critical narration of some specific themes: the spread of religions, the use of artistic manifestations to convey messages of faith, armed conflict (holy wars, jihad, and anti-Semitism), divisions (divergences and schisms) and, finally, the long road to the affirmation of the principle of full freedom of worship. We will refer, forcibly, to summary frameworks, which can be further deepened or declined according to specific educational objectives.

With regard to the first theme, the spread of religions, it should be remembered that religious sentiment is inherent in human beings; it has existed since individuals began to ask and then to try to answer the following questions, "who created us?" and "where do we go when we die?" In ancient times, polytheistic religions (from Greek: *polis* "much" and *theos* "god") were formed: that is, ancient civilizations believed in the existence of as many gods as there were "magical" and unknown aspects of the world around them; this was the religious horizon of the ancient Greeks and Romans, for example (Dillon, 2019).

Then, it was the turn of the great monotheistic religions (from the Greek *monos* "unique," meaning "believing in one God"), that is, from the oldest to the most recent, Judaism, Christianity, and Islam.

Space does not permit a detailed treatment of the development of the monotheistic religions here, however, it is worth mentioning, consistent with the inspiring principles of this volume, some points of contact between the Abrahamic faiths.

Already this adjective denotes a common characteristic, namely a spiritual relationship with Abraham (Stroumsa, 2011). He was, in fact, the first man to believe in one creator, judge, omnipotent, unknowable, and eternal God. Religious experience is based on divine revelation: it is God who makes himself known and manifests himself to mankind through the prophets, those who receive revelation and have the task of spreading it among the nations. The three faiths, therefore, have a significant prophetic tradition: Abraham about 4000 years ago made a covenant with God, later renewed around 1250 B.C. with all the Jewish people (Levenson, 2012); 753 years after the founding of Rome, in Bethlehem, Jesus, the son of God, was born, who preached God's love for mankind until his death and gathered a number of followers around him (Freeman, 2009; Ehrman, 2015). Finally, in the first half of the 7th century, a merchant named Muhammad was chosen by Allah to pass on his revelations and convert the then polytheistic Arab people to monotheism (Donner, 2010). The three religions were formed in a geographically and culturally bounded space: the eastern Mediterranean and the Near East. The Arabian Peninsula, although not directly facing the Mediterranean Sea, was part of the late ancient oine and was a participant in the economic and cultural exchanges of the area; in fact, numerous communities of Christian Jews had settled in Arab cities and, probably, it was also thanks to these mutual influences that the new monotheism developed (Crone, 2015, 2016), which, among other things, counts Jesus as a prophet of Allah and Ishmael, son of Abraham, as the progenitor of the Arabs. The city of Jerusalem plays a most significant role for the three faiths. It is considered a holy city for Judaism, Christianity, and Islam (before turning toward Mecca, Muhammad had pointed to Jerusalem as the point to which to turn at the time of prayer). The city's importance over the centuries is evidenced by the architectural treasures it holds: the Wailing Wall, sacred to Jews, what remains of the city's second temple after the destruction ordered by the Romans in 70 A.D., an event that triggered the Jewish Diaspora; the Basilica of the Holy Sepulchre, built in several stages on what is considered Golgotha: the mountain on which Jesus died and rose again, sacred to Christians; the Dome of the Rock, which holds the Foundation Stone, where, according to Islamic tradition, the prophet Muhammad ascended to Paradise, and the al-Aqsa Mosque, sacred to Muslims (Armstrong, 2002).

Regarding the issue of artistic manifestations, as the example of Jerusalem testifies glaringly, the religious heritage we have inherited represents a precious treasure to be enjoyed, preserved, and protected. But it is not only about the Holy City. UNESCO (2010) recognizes that about 20 percent of the sites on the World Heritage List have some "kind of religious or spiritual connection." But regardless of UNESCO recognition, religiously inspired architectural testimonies and artistic artifacts constitute a vast heritage, the result of the interconnectedness of cultures, feelings, and values that various peoples have ascribed to them over time. Just to give a few examples, by no means exhaustive, think of the Christian-Muslim legacies of the Mediterranean, such as the Mosque-Cathedral of Córdoba; the Alhambra complex in Granada, Spain; or the monuments of Arab-Norman Sicily; of the Jewish ghettos and legacies in many European cities; of Orthodox monasteries and Protestant cathedrals.

In the meaning of heritage, in fact, understood as "the heterogeneous and multiform set of legacies and resources, in which the environmental, historical-artistic, scientific and ideal characters, goods, values and knowledge collected and shared by human communities in their different territorial settings converge and sediment" (Dondarini, 2008), the ability to read current cultural heritage as the partial outcome of matrices, imprints and evolutions that have unfolded throughout history means placing at the center the lives of the generations who have lived there, those who live there and those who will live there, in a special synthesis of past, present, and future. Therefore, with the initiation of paths and activities related to the protection and enhancement of heritage, in its broadest sense, there is an opportunity to educate the younger generations to sensitivity and respect for these principles along with responsibility and civic and political commitment; these paths also allow for the assumption of an active role, on the part of male and female students, which proves effective in stimulating content learning and the adoption of critical research methodologies and tools, while promoting, at the same time, solidarity and cooperation among citizens for the preservation of what belongs to all (world heritage) and the enhancement of what belongs to each community (local or regional heritages).

Regarding the third and fourth themes, as mentioned above, the faithful have often come into conflict both among themselves, that is, among followers of the same religion, and by prompting a clash toward the "other."

Regarding the first case, the faithful generally accept the authority of certain sacred texts, traditions, and norms. However, interpretations of these teachings have ignited and still ignite intense debates. In the Jewish world, the first attempted schism was that of Korah, Datan, and Abiram who opposed Moses and were punished instantly by God. At the time of Jesus, the Samaritans, who had built a temple on Mount Garizim, were thought to be schismatics, and the Pharisees, loyal to official Judaism, avoided any relationship with them. The Essenes, who lived secluded in a desert area, represented a sect separate from official Judaism and rejected the corrupt clergy of Jerusalem (Clarke & Beyer, 2009). The Muslim community also split, a few years after Muhammad's death, into two opposing groups: the Sunnis and the Shiites. Shi'ism is the overall definition (derived from the Arabic *shi'a* "party, faction," implied by ʿAlī and his descendants) of the minority component of Islam, the root of which goes back to the civil war (*fitna*) that pitted ʿAlī ibn Abī Tālib against Muʿawiya, future Umayyad caliph, between 657 and 661. Sunnism, on the other hand, refers to the majority current of Islam, which distinguishes orthodoxy as opposed to dissenters (especially Shiites) and for the sake of obedience over custom (Hazleton, 2010; McHugo, 2017). Among the most important schisms (from the Greek "separation") within Christianity are the following doctrines: Arianism, which developed from the 3rd century and was condemned by the Council of Nicaea (325) and had a large following among the Germanic peoples between the 5th and 7th centuries; Nestorianism and Monophysitism, which emerged following the rejection of the provisions of the ecumenical councils of Ephesus (431) and Chalcedon (451); the one that sanctioned the separation of the Eastern Churches, called Orthodox, and the Roman-Latin Church following the mutual excommunication between Patriarch Michael Cerularios and the pope's representative, Cardinal Umberto of Silva Candida in 1054; the Protestant Reformation promoted by Martin Luther in Germany, which turned out to be a complex movement of renewal of faith and religiosity in the Roman Catholic Church (Cameron, 2012) and soon spread throughout Europe also thanks to the work of other reformers, such as the Swiss Zwingli and the French Calvin (Lewis & Lewis, 2009).

In a recent survey on discrimination in European Union member states (European Commission, 2019), nearly seven in ten respondents (69 percent) said they would not feel uncomfortable if the highest political office in their country was held by an individual of a different religion (although, however, the degree of agreement varied from 88 percent in the United Kingdom, 85 percent in Ireland, and 83 percent in Spain to 42 percent in Lithuania, 46 percent in Cyprus, and 50 percent in Greece). Eighty percent of respondents also said they would feel comfortable in the workplace with a Jewish colleague (96 percent in the Netherlands, 95 percent in the United Kingdom, 93 percent in Sweden, 53 percent in Romania, 63 percent in Bulgaria, and 64 percent in Austria), a percentage that drops to 71 percent with a Muslim colleague (93 percent in the United Kingdom, 91 percent in the Netherlands, 87 percent in France and Sweden, 35 percent in the Czech Republic, 37 percent in Hungary, and 47 percent in Lithuania). The Christian faith is generally well accepted, as 88% of respondents would feel comfortable having a colleague of that religion (proportions range from 97% in Greece to 74% in Romania). Finally, more than eight in ten respondents (83 percent) say they would feel comfortable with an atheist colleague (proportions range from 95 percent in the Netherlands to 57 percent in Romania). These data, although they can be considered quite positive, reveal some grey areas with respect to the full assumption of the principle of "religious tolerance," since quite a few respondents – especially in some countries – report a condition of discomfort in having a colleague of a faith different from their own. This situation can result in actual acts of discrimination, as evidenced by the same document (European Commission, 2019): 17 percent of respondents said that they had felt discriminated against, especially in public spaces, in the workplace and in job interviews, in the past year, and that in 38 percent of cases the discrimination was on a religious basis. As if that were not enough, the feeling of increasing violations to the concept of religious freedom seems to be confirmed by Fox's (2017) study, which identifies an increasing trend of religious discrimination in Western democracies, between 1990 and 2014.

It is understood that, despite the best efforts, violence and religious discrimination have been and unfortunately still are part of the European social horizon, although to a lesser extent than in the past. This situation has a historical origin which needs to be understood and analyzed. The divergences in question can be traced in part to the phenomena of jihad, holy war, and anti-Semitism.

Jihad is generally understood as the "effort" referring to the impulse to achieve a certain goal and can constitute the religious impetus of the individual to improve himself. However, jihad is also an armed endeavor that has as its intent the expansion of Islam or its preservation and defense: in the latter meaning, jihad can be translated as "holy war." The Qur'an and treaties of Islamic law prescribe that holy war is to be waged only against infidels, meaning pagans and polytheists, and that the war must be preceded by an invitation to convert to Islam: only upon a refusal can armed struggle proceed. In the case of holy war, the people of the Book are not obliged to convert but must pay tribute and accept the protection of Islam. In this sense, therefore, jihad has nothing to do with the violent actions carried out in Europe and in the Arab countries themselves by fundamentalist terrorists who claim to have launched holy war against the West and its allies (Cook, 2005; Barbero, 2015).

On the Christian side, among the best-known phenomena of the exercise of violence is that of crusade. Crusades are wars (but in the beginning they were "armed pilgrimages") called between the 11th and 13th centuries by the Christian peoples of Europe against the Muslims to liberate the Holy Sepulchre in Jerusalem and extend their political and social supremacy in the Holy Land. During the eight military expeditions, violence was not only directed toward Muslims but involved Christians themselves, as happened during the Fourth Crusade – with the siege of Zara and the sacking of Constantinople – and Jews, in Eastern Europe (Cardini & Musarra, 2019).

Phenomena of violence also occurred among Christians themselves in Europe. The most important example in this regard is the so-called religious wars that broke out in Germany, France, the Netherlands, and the countries of northeastern Europe following the spread of the Protestant Reformation (Nolan, 2006).

Anti-Semitism has represented, and still represents, one of the most enduring and execrable attitudes of racism in human history. It is based on intolerance, discrimination, and aversion to Jews. Anti-Semitism has a very ancient history, circulating as early as the time of the Roman Empire and acquiring further violence with Christians, who hurled against them the charge of deicide, that is, of having contributed to the execution of Jesus Christ. The French Revolution marked a break in the history of discrimination against Jews, which was explicitly condemned by the Constitution of 1791. During the 19th century, anti-Semitism re-emerged with new force, linking itself to racist theories built on pseudoscientific foundations and, particularly in the second half of the century, on nationalist political arguments (Germinario, 2011). Indeed, the Jew was accused of spiritually and culturally contaminating society. Anti-Semitism became a phenomenon of first magnitude in Eastern Europe (Russia and Poland), the Balkan Peninsula, and France in the late 19th century with the so-called Dreyfus Affair (in French "*Affaire Drefus*"), named after a French officer of Jewish origin, Alfred Dreyfus, who was unjustly accused of espionage and collusion with Germany. Anti-Semitism, which had already taken deep root since the First World War and become a mainstay in Hitler's Germany (between 1933 and 1945), became explicit in a systematic persecution of the Jews to its extreme consequences, their annihilation (by means of the so-called "final solution"): this was the Shoah, a word from the Hebrew language that denotes the genocide of the Jews in the Nazi death camps (Perry & Schweitzer, 2002; Poliakov, 2003).

Despite the violence and conflicts, in parallel, the principle of religious and religious freedom, closely linked to interreligious dialogue and respect, developed, and established itself, and this is the fifth narrative juncture in the history of religions that we propose.

Religious freedom consists of the possibility to freely convert or not to profess any religion, to manifest it in practice, worship, observance, or teaching, while retaining the same rights as citizens who have different faiths. It thus also includes the right for religious communities to witness and spread their faith in society without being subjected to oppression or persecution as a result. Therefore, contributing to the slow affirmation of the principle of religious freedom has been the historical and philosophical evolution of the concept of tolerance, that is, the condition – also legally guaranteed – of a coexistence between different faiths that, over time, has gradually become equal in rights and mutual respect.

In this sense, over the past 30 years religious authorities have moved toward actions of pluralism and dialogue. On April 13, 1986, Pope John Paul II and Rabbi Elio Toaff, considered the highest Jewish authority in Italy, met at the Great Synagogue in Rome: it was the first visit of the head of Catholic Christianity in two millennia and, at least symbolically, the watershed between a painful period of distance, misunderstanding, and persecution as well as the beginning of a path of dialogue and respect (Langer, 2015; Di Segni, 2021). With the same assumptions, on February 4, 2019, the Grand Imam of Al-Azhar (the most prestigious figure in Sunni Islam) Ahmad Al-Tayyeb and Pope Francis signed the document on Human Brotherhood for World Peace and Common Coexistence (2019). Another important testimony of interreligious dialogue is the October 13, 2007, open letter titled "A Common Word Between Us and You," signed and sent by 138 prominent Muslim personalities to Pope Benedict XVI, the patriarchs of the Orthodox Churches, and generally to all Christian religious leaders. The letter identified the "commandment of love toward God and neighbor" as the uniting point of the three religions in the book (*A Common Word Between Us and You. 5-Year Anniversary Edition*, 2012).

But the long road to tolerance has been long and bumpy, although in ancient times there was no real issue related to the principle of respecting and recognizing "other" religions: the Romans, for example, did not consider foreign gods a threat and were gladly included in the pantheon. In the Middle Ages St. Thomas Aquinas asserted that one could tolerate, that is, endure, differences in worship between Christians, Jews, and Muslims, borrowing St. Augustine's belief that faith, the work of grace, cannot be imposed by men; however, as we know, episodes of religious intolerance occurred with some frequency. In the Renaissance, intellectuals had dreamed of the project of a philosophical religion capable of settling conflicts between the followers of different religions. But it was in the Modern Age that the principle of tolerance, understood as acceptance of the plurality of religions and, consequently, the need for their independent and autonomous coexistence was formulated and took hold (Grell, 1999; Zagorin, 2003). During the Enlightenment, the road to tolerance led, in 1789, to the French Constituent Assembly promulgating freedom of conscience among the rights of man. In the 19th century, having acquired the right of the individual to profess faith and exercise worship, tolerance took the shape rather of the freedom of the church or churches in their relations with state power. Nowadays, the principle of religious tolerance, understood as pluralism of ideas, confessions, and lifestyles (Wrogemann, 2019) is still a right to be defended and on which to establish paths of active citizenship.

Historical concepts and goals

The historical frameworks outlined for each narrative theme – while being aware that the need for synthesis may undermine the restitution of the complexity of the phenomena – provide a guide for the teaching of European history through those of the religions that have furrowed the continent and are still practiced today.

The proposed narrative strands, through a transversal and chronologically contextualized approach, would allow addressing some traditional historiographical nodes, which accompany the political, cultural, and social development of Europe, as lenses to better read the principles that inspire our community today: the slow affirmation of religious freedom, temporal power and spiritual power, continuity and change in social phenomena, secularization, and armed conflict resolution are just a few keys to interpreting the historical meaning and value of democracy, secularism of the state, multiculturalism, and peace.

Conversely, with a view to education for active citizenship and in a historical-cultural dimension, it will be possible to design educational paths aimed at critically analyzing the contribution of religions to the development of knowledge and values; to recognize the interdependence between cults and religions and their local and global dimensions; to establish connections between different international religious traditions in an intercultural perspective; to be aware of the cultural value of religious heterogeneity, actively participating in the development and maintenance of the principles of freedom and tolerance as well as in the protection of architectural and artistic heritage; to evaluate facts and direct one's behavior on the basis of a value system consistent with the principles of the Constitutions and international human rights charters.

References

A common Word Between Us and You. 5-Year Anniversary Edition. (2012). The Royal Aal Al-Bayt Institute for Islamic Thought. https://rissc.jo/docs/20-acw/20-ACW-5.pdf

Alles, G. D. (Ed.). (2007). *Religious studies. A global view.* Routledge.

Antes, P., Geertz, A. W., & Warne, R. R. (Eds.). (2004). *New approaches to the study of religion* (Vol. 1–2). De Gruyter.

Armstrong, K. (2002). Jerusalem: The problems and responsibilities of sacred space. *Islam and Christian–Muslim Relations*, *13*(2), 189–196. https://doi.org/10.1080/09596410220128498

Barbero, A. (2015). *Benedette guerre. Crociate e jihad.* Laterza.

Bros, A. (1953). Aperçu historique sur l'histoire des religions. In *Histoire des religions* (Vol. 1, pp. 111–121). Bloud & Gay.

Cameron, E. (2012). *The European reformation.* 2nd ed. Oxford University Press.

Cardini, F., & Musarra, A. (2019). *Il grande racconto delle crociate.* Il Mulino.

Clarke, P. B., & Beyer, P. (2009). *The world's religions: Continuities and transformations.* Taylor & Francis.

Cook, D. (2005). *Understanding Jihad.* University of California Press.

Crone, P. (2015). Jewish Christianity and the Qur'ān (Part One). *Journal of Near Eastern Studies*, *74*(2), 225–253.

Crone, P. (2016). Jewish Christianity and the Qur'ān (Part Two). *Journal of Near Eastern Studies*, *75*(1), 277–314.

Dillon, M. (2019). *Gods in ancient Greece and Rome.* Oxford University Press. https://doi.org/10.1093/acrefore/9780199340378.013.104

DiSegni, R. S. (2021). *When Pope John Paul II came to the great Synagogue of Rome.* www.tabletmag.com/sections/history/articles/when-pope-john-paul-came-to-the-great-synagogue-of-rome

Dondarini, R., & Guerra, L. (2008). Un Patrimonio per il Patrimonio. In *Un patrimonio di esperienze sulla Didattica del Patrimonio*. Pàtron.

Donner, F. M. (2010). *Muhammad and the believers. At the origins of Islam.* Harvard University Press.

Durkheim, É. (1912). *Les Formes élémentaires de la vie religieuse*. PUF.
Ehrman, B. (2015). *After the New Testament: 100–300 C.E.: A reader in early Christianity*. Oxford University Press.
European Commission. (2018). *Eurobarometer 90.4: Attitudes of Europeans towards biodiversity, awareness and perceptions of EU customs, and perceptions of antisemitism*. European Commission
European Commission. (2019). *Special Eurobarometer 493. Discrimination in the European Union*. https://europa.eu/eurobarometer/surveys/detail/2251
European Commission. (2021a). *EU continues supporting education of refugees and addressing migration in Turkey with additional €560 million*. https://ec.europa.eu/commission/presscorner/detail/en/ip_21_6931
European Commission. (2021b). *Special Eurobarometer 508. Values and identities of UE citizens*. https://data.europa.eu/data/datasets/s2230-94-1-508-eng?locale=en
Filoramo, G. (2004). *Che cos'è la religione. Temi metodi problemi*. Einaudi.
Filoramo, G., & Menozzi, D. (Eds.). (2002). *Storia del Cristianesimo. Il medioevo* (Vol. 2). Laterza.
Filoramo, G., Giorda, M. C., & Spineto, N. (Eds.). (2020). *Manuale di Scienze della religione*. Morcelliana.
Fox, J. (2017). Religious discrimination in European and Western Christian-majority democracies. *Zeitschrift Für Religion, Gesellschaft Und Politik*, *1*(2), 185–209. https://doi.org/10.1007/s41682-017-0009-3
Freeman, C. (2009). *A new history of early Christianity*. Yale University Press.
Freud, S. (1927). *Die Zukunft einer Illusion*. Internationaler Psychoanalytischer Verlag.
Frobenius, L. (1898). *Der Ursprung der afrikanischen Kulturen*. Gebrüder Borntraeger.
Fugier, H. (1963). *Recherches sur l'expression du sacré dans la langue latine*. Ch.A. Bedy.
Germinario, F. (2011). *Argomenti per lo sterminio. L'antisemitismo e i suoi stereotipi nella cultura europea*. Einaudi.
Gräbner, F. (1905). *Kulturkreise und Kulturschichten in Ozeanien*. Verlag von A. Asher und Co.
Grell, O. P. (1999). *Toleration in enlightenment Europe*. Cambridge University Press.
Harrison, T. (2010). *Divinity and history: The religion of Herodotus*. Clarendon Press.
Hazleton, L. (2010). *After the prophet: The epic story of the Shia-Sunni split in Islam*. Anchor.
His Holiness Pope Francis & The Grand Imam of Al-Azhar Ahamad al-Tayyib. (2019). *A document on human fraternity for world peace and living together*. https://www.vatican.va/content/francesco/en/travels/2019/outside/documents/papa-francesco_20190204_documento-fratellanza-umana.html
Hubert, H., & Mauss, M. (1899). *Essai sur la nature et la fonction du sacrifice*. Alcan.
Hume, D. (1757). *Natural History of Religion*. A. and H. Bradlaugh Bonner.
James, E. O. (2007). *Comparative religion. An introduction and historical study*. Kessinger Publishing.
Jordan, L. H. (1905). *Comparative religion: Its genesis and growth, Edimburgo 1925*. Charles Scribner's sons.
Jung, C. G. (1970). *Psychology and religion: West and East. The collected works of Carl G. Jung*. Princeton University Press.
Kerényi, K. (1951). *Die Mythologie der Griechen. Die Götter- und Menschheitsgeschichten*. Rhein-Verlag.
Langer, E. (2015). Elio Toaff, rabbi who welcomed John Paul II to his synagogue, dies at 99. *The Washington Post*. www.washingtonpost.com/world/europe/elio-toaff-rabbi-who-welcomed-john-paul-ii-to-his-synagogue-dies-at-99/2015/04/20/48a611c0-e767-11e4-9a6a-c1ab95a0600b_story.html
Levenson, J. D. (2012). *Inheriting Abraham. The legacy of the Patriarch in Judaism, Christianity, and Islam*. Princeton University Press.
Lévy-Bruhl, L. (1922). *La mentalité primitive*. Alcan.

Lewis, J. R., & Lewis, S. M. (Eds.). (2009). *Sacred Schisms. How religions divide*. Cambridge University Press.

Lieberg, G. (1974). Considerazioni sull'etimologia e sul significato di religio. *Rivista Di Filologia Classica, 102*, 34–57.

McHugo, J. (2017). *A concise history of Sunnis and Shi'is*. Saqi.

Müller, F. M. (1892). *Anthropological religion*. 1st ed. Longmans, Green and Co.

Nolan, C. J. (2006). *The age of wars of religion, 1000–1650. An Ecyclopedia of global warfare and civilization* (Vol. 1–2). Greenwood Press.

Perry, M., & Schweitzer, F. M. (2002). *Antisemitism. Myth and hate from antiquity to the present*. Palgrave Macmillan.

Pew Research Center. (2017). Europe's growing Muslim population. *Pew Research Center*. www.pewresearch.org/religion/2017/11/29/europes-growing-muslim-population/

Poliakov, L. (2003). *The history of anti-semitism* (Vol. 1–3). University of Pennsylvania Press.

Rank, O. (1909). *Der Mythus von der Geburt des Helden: Versuch einer psychologischen Mythendeutung*. Deuticke.

Schaeffer, J. (2019). *Giambattista vico on natural law. Rhetoric, religion and sensus communis*. Routledge.

Schmidt, W. (1938). *Manaule di storia comprata delle religioni*. Morcelliana.

Stroumsa, G. G. (2011). From Abraham's religion to the Abrahamic religions. *Historia Religionum, 3*, 11–22.

Tylor, E. B. (1994). *The collected works of Edward Burnett Tylor*. Routledge.

UNESCO. (2010). Heritage of religious interest. *UNESCO initiative on heritage of religious interest*. https://whc.unesco.org/en/religious-sacred-heritage/

United Nations High Commissioner for Refugees. (2022). *Ukraine refugee situation*. United Nations High Commissioner for Refugees. https://data2.unhcr.org/en/situations/ukraine

Whaling, F. (Ed.). (1985). *Contemporary approaches to the study of religion* (Vol. 1–2). De Gruyter.

Wrogemann, H. (2019). *Intercultural theology: A theology of interreligious relations*. Ivp Academic.

Zagorin, P. (2003). *How the idea of religious toleration came to the west*. Princeton University Press.

EPILOGUE: "WE WANNA LEARN LIKE COMMON PEOPLE WHATEVER COMMON PEOPLE DID"[1]

Juan Ramón Moreno-Vera

"Lisa the iconoclast" is the 16th episode of the 7th season of *The Simpsons*, originally aired on 18 February 1996. The episode showed a well-known tension among history educators: to maintain the official narrations of history versus the implementation of research-based history education and active-learning methodologies.

As Springfield celebrated the bicentennial of founder Jebediah Springfield, Miss Hoover (Lisa's teacher) assigned the students to write an essay on that relevant character's life. Lisa started her research going to the historical society where she founded a document that evidenced that Jebediah Springfield was not a national hero; he was a cruel pirate that tried to kill (and failed) George Washington.

Lisa tried to convince the townspeople the truth of Jebediah showing them the recent discovered primary source, but she only found disbelief and hostility. Miss Hoover gave Lisa a failing grade and, even the historian working in the historical society, Mister Hurlbut, tried to protect the glorious myth of Jebediah Springfield and, with that, the dignity of the whole town.

Is this situation still happening today in our history classes?

When, in the 19th century, many of the educational systems were established, history education was a very important tool to consolidate the recently-created liberal nation-states. As López Facal and Schugurensky commented, textbooks, public memory and school programs maintained this perspective (and still do today) inspired by scientific positivism, patriotic history (myths, flags, wars, anthems, etc.) and the elite's interests and needs.

But what is history's purpose today? For sure, history could not be a simple chronological account of the glories that happened in the past. Instead of that, history education must provide the students a critical analysis of what happened based on the use of credible (and compared) sources and data to build their own interpretation and historical conceptual knowledge.

Students need to interpret the past in order to understand the present and, therefore, to guide correct decisions in the future.

It is important, in terms of history education, to respond positively to the current needs and problems of our European society: globalization processes affecting economy, social relations, rights, wars and democratic values. So, history education has to face new challenges: from the nation-state and the elite's needs to the history of common people as Hobsbawm recommended.

Why do we have to assume this new paradigm in history education? Because living in democracy implies that all the people have the same rights and duties and demands respect for all and the dignity of each person. As indicated López Facal and Schugurensky, the privileges of a few and the exclusion of many are incompatible with democratic societies and values.

In that sense, teaching history will help our students to keep democratic values and equality in the future. Paragoning the lines from Pulp's 1995 song "Common People": "we wanna learn like common people whatever common people did".

To reach this goal, authors like Seixas, Peck or Morton proposed to learn a deeper history. First-order concepts are important; students will need to know the dates, ages, periods, important facts and characters to build a correct historical structure in their minds. Second-order concepts, they called them "historical thinking competencies", allow students to think critically, to use primary sources, to make historical argumentations and discussions and, generally, to understanding historical complex processes.

Gómez Carrasco and Sáiz Serrano indicated the important growth of studies on historical thinking competencies, in different countries and research groups, developed in recent years. In this sense, it is important to link learning processes with historical consciousness which reflects on the social functions of history, identity, public history, memory and ethical dimension of history.

In other words, to learn history is much more than memorizing facts, dates and characters with patriotic purposes. Our students need to learn what is history, how history is built, to be critical with information sources and how to use historical knowledge to interpret the present public life and exercising civil rights.

Learning historical thinking competencies and historical consciousness is not natural as Sam Wineburg's *Historical thinking and other unnatural acts* reminds us. Gómez Carrasco and Sáiz Serrano said it clearly: learning history implies a well-designed instruction process.

But, this historical instruction process, guided by the teacher, must be based, as Kuhn, Lakatos or Bunge indicated, on the scientific method, the search of evidence, the use of primary sources and students' cooperative research. On 30 April 2020, during the COVID-19 pandemic caused by SARS-CoV2 and under a severe isolation, Italian first minister, Giuseppe Conte commented the importance to distinguish, like the old Greeks did, between "doxa", that is the opinion based on personal perceptions and values, and "episteme", that is the knowledge based on scientific evidence.

The use of evidence and sources are important in history education. It helps the students to be more critical and to fight against new threats like post-truth and fake news. As Agnes Heller suggested, in social studies education we have to take in account the concept of hermeneutics and, also, try to teach our students to think and interpret the reality we are living in.

In this book, the authors recommend three new approaches to implement activities based on historical sources: narratives, digital sources and heritage.

Stéphane Lévesque explored the concept of narrative competence but not as a closed account of the past, but with the intention of understanding what insight the study of narrative in history can offer to education. Are historical narratives truthful representations of the past? Authors like Seixas or Rüsen highlighted that a historical narrative is a construct that provides the past with a sense of coherence and direction, but narratives are not direct truthful copies of the past but rather "representations" of it.

To build those representations of the past, teachers could select primary or secondary historical sources to make their students research and ask critically what happened in the past. Obviously, official or domestic documents, archives, museums, works of art, heritage, videos, films, photographs, common and historical objects, archeological pieces, sounds, discourses or oral expressions could be valid sources to teach and learn history.

In this sense, Colomer Rubio and Pons Pons explored two issues: on one hand, the changes in history education with different digital resources and the problems that arise from their use in the classroom and, on the other hand, the non-neutrality of the digital space, the digital historical sources and how public policies promote their use and instruction developing media and historical literacy far from the idea of "technological panacea".

Sampedro-Martín, Arroyo-Mora, Cuenca-López and Martín-Cáceres reflected around other kind of historical sources that are present in most of our European cities, villages and landscapes: heritage. In their words, the use of heritage as an historical primary source is crucial to suggest educational experiences to integrate a critical view of history and a participative eco-citizenship democratic education. To reach that goal, they proposed not just using cultural heritage but to use, as well, controversial heritage that promotes innovative, interactive, dynamic and participatory visions of citizenship, socio-environmental problems and controversial issues of the past and present and their possible future solutions.

To implement these kinds of resources in history lessons, the authors of the book also propose new approaches to European history through transversal topics that overcome the traditional chronologic axis of relevant facts. These new approaches try to show a wider look on European history, making visible the daily history of hidden common groups: rural areas, women, working-class, religions, families, travelers or those persecuted by justice.

The history of peasantry is present in Fernández Prieto's and Cabo Villaverde's chapter and also in the chapter by Moreno-Vera and Monteagudo-Fernández. In the first case, the authors reflected on the history of countryside and the relation between us, the landscape and nature. In the second case, the authors commented the inequalities, in terms of history education, of elite groups and bourgeoisie living in the cities (the centre of political power) and peasantry living in rural areas that have been continuously invisible in history textbooks.

Invisibility is also represented in the book in the chapter by Danielsson Malmros and Sjöland and the chapter by Sánchez-Ibáñez and Irigoyen-López. Regarding women's invisibility in history education, Danielsson Malmros and Sjöland emphasized different themes in a chronological overview, reflecting on historical consciousness, empathy and the importance of teaching history in present-day society under a gender-equality point of view.

Linked to that topic, Sánchez-Ibáñez and Irigoyen-López reflected on the scarce presence of the daily life of families in historical official narratives. Family was supposed to be the historical context for women, children and elderly. Social groups far from political decision making spaces. Moreover, families' daily life was underestimated in history education although the importance of families to understand social changes, economy and legislative changes in European society increased over time. Family diversity, legal changes and new social rights won in the last decades (abortion, divorce, equal gender marriage, adoption, etc.) have to be explained to prepare the students to future challenges as family models, demographic changes, migration, economic inequalities or poverty.

In terms of inequalities, we can find a discussion in three different chapters. The one from Rodríguez-Pérez, Miralles-Martínez, Precioso-Izquierdo and Miralles-Sánchez is linked to the social and economic impact of the technological revolutions in Europe. Revolutions, from prehistory to the present times, imply an enormous impact in terms of elite's world domination at a political, economic and cultural level. Industry and technology can explain the consequences of various empires, the economic differences between North and South but, also, the concentration of wealth and inequalities.

Close to that concept, it is important for authors like Felices de la Fuente, Cózar Gutiérrez and Chaparro Sainz to reflect about the concept of power since these structures have been decisive in the construction of European history. Prominent groups have a close relationship with political power, economic decisions, democracy interests and the protection of nationalism and nation-states to keep their privileges.

In regard to the concept of power inequalities we finally find the chapter by Galletti and Ghizzoni about churches and religions in Europe. In words of these authors, to consciously design the key tools of global citizenship, the history of religions constitutes a relevant thematic area, combining social, economic, institutional and cultural history. For them, the use of artistic manifestations to convey messages of faith, peace, armed conflicts, divisions and unions is important to design educational pathways recognizing the interdependence between cults and religions (in a local or global perspective) and making connections between different faiths until arriving to the principles of freedom, tolerance and protection of cultural heritage.

Due to the consequences of political, social, economic, cultural and religious inequalities and differences, we can find two chapters that reflect on terror, violence and conflicts in European history. For Pinto Ribeiro, Marques Alves, Vieira, Moreira, Martins, Magalhães and Lopes, war, violence and terrorism are some of the most present elements over different times. But, in the historical implications in terms of political issues, the authors point of view is based on the interpretation of invisible historical characters as testimonies, victims, participants and observers to build a multiple and never univocal interpretation. It is important for the authors to reflect about the consequences of violence for common people that suffered genocides, hunger, poverty, diseases and rapes instead of focusing the concept of war from the point of view of national heroes, national pride or the glory of the victor.

Related to that topic, van Boxtel reflected about outsiders, rebels, criminals and those persecuted by justice and powers. Punishments appear, as the author comments, in the history of Europe especially for those who used violence and rebellion to face the powers, institutions or bourgeoisie's economic interests.

Finally, we can find an interesting transdisciplinary approach for a history of Europe by Borghi and Smurra. They based their educational proposal on travel stories and travelers. This topic is centered on active citizenship education as analyzes itineraries, routes and cultures. From routes of faith to the ones of conflict. From trading or migrations to conquests and wars. These travels and travelers created international networks of exchanges: foodstuffs, metals, timber, grain, spices, textiles, men, women, slaves or workers. These cross-currents explained the construction of the history of Europe and the relationships with the rest of the world and cultures to promote tolerance and solidarity as basic democratic values for European citizens.

In conclusion, the main target of this book was to show new paths and approaches in history education. It is important to overcome the traditional power-nation-state narration, with its positivist account of historical events, and focus history education on the development of historical thinking competencies; the use of sources, documents, pictures or objects; encouraging the students to use research-based active methodologies to find scientific evidence, and, above all, to transmit European democratic values to show the invisible histories, the daily life of common people and the importance of keeping democracy, equality and human rights.

Note

1 This chapter is a result of projects "HistoryLab for European Civic Engagement: open e-Toolkit to train History Teachers on Digital Teaching and Learning", funded by SEPIE on call ERASMUS + KA226 [2020–1-ES01-KA226-HE-095430], and research project PID2020–113453RB-I00, funded by Agencia Estatal de Investigación of Spain (AEI/10.13039/501100011033).

INDEX

5G 105

abolitionism 198
Abulafia, D. 193
acculturation 3, 4, 109
agency 58, 71, 180
agriculture 86, 93–94; capitalism and 92–93; green revolution 95–96; liberal agrarian revolution 94; technology and 101; *see also* peasantry
Al-Tayyeb, A. 215
Altieri, M. 85
American Historical Association (AHA) 44
analepsis 57
Ancien Régime 133, 143
Anglo-American school 26–27, 28–29
Annals school 125
anti-heritage 72
anti-Semitism 214
Arendt, H. 154
Argar culture 139
argumentation 31
aristocrats 138, 139, 140
armed conflict 154, 155–156; *see also* war
Arroyo-Mora, E. 8, 221
artisan workshops 103
Ashby, R. 58
Assadourian, E. 70, 71
assessment 34, 59
authoritarianism 16

bagaudae 117
Bakunin, M. 170
banishment 166

'banking education' 19
Barbagli, M. 126
Barca, S. 87
Barthes, R. 56
Barton, K. C. 28, 61
Bauman, Z. 105
Bayly, C. 194
Beard, M. 138
Beccaria, C. 165–166
Becker, C. 54
Belew, K. 50
belonging 125
Benchmarks of Historical Thinking Project 28–29
Berger, J. 90
Berque, A. 85
Betrán, J. L. 120
Bevilaqua, P. 85
Bielefeld school 17
Biesta, G. 174
birth rate 133
Blanning, T.C.W. 137
Bloch, M. 84, 194
Bokova, I. 74
Boltvinik, J. 115–116
borders 153–154
Borghi, B. 223
bourgeoisie 115, 116–117, 119, 127, 142, 143, 184; gender relations 187; revolutions 143
Braudel, F. 197; *The Mediterranean and the Mediterranean World in the Age of Philip II* 84, 193
British model 99

Bruner, J. 5, 16, 58
Brzezinski, Z. 149
Burkholder, P. 44
Byzantine Empire 151; gender inequality 118

Cabezos de Huelva 73
Cabo Villaverde, M. 221
Cambridge Group for the History of Population and Social Structure 125–126
Cambridge History Project 27
Cameron, R. 101, 106
camps 168
Canada 17, 18, 26, 28, 60, 62
capital punishment 166
capitalism 15, 92–93, 103, 107, 109–110, 184; consolidation of smallholdings 94–95
Carr, D. 54
Carr, E. H. 53
celibacy 127, 128
Celts 3
Centre for the Study of Historical Consciousness 28–29
change 180–181, 187
Chaparro Sainz, A. 222
Chapman, A. 55, 58
Charles III 151
China 105
Chomsky, N. 105
Christianity 4, 142, 208; crusades 214; schisms 212
Christides, B. 118
church, the 1, 137–138, 140–141, 142; gender relations and 183–184
citizenship 7–8, 186
citizenship education 22, 28
civic education 7
civic skills 109
Clark, P. 5, 6, 58
classroom, traditional model 19
Clausewitz, C. 149
Clovis 4
Clube de Roma 84
Code of Hammurabi 163
cognitive psychology 16, 17
Cold War 1, 15, 107, 144, 156
Coleman, M. J. 126
collective action 121
Coller, I. 193
Collingwood, R. G. 54
Colomer Rubio, J. 8, 220, 221
colonialism 15, 75, 107, 156, 158–159
coltan 102

competencies, historical thinking 29–30
concepts 180; meta- 31; second-order 58, 220
Concepts of History and Teaching Approaches 7–14 (CHATA) 27
conjunctures 201
Constitutionalism 143
constructivism 16, 20, 60, 62
consumer society 101
Conte, G. 220
content/story 56–57
continuity 181, 187
controversial topics 21, 68; heritage 69–70; socially acute questions 159–160
Coornhert, D. V. 164
corporal punishment 165
Council of Europe 69
Council of Trent 142
Covid-19 pandemic 6, 7, 16, 47, 132, 220
Cózar Gutiérrez, R. 222
craftsmanship 102
crime 162; cyber 164; motives 164; organized 164; rape 189; sin and 163; teaching about 171–172, 174–175; white-collar 164
critical literacy 21
Croce, B. 4, 54
Crosby, A. 84
cruelty heritage 72–73
Crusades 151–152, 214
Cucuteni-Trypillia culture 139
Cuenca-López, J. M. 8, 221
curiosity-driven learning 21
curriculum 34; traditional model 19
cybercrime 164

Danielsson Malmros, I. 222
Danto, A. 54
Darwin, C. 83
Davis, N. Z. 43, 85
de Coulanges, F. 53
de Miguel, R. 50
de Molina, M. G. 85
de Valera, E. 91
death rate 133
democracy 13, 22, 68, 107, 112, 140, 143, 145, 220
democratic erosion 15–16, 22
democratic model 20–22; pedagogy 21; principles 20–21
developmental psychology 16
dialogue 16
Díaz, M. 43
'digestive' pedagogy 19
digital divide 47

digital literacy 49, 50, 109
Digital Revolution 104
digital technology 42–43; media literacy 46–47
discourse 57
doxa 220
Dreyfus, A. 214
Dursteler, E. 193
Dutch school 27, 30–31
Dwyer, P. 138

economic inequality 112, 119, 120, 122, 131–132
ecosocial citizenship education 76; dependence on the Earth 70; interdependence 70–71
elites 139–140
ellipsis 57
Emerging Sources Citation Index (ESCI) 32
enduring issues 174–175
Engels, F. 121
England 26, 27, 58, 116, 120; agricultural revolution 93–94; first Industrial Revolution 105; new poor law 162
Enlightenment 143; gender relations and 185–187
environment and environmentalism 15, 84–85, 88, 89; natural park 87; Place-Based-Education projects 96
episteme 220
EPITEC project 69
Estepa, J. 72
ethics of care 70–71, 73, 74
ethnolinguistic groups: Celtic 4; Germanic 3–4; Slavic 4
Eurocentricism 9
Europe 1, 5; borders 153–154; bourgeoisie 116–117; family studies 126; migrations 2–3, 4; myths 3; peasantry 85–87, 90–92; population growth 128–129, 199–200; rural society 118; urbanization 114; war 152–153
European Union (EU) 112, 131, 144–145, 156, 206; Digital Education Action Plan 46
Evans, R. J. 126, 137
evidence 220–221
extended family 129–130

Facal, R.-L. 7
fake news 16, 105
family 129, 186, 222; extended 129–130; marriage 127–128; matriarchy 130; non-traditional 130; nuclear 129–130; patriarchy 129, 130, 139; roles 130
family studies 125–126
Faro Convention 69
Fauve-Chamoux, A. 127
Felices de la Fuente, M. 222
Feliú, M. 72
feminist movement 15, 122, 188
Fernández Prieto, L. 221
Ferro, M. 161
fertility rate 133
feudalism 103, 110, 141
first Industrial Revolution 105
First World War 144, 155–156, 189
Fitzgerald, D. 85
focalisation 57
food riots 169
forced migration 198
Fourth Industrial Revolution 100, 104
Fraga, X. 90
France, economic inequality 131
Francis, Pope 215
Frankfurt school 17
Freire, P. 19
French Revolution 74, 152, 155, 169, 170, 187, 193, 214
FUER model 29, 59–60

Gambi, L. 193
gamification 47
Ganong, L. H. 126
Gardner, H. 43
Gatell, C. 50
Gebhardt, M. 189
gender and gender history 15, 179; ancient societies 183; Enlightenment 185–187; genealogic perspective 181; global perspective 181–182; heritage and 74; industrialisation 185; inequality 117–118, 119, 120, 121, 122; intersectional approach 180, 182; Middle Ages 183–185; nineteenth century 187–188; power 180; prehistory 182; Renaissance 184–185; sex change legislation 130–131; twentieth century 188–190
genealogic perspective 181
genealogy 4
Genette, G. 56
Geneva Convention 197–198
genocide 159; Holocaust 189
geographical determinism 83, 89
geopolitics 138
German school 27, 28–29, 30, 59

Germans/Germany 3–4, 17
Giddens, A. 71
Ginzburg, C. 85
Global Survey of Teachers 13–14
globalization 15, 19, 20, 199; scramble-for-land revolution 95
Gómez Carrasco, C. 8
González-Reyes, L. 70
Greece: aristocracy 140; urban planning 114
green revolution 95–96
Grever, M. 6
guilds 119, 140

Han, B.-Ch. 105
Hangen, T. 49
Harris, L. M. 5
Harrison, D. 184
Hazen, C. 138
Hecataeus of Miletus 207
hegemony 107
Heller, A. 221
Henry VIII 142
heritage and heritage education 69–70, 160, 203, 221; anti- 72; artistic 74; of cruelty 72–73; eco-citizenship 71; gender perspective 74; inclusive 74–75; interested 73; religious 211–212; silenced 73–75; subjected-rescued 75; in transition 76
Hernàndez-Cardona, F. X. 72
Herodotus 207
Herrero, Y. 70
Hill, C. 85
Hilton, R. 85
historical awareness 17, 18
historical consciousness 5–6, 7, 14, 17, 21, 25–26, 27, 37, 59, 60, 179, 220
historical empathy 34, 180, 181, 183, 186
historical interpretation 59
historical knowledge 51, 157–158; geographical determinism 83
historical memory 17
historical narrative 53–54, 57, 59, 221; plausibility 55; tasks 55, 56
historical reasoning 27, 30–31
historical subject 30
historical thinking 5–6, 8, 17–18, 25–26, 37, 48–50, 58, 60, 62–63; academic production 32, 34, 35; Anglo-American school 26–27, 28–29; assessment 34; competencies 29–30, 220; conceptual framework 29; criticism 29; curriculum 34; Dutch school 27, 30–31; English research 27; FUER model 29; German school 27, 28–29, 30; primary sources 34; Web of Science (WOS) 31–32, 34, 35, 36, 37
Historical Thinking Competencies in History (HITCH project) 29
Historical Thinking Project 18, 29
historicism 13, 15
historiography 15, 16, 59, 84, 85, 200
history 4, 160; 'from below' 166–167; conjunctures 201; learning 25–26; of religion 208–209
History 13–16 Project 6
history education 5, 6–7, 8, 13, 17, 31, 51, 58, 59, 96–97, 219–220; democratic model 14, 20–22; English tradition 58–59; evidence 220–221; multicultural approach 7, 9; research 18; traditional model 14, 18–20; see also teaching history
History Education Group 45
HistoryLab 122
"HistoryLab for European Civic Engagement" 6–7
Historypin 50–51
Hobsbawm, E. 85, 112, 113, 116
Holmes, B., *Gender: Antiquity and its Legacy* 182
Holocaust 189
human rights 143, 157
human trafficking 164
Humanities Curriculum Project (HCP) 16
Hume, D. 208

Ibagón, N. J. 68
identity 20, 61, 62, 183; national 19; religious 209; see also heritage education
imperialism 158–159
inclusive heritage 74–75
independence movements 156
Industrial Revolution 100, 102, 104, 105, 108, 110, 128; urbanization 113
industrialisation 93, 95, 101, 102; gender relations and 185; see also technological revolution
inequality 16, 107–108, 126, 181, 221; economic 112, 119, 120, 122, 131; gender 74, 117–118, 119, 120, 121, 122, 130–131; power 222; social 7, 131
infant mortality 133
information 49, 51, 100, 104, 105
Information and Communication Technology (ICT) 42
innovation 103–104

inquiry-based learning 174
interdisciplinary approach 21
interested heritage 73
international conference on historical consciousness 18
Internet 44, 46–47, 48–49, 105; history education and 45–46; learning history 28; online platforms 104; privacy and 106
intersectionality 182
invisibility 222
Ireland, Magdalene laundries 167
Irigoyen-López, A. 222
Islam 211, 212; gender inequality 118–119; jihad 213; marginalised groups 119
Islamism 171
Italy 131

James, L. 138
jihad 213
John Paul II, Pope 215
Jones, R. B. 17
journeymen 103
justice 162, 185; penal codes 163
Justinian I 118

KA226 Erasmus + project 6
Kalifa, D., *Vice, Crime, and Poverty: How the Western Imagination Invented the Underworld* 167
Kallifatides, T. 92
Kent, S. K., *Gender: A World History* 182
Kertzer, D. I. 126
keyword co-occurrence analysis 32
knowledge 7, 16, 17, 19, 20, 27, 63; digital sources 44; historical 13–14, 17, 21, 23, 26, 28, 51; "powerful" 31; second-order concepts 58
Koning, N. 85
Körber, A. 26, 29, 63
Kriesberg, L. 126

labour movement, women and 188
landscape 85
language 3, 4, 180; *see also* ethnolinguistic groups
Laslett, P. 125
learning 23, 62–63; history 25–26, 28, 220; inquiry-based 174
learning theory 16
Lee, P. 35, 58
Leeds, A. 115, 116
Lefebvre, H. 138
Lemkin, R. 159
Létourneau, J. 60

Lévesque, S. 5, 6, 8, 26, 32, 35, 48, 58, 221
Levi, G. 85
Levstik, L. 28, 61
LGBT Pride Day 74–75
liberalism 143, 144, 152, 155, 156
life cycle 129, 133
literacy 43; critical 21; digital 46, 49, 50, 109; historical 5–6; media 43, 45, 46–47
Locke, J. 165
López Facal, R. 35, 219
Los Millares 139
Lovelock, J. 84
Luddite movement 102–103, 121

Macron, E. 1
Maderuelo, J. 85
Magalhães, D. 222
Magdalene laundries 167
Malthus, T. 128
Mann, S. A. 115–116
marginalised groups 166, 172; camps 168; "fallen women" 167; vagabonds 167
Margulis, L. 84
maritime trade 104–105; piracy 194, 197, 203–204; ports 195–196; slaves 200
Marques Alves, L. 222
marriage 127–128, 184, 187; 'Stockholm' 187
Martín, D. 120
Martín-Cáceres, M. J. 8, 72, 221
Martins, D. 222
Marxism 15
material culture 133
matriarchy 130
matrimonial endogamy 133
matrix of historiography 59
Maynes, M. J. 126
McConnell, R. C. 126
Meade, T. A., *A Companion to Global Gender History* 181
Meaning of History, The: Toward a Rethinking of the History and Citizenship Education Program in the Secondary III and IV 60–61
media literacy 43, 45, 46–47
Megill, A. 55, 56
memory and memorization 19, 25, 28, 49, 160; resentment 159
merchant capitalism 184
meta-concepts 31
Metzger, S. A. 5
Michel, J., "Le devoir de mémoire" 160–161
middle class 117, 187

migration 2–3, 129–130, 133, 187, 193, 199, 200, 206–207; Celtic 3; forced 198; Germanic 4; internal 101; Slavic 4; *see also* travel and travelers; urbanization
Mink, L. 55
Miralles, P. 68
Miralles-Martínez, P. 222
miscegenation 2–3
modernisation 88
monarchy 137–138, 141–142, 143
monotheism 210–211
Monteagudo-Fernández, J. 221
Monte-Sano, C. 32
moral economy 92
Moreira, A. 222
Moreno, J. R. 120
Moreno-Vera, J. R. 221
Morin, E. 157
Müller, M. 208
multicultural approach 7, 9
Mumford, L., *Technics and Civilization* 106
Munslow, A. 57, 58; *Narrative and history* 56
Museo do Pobo Galego 76

Napoleonic Code 186–187
narrative 53–54, 55, 59, 160, 183; content/story 56–57; discourse 56, 57; focalisation 57; narrated time 57–58; one-sided 172, 174; theory of agency 58; voice 57; zero focalization 57
narrative competence 8, 30, 58, 59–60, 221; teaching 61–63
nationalism 3, 14–15, 143–144, 155
nation-state/s 14, 15, 19, 94, 143; sovereignty 143
natural increase 133
natural park 87
nature 88
Neal, L. 101, 106
Neanderthal 2
Netherlands 6
New History 17
New Regime 143
Newark, T. 149
nobility 141, 142
nuclear family 129–130

Oakeshott, M. 54
O'Connell, M. 193
oligarchy 140
online platforms 104
organized crime 164
Ortega y Gasset, J. 102
other/s 19, 68

paganism 208
Pankhurst, E. 188
patriarchy 129, 130, 139, 182
patrimonialisation 76
patronage 142
Peace of Westphalia 154
peasantry 85–87, 88–89, 90, 92, 94, 95, 115–116, 221; *bagaudae* 117; emigration 91; politics 91; production 91; refeudalisation 120–121; revolts 119–120, 121, 168–169
pedagogy 8, 14, 16, 18, 43, 47, 63; democratic model 21; 'digestive' 19
penal codes 163
Pennacchi, A. 90
People's Will 170
philosophy 17, 29
Piaget, J. 16
pilgrimage 202–203
Pinto Ribeiro, C. 222
piracy 194, 197, 203–204
Place-Based-Education projects 96
plausibility 55
Polanyi, K. 85
political parties 143
politics: geo 138; peasantry and 91; sustainability 96
polytheism 210
Pomian, K. 153
Pons Pons, A. 8, 221
population growth 128–129, 199–200
Portass, R. 115
ports 195–196
Portugal 158; economic inequality 132
positivism 53, 219
post-colonialism 15
poverty 131; *see also* economic inequality
power 14, 15, 136, 167; aristocracy 140; Church 137–138, 140–141, 142; elites 139–140; emotional aspect 138; female 138, 180; inequality 222; monarchy 141–142, 143; oligarchy 140; patriarchy 139; political 140; in prehistoric societies 139; research 137–138; sovereignty 140, 141, 143; totalitarianism 144
"powerful knowledge" 31
Precioso-Izquierdo, F. 222
prehistory, gender relations 182
primary sources 34
privacy, technology and 105–106
privateer 197
producing society 101
production 91, 93, 102; English agricultural revolution 93–94; smallholders 94–95
progress 84, 94, 143, 164

prolepsis 57
proletariat 85, 112, 121
propaganda 159
proto-Indo-European theory 208
Publius Tacitus 3–4
Puig de Sant Andreu de Ullastret 73
punishment 162, 164; banishment 166; capital 166; corporal 165; imprisonment 167; teaching about 171–172, 174–175; for vagabondage 167; workhouses 165–166; *see also* justice
Putin, V. 1

racism 84; anti-Semitism 214
Rappaport, D. 170–171
raw materials 84, 102
reasoning 5, 7; *see also* historical reasoning
Redgrave, R., *The Outcast* 162
refeudalisation 120–121
reflection 7, 14, 174–175
Reisman, A. 32
religion/s 137–138, 141, 206, 216, 222; art and architecture 211; conflict and 212; crime and 163; discrimination and 213; gender relations and 183–184; history of 208–209; identity and 209; monotheistic 210–211; pagan 208; pilgrimage 202–203; polytheistic 210; spread of 210; terrorism and 171; violence and 207, 213–214; war and 152
religious tolerance 212–213, 215
Renaissance 137
research: historical thinking 31–32, 34, 35, 36, 37; history education 18
resentment 159
revolt 141–142, 168; peasant 119–120, 121
revolution 143, 222
Ricoeur, P. 54, 55
Ringrose, D. 137
Ritter, C. 83
Rodríguez-Pérez, R. 222
Roman Empire 140; ruralisation 114; social inequality 117–118; war 150–151, 155
Romanticism 3, 4
rural society 90, 96, 112, 113, 114, 118; consolidation of smallholdings 94–95; eighteenth century 93–94; liberal agrarian revolution 94; *see also* peasantry
ruralisation, Rome 114
Rüsen, J. 6, 17, 26, 29, 54, 57, 59
Russia 1, 2, 144; peasantry 92; refeudalisation 120–121

Sáiz, J. C. 35
Sáiz Serrano, J. 220
Salort i Vives, S. 100
Sampedro-Martín, S. 8, 221
Samuel, R. 85
San Domingos de Bonaval park 76
Sánchez-Ibáñez, R. 222
Santisteban, A. 45, 68
Sartre, J.-P. 19
Schaffer, D. 44
school 18–19
School Council History Project 58
school/s, democratic model 20
Schugurensky, D. 219
Schwab, K. 100
science 95; skills 108–109
Scott, J. W., "Gender: A Useful Category of Historical Analysis" 181
Second World War 144, 156, 189–190
second-order concepts 58, 220
sedentism 101, 113
Seignobos, C. 49
Seixas, P. 6, 18, 26, 28, 32, 35, 36, 54, 60
serfdom 103
Serres, M. 102
Seven Years' War 152
sexuality 183
Shemilt, D. 17, 36
Sieferle, R. P. 85
Simonneaux, J. 159–160
Sjöland, M. 222
skills: science and technology 108–109; social and civic 109
slavery and slave labor 103, 107, 110, 197–198, 200; uprisings 169–170
Slavs/Slavic culture 4
smallholders 94–95, 118
smartphone 103, 106
Smil, V. 85
Smurra, R. 223
Sobrino, D. 50
social Darwinism 83
social homogamy 134
social inequality 7, 126, 131; Early Middle Ages 118; Medieval Age 118; refeudalisation 120–121; Rome 117–118; technological revolution and 100–102; *see also* bourgeoisie; peasantry
social justice 16, 71, 75
social mobility 129
social networks 44, 110, 145
social stratification 134
social studies 17
social technology 106, 110

socially acute questions 159–160
Sostegno per l'Inclusione Attiva (SIA) 131
sovereignty 140, 141, 143
Soviet Union 144, 156
space 138
Spain 34, 35, 37, 91; *Cabezos de Huelva* 73; economic inequality 131–132; *Museo do Pobo Galego* 76; Portomarín 75; *Puig de Sant Andreu de Ullastret* 73; *San Domingos de Bonaval* park 76; social inequality 131; Valley of the Fallen 72
Spanish flu epidemic 128, 133
Spector, U. 113
Spencer, H. 83
Spengler, O. 83
standardized tests 20
Standford, M. 57
steam engine 105
Stenhouse, L. 16
story 57; *see also* narrative
structure 180
subjected-rescued heritage 75
suffrage 143, 188, 190
surveillance 105–106
sustainability 84, 95, 96
Sustainable Development Goals 71, 131
Sutherland, E. 163–164
Sweden, economic inequality 132
synoptic judgment 55

Tardón, M. 70
teachers 22, 43; digital literacy 46
teaching history 5, 48, 96; multicultural approach 7, 9; narrative competence 61–63; research 18; technology and 43–46
technological revolution 99–100, 100–102, 108, 110; social inequality and 100–102; work organization and 102–104
technology: craftsmanship 102; history education and 43–46; innovation 103–104; Luddites 102–103; privacy and 105–106; resources 106; skills 108–109; smartphone 103, 106; social 106; society and 106; *see also* digital technology
temporal orientation 30
territorial intelligence 71
terrorism: anarchistic wave 170; anticolonial wave 170–171; Islamism 171; new left wave 170–171; religious wave 171
textbooks 5, 22, 44, 45–46, 48, 50, 172; traditional model 19
Theodora 118

Thirty Years' War 152
Thompson, E. P. 85, 92, 106
timocracy 140
Toaff, E. 215
total war 159
totalitarianism 144
trade 185, 194, 199; maritime 104–105, 197; ports 195–196; slave 198, 200
trade unions 103, 121
traditional model 18–20
trajectory dependency 88
transdisciplinary approach 21
transoceanic routes 104–105
travel and travelers 201; pilgrimage 202–203
Treaty of the Pyrenees 154
Trevelyan, G. M. 54
trial by ordeal 163
Twitter 50–51
Tylor, E. B. 208

Unetice culture 139
United Kingdom 6
United Nations 156, 159
United States 17, 18, 26, 28, 35, 104, 107, 144
unwed mothers 162
uprisings 174; enslaved people 169–170; peasant 168–169; urban 169
Urban II, Pope 151–152
urban planning 115, 122; Greece 114
urbanization 101, 102–103, 110, 112, 113; economic inequality 120, 131; Europe 114; housing 115; *see also* rural society

vagrancy 167
Valley of the Fallen 72
van Boxtel, C. 31, 223
van Drie, J. 31
VanSledright, B. 35, 62
Vico, G. 208
Vieira, H. 222
Vikings 151, 196
violence 163, 223; jihad 214; piracy 194, 203–204; politically motivated 168; rape 189; religious 207, 213–214; teaching about 171–172, 174–175; terrorism 170–171; uprisings 168–170
voice 57
von Humboldt, A. 83
von Ranke, L. 54
VOSviewer 32
Vygotsky, L. 16

Waldis, M. 61
Waltner, A. 126
war 149, 222–223; Crusades 151–152, 214; discussing in the classroom 157–160; in Europe 152–153; First World War 155–156; Roman Empire 150–151; Second World War 156; total 159
Warwick-Booth, L. 126
Web of Science (WOS) 31–32, 34, 35, 36, 37
White, H. 54
white-collar crime 164
Wiesner, M. E.: *A Companion to Global Gender History* 181; *A Primer for Teaching Women, Gender & Sexuality in World History* 182
Wikipedia 46–47, 48–49
Willoughby, U. E. 182
Wilschut, A. 5
Wilson, C. 85, 90
Wineburg, S. 6, 28, 32, 35, 49; *Historical thinking and other unnatural acts* 220
Wollstonecraft, M. 186
women 222; "fallen" 167; marriage 127–128; and power 138, 180; rape 189; salary gap 129; suffrage 188, 190; unwed mothers 162; *see also* gender and gender history
work 103
workhouses 165–166, 167
World History 15, 200–201
Worster, D. 84–85

xenophobia 16, 20

Young, M. 31

zero focalization 57

For Product Safety Concerns and Information please contact our EU representative GPSR@taylorandfrancis.com
Taylor & Francis Verlag GmbH, Kaufingerstraße 24, 80331 München, Germany

www.ingramcontent.com/pod-product-compliance
Lightning Source LLC
Chambersburg PA
CBHW051355290426
44108CB00015B/2020